Women in Islam

Women in Islam

Wiebke Walther

WITH AN INTRODUCTION
BY GUITY NASHAT

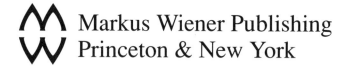

Markus Wiener Publishing
Princeton & New York

Translated from German by C.S.V. Salt in 1981.
Copyright © 1981 by Edition Leipzig.
Copyright © 1993 by Wiebke Walther for the updated text.
Copyright © 1993 by Guity Nashat for the introduction.

For information write to: Markus Wiener Publishing, Inc.
114 Jefferson Road, Princeton, NJ 08540

Library of Congress Cataloging-in-Publication Data

Walther, Wiebke.
    [Frau im Islam. English]
    Women in Islam: from medieval to modern times/byWiebke
Walther; introduction by Guity Nashat.—Rev. ed.
    Includes bibliographical references and index.
    ISBN 1-55876-052-0
    ISBN 1-55876-153-9 (pbk.)
    1. Women, Muslim—History. 2. Women, Muslim in art.
3. Art, Islamic. I. Title.
HQ1170.W2813 1992   92-20971
305.4'0917'671—dc20   CIP

Book Design by Cheryl Mirkin

Printed by Princeton University Press on acid-free paper

Contents

Foreword

I n the early years of the 1990s, there were over one billion followers of the Islamic faith, a large number of them living in traditional Islamic countries, which are becoming the focus of increasing international interest.

Over the last hundred and fifty years, the situation of half of these several millions—the women of Islam—has repeatedly caught the attention both of non-Islamic authors, who usually display a critical turn of mind, and of Muslim apologists. This book examines the issue of women in Islam from a largely historical standpoint.

It focuses on the central Islamic countries, i.e. the Arab world, Turkey, Iran and Mughal India. The subject of Islam in Black Africa and in East and Southeast Asia requires special treatment, and has not been covered here. Even with these restrictions, it is possible only to skim the surface of the wealth of available material.

Still, in dealing with the wide-ranging and many-sided subject of women in traditional Islamic countries, every effort has been made to draw a well-rounded picture, to avoid sweeping generalizations, and to give adequate justification for any statements and conclusions.

Since the book has been written for a wide range of readers, the scholarly transliteration of Arabic, Persian and Turkish names and terms has been dropped in favor of one that takes pronunciation into account, yet the results are still only approximations, due to differences in the phonetic systems. For the benefit of the expert, however, the scholarly transliteration has been retained in the titles of original works listed in the bibliography.

I would like to thank my Muslim colleagues in Egypt and Iraq

1

who, in letters and in conversations, readily answered the questions I put to them in the course of two study trips. I respect and honor their views. At the same time, I hope they will understand that I, as a non-Muslim, do not always share them. This difference in viewpoint can be seen in the very title of this book. In contrast to the position of many Muslims today, orientalists see Islam as more than a religion. Unlike any other religion in history, they point out, Islam has penetrated and shaped the politics and culture of the countries dominated by it, and has molded the lives of those who profess it. Thus, in this book, the title "Women in Islam" not only covers the position of women in religion and religious law, but also in social life, history and culture.

Wiebke Walther

Introduction

BY GUITY NASHAT

Our knowledge of women in Islamic society has benefitted from the burgeoning studies on women in the West. This interest has resulted in excellent monographs, essay collections, scholarly and popular articles, and translations of works by Muslim women into Western languages, particularly English. The role of women and their contributions to society are being investigated by scholars in various fields ranging from anthropology to literary criticism. These studies are beginning to provide a more accurate picture of Muslim women than the stereotyped images projected by Orientalists* and missionaries of the past century—still to be seen in the popular press, the media, and Hollywood films. Women's mass participation in many of the recent political events in the Middle East has also contributed to shaking these myths, though it has not effectively shattered them.

Many recent studies have focused on Muslim Middle Eastern women in the twentieth century. The availability of additional sources is one of the reasons for the greater focus on the more recent period, particularly the post-1950s. Also, travel to the region is now much easier, which has helped anthropologists to lead the way in serious work in this area. In addition, women have become more visible and articulate. Many have entered professional life, including the social sciences; thus, they have themselves contributed valuable studies on women.

---

* Despite the shortcomings of the terms Orient and Orientalistic, they are both employed in this book because of their continuing currency. See Edward W. Said, *Orientalism* (New York: Random House, 1978)

Despite the progress made in our knowledge of Muslim women in the twentieth century, which can be attested to by the accompanying bibliography, the study of women prior to the modern period is still in its infancy. Various reasons account for the dearth of serious studies on the pre-modern period. One reason, true also of the study of women in other areas, is that historians are drawn to those social and political processes that result in change. Women everywhere have been generally excluded from having the power to initiate or contribute to these types of processes. Another reason, unique to this region and other Muslim countries, is that until recently, society was divided vertically along gender lines into the public world of men and the private world of women. In addition, even in periods such as early Islam, when women were active in society, with a few exceptions, they played secondary roles. The major decisions were made by men.

As social mores restricted women's visibility in public life, with the exception of information on women in the first Islamic century, standard sources gradually became more reticent about conveying information on individual women. However, their exclusion from the sources did not mean that they ceased to play a major role in society or that their contributions became less important than the men's. In fact, written accounts continued to contain information on many aspects of Islamic life, which can be used to reconstruct many aspects of women's lives and their role in society.

These sources reveal that Muslim women during the first century of Islam, including the Prophet's period (570-632 A.D.), were more active in public life and that they became more restricted later. Furthermore, we learn that many of the basic features that characterize the treatment of women in Islam (such as their seclusion, the veil, and their subordination to men) pre-date the advent of Islam in the seventh century. A widespread misconception, which attributes many of these practices to Islamic teachings, stems from the traditional periodization of Islamic history, whereby the rise of Islam (610 A.D.) is treated as a new beginning. Whatever occurred since the seventh century is treated as the domain of Islamic or Middle Eastern history, and whatever occurred prior to that period is relegated to the realm of ancient Near Eastern history. Many Islamicists have followed the periodization of early Muslims, who believed that their pre-Islamic traditions belonged to the time of ignorance, and were therefore worthless. Although most historians are aware that the majority of those who embraced Islam within a century after its advent lived outside of Arabia, in regions deeply steeped in much older and highly-developed cultural traditions, few scholars have systematically looked for continuity between these cultures and post-Islamic developments. This approach is particularly inadequate for the study of women, whose treatment and status were greatly influenced by the pre-Islamic attitudes of the non-Arab converts, the majority of Muslims within a century.

Recent studies suggest that the salient features generally associated with the treatment of women in Islamic society had already developed by the seventh century, when Islam was revealed. The subordination of women and the discrimination practiced against them resulted from the gradual evolution of the social and economic conditions that existed in the Middle East since neolithic times. In much of the region, as agriculture assumed a larger share as a source of revenue, the use of the plough and the aridity of the land encouraged greater division of labor in the early communities, with men playing an increasingly large role in the field and women devoting more time to childrearing and domestic activities. The rise of urban life, which appeared first in Mesopotamia (present-day Iraq) accelerated the existing division of labor between women and men. It further reduced women's social and economic power, fostering a development of attitudes that held them to an inferior position.[1]

The dramatic reversal that occurred in the role of women within two centuries after the rise of Islam, reflects the radically different social and economic conditions that prevailed in the two periods. Islam was revealed in the city of Mecca, which was an active com-

---

[1] For more detail see Guity Nashat, "Women in the Middle East 8,000 B.C. - A.D. 1800" in *Restoring Women to History: Teaching Packet for Integrating Women's History into Courses on Africa, Asia, Latin America, the Caribbean and the Middle East,* ed. by M. Strobel and C. Odim Johnson (Bloomington: Organization of America Historians, 1988).

mercial center, but the mores of Meccans reflected Arabia's pastoral lifestyle. Arabian society needed the contribution of women in social and economic life; thus, it allowed them corresponding visibility and social power. To be sure, women were not seen as equal to men, but they had greater freedom and social power than elsewhere in the region.[2] Not surprisingly, women were more active socially when Islam was predominantly the religion of the people of the Arabian Peninsula.

A few decades after the Prophet's death in 632, the Arabian Muslims conquered much of the Middle East. In the conquered territories, which included much of the Byzantine and all of the Sasanian empires, women, particularly in urban areas, played a role that was more restricted to household activities and childrearing. As an ever-increasing number of the population of the conquered areas embraced Islam, the status women had enjoyed in the beginning of Islam began to be undermined.

Not surprisingly, the ways of the conquered population, who vastly outnumbered the early Muslims of Arabian origin, prevailed. Although many of those living in the regions outside of Arabia had converted to Islam, the coming of the pastoral Arabs did not change the socio-economic conditions in the conquered territories. These remained urban and agrarian; consequently, the attitudes and the value system those conditions had generated remained equally unchanged. Women continued to be viewed as inferior to men, descent through the father continued to be emphasized, effort was made to minimize contact between male strangers and women, and women's activities were relegated to tasks within the household and raising of children. Many of the theologians who were interpreting and developing the religious law were themselves of non-Arab stock.[3] In their debates over the proper mode of behavior for Muslim women, they insured that the discussions of the Koranic references to women would be interpreted in a manner that reflected the older cultural

---

[2] M. Watt. *Muhammed at Medina.* Oxford: The Clarendon Press, pp._
[3] Ibn Khaldun, *The Muqaddimah: An Introduction to History,* trans. Franz Rosenthal, ed. (Princeton: Princeton University Press, 1989).

value systems. This explains why in many cases the Koranic statements regarding women are less restrictive than the eventual provision that appeared in the *Shari'a*.

The gradual restrictions placed on women's public role are reflected in the discrepancy of some statements affecting women between the two most important sources of the *Shari'a*, Islamic law; the Koran, which Muslims view as direct Divine Revelation, and *hadith*, the sayings attributed to the Prophet. In every case, the Koran is less restrictive towards women than *hadith*. This discrepancy arose because the Koran, which was collected in the two decades after the Prophet's death, and considered direct Divine Word, would not leave room for human tampering; *hadith* was written down at least a century later and its authenticity was challenged from the beginning. The provisions regarding the veil and punishment for adultery reveal that both became stricter by the time of Imam Shafi'i, the great Islamic jurist (d. 824 A.D.). He was instrumental in developing arguments that justified the more restrictive provisions by arguing that even though the Koran did not require them, the Prophet's enactment of them should give them the force of law.[4] Eventually, the *Shari'a*, the religious law that derived from these and other sources, began to be treated also as infallible. The fact that for many centuries, conditions in the Middle East changed only slowly, enhanced their authority.

However, the renewed contact between the West and the Middle East at the end of the nineteenth century, thrust many of the practices concerning women into the limelight. The challenge to Muslim treatment of women came from Western Europeans, who, in the course of the eighteenth century surpassed other groups in the world, including their Muslim Middle Eastern neighbors, in economic, military, and scientific fields. In the nineteenth century, Europeans exploited their new-found power to extend hegemony over much of the world. In the Middle East, the treatment of women provided Europeans with an excuse to declare the inferiority of Muslims and their religion, and

---

[4] For excellent discussion of Islamic law and Shafi's role see Joseph Schacht, *The Origins of Muhammadan Jurisprudence* (Cambridge, England: The Clarendon Press, 1950).

also justification for Europe's imperialist and colonialist policies and practices. Many popular and scholarly articles portrayed Muslim women as one of two extremes: as voluptuous objects of desire, surrounded by servants and slaves, or as abject and submissive victims as the mercy of tyrannical husbands and fathers.

To be sure, women in the Middle East suffered from many inequities and abuses. But most of the European critics were not in a position to perceive these abuses, much less to correct them. At worst their criticism was designed to promote their own aims; at best, it stemmed from self-righteous indignation and masked their feelings of superiority. They condoned very little and condemned every practice that differed from what was common in their tradition. Their attitude toward divorce was typical: it was found to be barbaric and to foster the abandonment of women. But they rarely acknowledged the advantages Muslim women enjoyed under the law: full control of their assets, some power to initiate a divorce, the right to inherit, and the recognition of women's sexual rights within marriage.

European use of women's status to denounce Islam, in turn, aroused the wrath and fear of traditional sectors, led by the clergy, who equated change in the status of women with efforts by enemies of Islam to undermine the religion and their way of life. Though the decline of Western power after World War II laid these fears to rest, they have emerged as powerful themes in more recent decades. It was an argument effectively used by Ayatullah Khomeini to mobilize the traditional sectors in Iranian society against the Shah. His success is an indication of its great appeal.

The defensive posture of traditional groups was not the only reaction to European criticism of the treatment of women. By the turn of the new century, it met with growing tacit approval of Westernized intellectuals, government officials, and members of the upper and middle classes of society. In retrospect, their writings seem naive and simplistic. They had preconceived notions about European society, and idealized the seeming freedoms women enjoyed there. They neither knew the European abuses from which European women suffered, nor did they have any understanding of the plight of women in their own societies. As a rule, they were Europhiles. They criticized those aspects of the treatment of women that did not correspond to practices prevailing in the West. While some were among the most vocal opponents of European colonialism in the region, they reveal and unbounded faith in European's good intentions. They tacitly blamed Islam for many of the ills from which women suffered.

Finally, mention must be made of the ideological dimension of the treatment of women in Islam. Though its origins date back to the European writings on Muslim women, the treatment of women has been used by various groups to buttress political and nationalist ideologies. The apologists present an idealistic picture of women in Islamic society, and in their effort to justify how women were treated, they defend even obvious abuses, such as child marriage, seclusion of women, the veil, and polygamy. The critics portray women as totally helpless and exploited victims of a harsh patriarchal religion. Though undeniably, Muslim women to this day are victims of discrimination and abuse, their history is not primarily one of disadvantage and degradation. The study of women is also distorted by nationalist writers, from among the three major ethnic groups—Arabs, Iranians, and Turks—of the Middle East. Advocates in each group place the blame for the disadvantages in women's conditions, in both the past and the present, on other groups.[5] Undoubtedly these controversies do not make the study of women's past, and developments that affected them, any easier.

There is a need for greater attention to the study of Muslim prior to the modern period. Much more work needs to be done before any of the major problems that have affected women in this region for millenia can be fully understood. However, even partial answers will be useful, and a step in the right direction. For example, we may not have all the evidence yet about the origins of the veil, or the reasons for the seclusion of women. But a better understanding of why some of these practices were firmly institutionalized in the *Shari'a* would provide important insights.

---

[5] For example, see 'Abd Ar-Raziq, Ahmad. *La Femme au Temps des Mamlouks en Egypte.* Text Arabes et Etude Islamiques, Tome V, 1973. The author presents a rosy picture of Egyptian women under the Mamluks and blames many of the inequities to which Egyptian women were subjected under the Ottomans.

Thanks to the cultural flowering in the early Islamic centuries, a rich body of sources is at our disposal. The need of the non-Arabic speaking converts to understand the sacred text, the Qur'an, meant that writing and other literary activities occupied a special place in the newly-emerging civilization. These range from theological works to legal discussions, Qur'anic exegesis, *hadith* analysis and discussion, a wide variety of historical and literary works, literary criticism, manuals of government, and even such mundane activities as cooking. Sometimes, women are prominent as narrators and subjects of these works. These sources shed light on many aspects of women's lives and activities, though less on individual women.

But a word of caution needs to be sounded: access to and utilization of this information requires special skills. The researcher must have training in the languages of Islam, especially Arabic, and a thorough knowledge of the history of the period of his or her interest, as well as an appropriate methodology to synthesize diverse prespectives. To these, a scholar must bring an appreciation of the importance of women's contributions to the evolution of society and civilization. The materials on women need to be culled from a wide variety of sources. One must also have knowledge of the historical and literary works through which the material and references about women are scattered. Is it any wonder that the number of studies dealing with women has remained so small?

Dr. Wiebke Walther's *Women in Islam*, which focuses on premodern women, is a welcome contribution to scholarly research on women. Dr. Walther's qualifications are admirably suited to the task at hand: she has a doctorate degree in Islamic cultural history, and her work reveals an extensive knowledge of the vast spectrum of intellectual and artistic activitites—law, theology, literature, and art, to mention a few—which she has utilized to depict a complex and multifaceted account of the role of women in Islamic society. She does not limit the discussion to the contribution of elite women, but also includes the less visible women in towns and rural areas. She ably presents a general overview of the evolution of the role of women over the centuries and the geographical region in which Islamic civilization flourished.

Dr. Walther has synthesized materials from across a wide field to bring us a coherent picture of how women lived. Her approach goes beyond the life and role of women of the upper classes and provides some understanding of women in other strata of society. She also examines women's lives and their roles within the larger context of contemporary society.

The author's use of literature and Islamic high culture, and many reproductions of Islamic art, renders the book interesting for the general public as well as serious students in the field. Her study provides a useful precedent for others to follow. Her portrait is compelling evidence of the important role women played in Islamic society and of the recognition they were given by that society. It should help debunk the myths and misunderstandings so widespread among Westerners about the lives of Muslim women.

Chicago, May 1992

1

This highly realistic Arab miniature of 1237 depicts the arrival of two travelers in a small town. Everything is shown: the mosque and minaret, various domestic animals at the waterside, hen and cock on the dome-shaped roofs of houses in what is probably the sūq or market. On the right is a view of the town gate and the guard with his long halberd. In front of it sits a woman with a distaff under her arm. The clothing of all the persons shown is decorated with the strips of lettering known as tirāz, as are the saddlecloths of the camels.

Preface

TO THE AMERICAN EDITION

I n her introduction, Guity Nashat makes remarks about my book that are both necessary and complimentary, I am grateful for her kind words; but let me add some words of my own.

First of all, I wish to express my gratitude to Markus Wiener for publishing a revised and emended version of this book, which I wrote in German over twelve years ago. As Guity Nashat points out, gender studies on Muslim women have advanced since that time, along with gender studies in general. A number of studies have been published, especially on modern Muslim women in different regions of the Islamic world. Some of them are more informative than others. Of those dealing with sociological or ethnological problems, many are based on immediate field studies; some are based on original sources, particularly when the focus is on historical and cultural questions.

When I began to concern myself with the situation of women in Muslim countries, I was well-read in modern Arabic literature, which since its very beginning has focused on the role of women, or more precisely, on the social repression of women in a strongly male-dominated society. Being an Islamicist, I am also familiar with works of modern and classical Persian and Turkish literature. The literature of both countries concerns similar problems; one can conclude that such topics are typically Islamic, rather than bound to individual countries. Some typical examples include the right of a man to marry more than one wife, when the first one cannot bear a child; marriage (always arranged by the father) of a poor and very young girl to an old man; or the circumcision of girls. This is still prevalent in some Arab countries such as Egypt, despite the fact that it has been prohibited by law

13

for many years. The cult that has formed over the issue of virginity is to be found in the entire Mediterranean area, but one tradition or social convention that seems to be typically Arabo-Islamic is the *ghusl al-ʿār,* the "washing of dishonor by blood." The father, brother, or another near male relative of an unmarried girl is socially obliged to kill her if there is the slightest suspicion that she has lost her virginity. He has to reestablish the presumed lost honor of his family—lost by the very idea of the girl's losing her virginity without marriage—not by calling to account the seducer, but by killing the victim, the girl.

This and other customs cannot be justified by original Islamic beliefs. In reality, not every social phenomenon or value that affects the lives of girls and women in Muslim countries is caused by Islam, or can even be explained by it. More than any other religion, Islam claims to penetrate and shape the lives of its adherents. For centuries, it has met this claim to a great extent, but as in every religion, in every ideology, there is a difference between the ideal and the reality. As I have said, there are traditions that have been followed for many centuries, standards of value, which are not codified in early Islam and do not have their roots in it. Many of the cultural, political, social, and administrative traditions of the countries of the Ancient Near East were absorbed by and integrated into Islamic culture and social life, beginning at least with the so-called Abbāsid revolution of 750AD. There were influences from the neighboring countries as well.

One must not disregard the historical and economic situation of the country or region, or the social and economic position of the family to which a girl or a woman belonged. Her individual abilities, intelligence, and education (which usually depends greatly on the social position of her family), as well as her beauty could influence her fortune. Beauty, however, was regarded ambivalently. Even early Arabic sources define women as *fitna,* today a woman's name, which means a whole range of things from "charm, attractiveness" to "intrigue, riot, dissension, civil strife." Perhaps a woman's personality has to develop in a struggle against outside factors; at least she cannot be seen separately from them, which may fascinate her male counterparts or an outside observer.

Regarding the title of my book, I want to emphasize that there is a whole network of factors, indistinguishable from the all-embracing cover of Islamic religion, in which the lives not only of Muslim women but all women in Muslim countries are embedded. (I include Christian and Jewish women as well, based on the following: when Muslim women in an Islamic country—the overwhelming majority—are veiled, Jewish and Christian women veil themselves as well. It is not only that they cannot evade the ruling social system, but that they want to follow it along with all other women.)

When I first wrote this book, I focused on the time before the nineteenth century and gave only a short survey of developments since that time. Since most of the studies on Muslim women done since the publication of my book have focused on the present, I have made some necessary emendations in the last chapter as I did some emendations and supplements in the chapters before, for which I used Arabic sources and a large part of the titles mentioned in the Recent Bibliography by Fariba Zarinebaf-Shahr. So I here enclose additional titles not mentioned in this bibliography, titles in Arabic, German, English and French, and refer to some recent publications from my pen, in which I give condensed informations about the topic "Women in Islam" and "Women in the Arabian Nights", all of them in German. I believe that the last chapter is valid in its basic features, and is, although still only an abridgment, needed to complete the picture. As to the other chapters I tried to give evidence by statements and informations from original sources in translation, abstaining mostly from giving judgements or theories, but trying here and again to refer to similar or at least resembling conditions in Europe.

Wiebke Walther
Bamberg, July 1992

2

A miniature from a collection of legends of the Prophet. The Koran also contains the Old Testament story of Noah and the ark. Noah is shown with a nimbus of flames, since, according to the Koran, he is a prophet; his three sons and daughters are depicted here as Moslems of the second half of the sixteenth century. Animals can be recognized in the hull of the ship, and the water is rising over a dome and two minarets.

3

One of the most delicate of all Islamic miniatures shows the arrival of Prince Humāy at the residence of Princess Humāyūn and her ladies. The golden crescent of the moon and the stars stand out against the blue of the night sky, but the blossoming shrubs and trees in the garden and the gowns of the ethereal figures shine forth with all the colors of daylight.

4

A scene from a Persian romantic epic—a prince visiting a princess in her pavilion—shows the room's splendidly decorative interior. Not only are there colored tiles on the walls but also delicate murals, which, according to Islamic traditions, are not really permissible. On the floor, under the glittering golden throne of the king, is a brilliant red carpet.

5

There are sorceresses, female demons, and good and wicked fairies in the literature of the Islamic countries, but Islam has never experienced anything like witch-hunting. Here is a scene from the Shāhunāmeh, *the Iranian national epic: the killing of a sorceress.*

6

A colorful scene before the gate of an Indian city on a miniature painted in 1617 for the library of the Emperor Jahāngīr. In this miniature, we see a baker in his shop, a wood seller, a water carrier, gardeners at work and, screened by trees and a wall, women making lace at the side of a watercourse. Within the city, Koran readers can be identified on the roof of a house, in the interior of which two women are gesticulating while two others are talking in the harem garden. The guardian of the gate looks down from above.

7

This is how a Persian miniaturist of the sixteenth century imagined Muhammed's first meeting with Khadīja, who was to become his wife. As a sign of the saintliness which was later attributed to him, the Prophet is surrounded by a nimbus of flames. He is also wearing a veil, which completely hides his face.

8

According to the Koran—this is a miniature from a later collection of legends about the prophets—Jesus was not born in a stable. Mary was overcome by labor pains under a palm tree, which provided her with fresh dates to eat and under which there flowed a streamlet with cool, clear water. (19:23ff.) The Holy Child is also surrounded by a nimbus of flames since Islam regards Jesus as a prophet, too. He is wrapped in the manner that was probably customary for infants at that time in Iran.

9

The sharī'a *allowed a man to take up to four wives at the same time, provided he treats them justly and as many concubines as he wished from among his slaves. Thus rulers and other powerful personages could establish large harems in which close watch was kept over the women.*

10

With the roguish faces of children, Adam and Eve leave the garden of Paradise. Two guards and a virgin of Paradise watch them go; others observe them from a building. In the foreground, a peacock and a snake symbolize human vanity. In the Koran, it is not Eve who seduces Adam; rather, Satan, at the front of the picture, leads both of them astray.

11

The Queen of Sheba is mentioned in the Koran (29:22ff.) as a pagan, but without any of the negative comments I sometimes made about women rulers. In this miniature, she is painted as an Iranian princess of the sixteenth century with the tāj-kulāh, the "crown hat," on her head, and she is surrounded by winged genies bearing refreshments or playing music. In the foreground, from the realm of fantasy, are Satan and a herd of steeds and other animals, which, according to the Koran, and the vast legendary material about Solomon were created by God from divine spirits to obey Salomon's, the Queen's lover's orders.

12

Among the Sūfīs, the Islamic mystics, women were more highly esteemed than in Orthodox Islam. A Persian miniature from the mid sixteenth century shows women taking part in a service in a mosque from a position in a gallery of their own, as prescribed by the Sunna.

13

To offend the honor of a married women was considered an insult worthy of harsh punishment. This is a scene from the Kalīla wa-Dimna *collection of fables: A falcon is trying to peck out the eyes of his falconer, who had several times attempted—in vain— to win the favor of the wife of the Governor of Balkh. The latter is depicted here endeavoring to drive off the falcon with a stick. The woman is wearing a brightly patterned gown with the typical wide sleeves of the time.*

14

Layla and Majnūn fell in love at the Koran school. Boy and girl pupils are kneeling before the teacher, also on his knees, on brightly colored mats; the copies of the Koran are on the typical lecterns. In the left foreground, a pupil is being given the bastinado while on the right a school servant is grinding ink. As usual, the lesson is being held in a mosque.

15

A scene from the Shāhunāmeh. *Rūdābeh, shortly before the birth of Rustam, has fainted since the size of her stomach seems to preclude the possibility of a birth. An old woman, her mother, scatters perfumed water over her to refresh her. In the foreground an eunuch hands a fortifying meat dish to a maid-servant. On the roof, the father of the child, the white-haired Zāl, asks his protector, a magical bird, for advice. The bird describes the Caesarean section by which the child must be born, and the* Mōbed, *the wise man who will perform it, is already coming through the door.*

16

According to the Iranian saga, it was the legendary King Jamshīd who taught his subjects the various crafts. Smiths, dyers, tailors, and weavers are to be seen. The only craft carried out by a woman is spinning. Here, in the Iran of the second half of the fifteenth century, it is the spinning-wheel that is used and no longer the distaff depicted in earlier pictures.

17

A lady of the harem is unwell; the physician has been called, and he is now feeling her pulse. He is attended by a colleague. The patient is held by another member of the harem. The master of the house watches the scene from a window opening. In the foreground, medicine is being prepared by one of the inmates.

18

A scene from a popular novel. Men stoning an adulterous pair. On the right, a second scene: the Abyssinian who seduced the woman is sitting in a crate.

Historical Background

In about 610 AD, when he was some forty years of age, the merchant Mohammed, from an impoverished branch of the Qoraysh, the main tribe of the Arab trading city of Mecca, had a vision. His subsequent interpretation of this vision, which came after much reflection and searching for God, was that the archangel Gabriel had brought him a message from Allah. In seventh-century Arabia, Allah was the name given to the supreme God of numerous divinities and demons. Moslem theologians disagree on which verses Muhammed heard first, since the Koran (Qor'ān, "recitation") was written down only after his death and arranged according to the length of its *Sūras*, or chapters.

It is quite certain, however, that the first messages proclaimed by Muhammed as the revealed word of Allah were a warning to the arrogant merchant caste of Mecca, a warning of the Day of Judgment and the End of the World. Muhammed's message urged the merchants to do good and pious deeds, to abandon polytheism and to praise the goodness, mercy, justice and power of Allah; later they also announced the joys of Paradise awaiting the faithful.

These revelations were presented in rhymed prose, a stylistic device used by ancient Arabic soothsayers. Considered to be the word of God, the sacred writings were and are of such majesty that Moslems throughout the ages have regarded the Koran as a stylistically inimitable miracle which, in the Orthodox view, must not be translated. They have been translated, however, and Arberry's translation of one of the oldest *Sūras* conveys an impression of this form: "Recite: In the Name of thy Lord who created—created Man of a blood-clot.—Recite: And thy Lord is the Most Generous—who taught by the Pen—taught Man, that he knew not." [1] The wealthy merchants of Mecca paid no heed to Muhammed's message, since the caravan trade was not their only source of income; they also made money from the cult of the Ka'ba in Mecca, where the Black Stone was revered and which attracted numerous Bedouin tribes of the Arabian Peninsula. The merchants were quick to detect a threat to their privileges and prosperity and persecuted Muhammed and his early followers, treating them with scorn and contempt. Among these first followers were Muhammed's wife of the time, Khadīja, of whom we will hear more, and members of Mecca's lower and middle classes.

The pressure exerted by the commercial aristocracy on the followers of the new faith became increasingly severe, and ultimately Muhammed was compelled to accept an invitation from the Arab tribes of Aus and Khazraj which occupied the date oasis of Yathrib, some three hundred kilometers from Mecca. These two tribes were enemies and hoped to find a mediator in the founder of the new religion.

In 622, Muhammed and his followers made the migration *(hijra)* from Mecca to Yathrib, which was renamed Medina from the Arabic *Madinat an-nabiy*, "the city of the Prophet." This very year 622 marks the beginning of the Islamic calendar, which, unlike the Roman calendar, is based on lunar years.

Muhammed now became the religious and political head of a community, and Islam, at least in theory, has preserved this unity of political and religious leadership throughout the centuries. His revelations from this period no longer possess the passion of the first *Sūras* of Mecca. They contain rules designed to govern the life of the new community and the relationship between the muhājirūn, the "emigrants" from Mecca, and the *Ansār*, their "helpers" in Medina, for the bonds of tribal adherence, deriving from kith-and-kin relationships, were now to be replaced by the *umma*, the "community" of the

---

[1] Translated by A. J. Arberry. All other quotations from the Koran are taken from Richard Bell's *The Qur'ān* (Edinburgh: T. & T. Clark, 1937. Reprinted in 1960). Subsequent citations will be indicated by numbers in parentheses ( ), with the first number designating the *Sūra*, the second the verses.

faithful." In modern Arabic, *umma* means "nation."

The *Sūras* of Medina also deal with questions relating to Judaism and Christianity, since several Jewish tribes lived in Medina and since Christians were to be found close by, principally among some Bedouin tribes of the Arabian Peninsula but also in areas bordering states with a higher level of civilization. Muhammed saw himself as the last in a series of messengers sent by God, perfecting the revelations He had made to Jews and Christians. At first, Muhammed believed that the Jews of Medina would acknowledge him as a prophet. When this did not happen, his reaction was harsh. He decreed that his people should pray toward the Ka'ba in Mecca instead of toward Jerusalem, thus acknowledging the Arab Ka'ba cult as a central element in the new faith.

Muhammed gradually acquired followers among the Bedouin tribes of the Arabian Peninsula. Over a number of traditional Bedouin raids, he achieved material benefits for his followers and was ultimately able to gain the upper hand over his adversaries among the merchant aristocracy of Mecca. In 630, Muhammed and his followers entered Mecca in triumph. When he died in Medina in 632, most of the Bedouin tribes and the inhabitants of the few Western Arabian cities were followers of Islam, the new faith which was more appropriate than Christianity or Judaism to the social conditions prevailing in those areas at that time. In the centuries that followed, Islam demonstrated a capacity to absorb new elements and to adapt to more highly-developed social and cultural structures.

The governing maxim of the Islamic faith is: *Lā ilāha illā' llāh wa-Muhammad rasūl Allāh,* "There is no god but Allah, and Muhammed is the messenger of Allah." In contrast to Jesus, who called himself the Son of God, Muhammed says of himself, "I am only a human being like yourselves." (18: 110) Muhammed is the instrument of revelation, of the divine message revealed in the Koran. The Koran has remained unchallengeable for Muslims to the present time; a believer considers it self-evident that God does not err, and that the Koran is the word of God. Later, Muhammed's community, probably taking their lead from the Christian view of Jesus, came to believe that he performed miracles. He regarded himself as the Seal of the Prophets; that is, the last in a line of prophets that included Adam, Abraham, Moses and Jesus, all of whom had proclaimed divine doctrines; he had brought God's message to the Arabs. This recognition of earlier prophets and above all of "religions of the book" like Christianity and Judaism, which like Islam possess holy scriptures, allowed Islam to be tolerant toward other religions in the Middle Ages. At times in the history of Islam, Jews and Christians played a prominent role in the public life of Islamic countries. They were physicians, court secretaries, translators and money changers. Still, they had to pay higher taxes, and in that respect at least were always second-class citizens.

Islam means "surrender to God's will"; a believer is a Muslim, "one who surrenders to God's will." The concept of Islam, the outward profession of this religion, also includes that of *iman,* "profound belief coming from the heart." Surrender to God's will presupposes *husn az-zann,* the belief that God (Allah) is good, and that He can be trusted to know what is best for Man.

The duties that Islam imposes on the faithful are prayers five times a day in the direction of Mecca. The alms tax is to free the rich from excessive wealth and to indicate their financial responsibility for poorer citizens. In the month of Ramadan, the practicing Muslim must fast from dawn till dusk; in addition, he must make the pilgrimage to the Ka'ba in Mecca at least once in his lifetime.

Unlike Christianity, Islam has no priests, no body of religious officials to undertake tasks that cannot be entrusted to ordinary members of the faith. Just as Muhammed was both a political and a religious leader, his successors had a similar dual status and initially called themselves *Khalifat rasūl Allāh,* "successor to the envoy of Allah." Of course, an *imām* or prayer-leader had to fulfill his function in the various mosques, but he was not ordained as is, for example, a Catholic priest.

Within a few decades after Muhammed's death, Arab troops—semi-nomads and religious warriors—had conquered the entire area surrounding them, an area made up of highly-civilized states. They put an end to the Sassanid Empire in the East, and conquered a large part of the area in the West occupied by the other great power of that time, Byzantium. In these conquests, religious fervor was not the only source of strength for the Muslims. Rich booty fell into their hands, and their success seemed to confirm the correctness of their doctrine, as well as their belief that Allah was on their side.

But while Abū Bakr, the first Caliph after Muhammed, still distributed the spoils equally among the Muslims, the next in line, Umar, introduced social distinctions according to the intensity of one's profession of faith. Since this qualification was difficult to assess, the degree of relationship to the Prophet and the date of conversion to Islam became the decisive criteria. Contrary to the Islamic doctrine of equality among all believers, an oligarchy emerged, and the first social protests occurred, expressed in religious schisms. Othman, the third of the first four Caliphs whom most Muslims exalt to this day as "the rightly guided," was murdered, as was his successor Alī. Alī's followers in Iraq formed the Shī'at Alī, the *party of Alī,* or the Shi'a as it was later known, a faction which recognized only Alī and his descendants as legitimate claimants to the title of Caliph. At the present time, the Shī'ites live mainly in Lebanon, Iraq, South Yemen, Iran, and India. They account for about ten percent of all followers of Islam. Most Muslims describe themselves as Sunnites, people who regard the *Sunna* or "custom" of the Prophet as their model, and remain true to the community of the faithful.

In 661 AD, the Arab dynasty of the Umayyads came to power, in the person of the Caliph Mu'āwiya. He made Damascus the capital. As a result, Central Arabia, with its two holy cities of Mecca and Medina, gradually regained the status of a minor province.

When the rule of the Umayyads was ended by the Abbāsid Revolution in 750, the *dār al-Islām*, or "House of Islam," stretched from the Pyrenees to the Indus valley. Social relations in the conquered territories were generally left unchanged by the Arabs. Early feudal structures continued to exist in countries at a higher level of civilization, whereas, in the deserts and steppes of the Caliphat, Arab and Berber nomads relied on cattle breeding. The conquered people were mostly peasants, artisans, merchants, officials of the administrative apparatus (which the Arabs left intact) and great landowners, who, unlike the European feudal lords of the Middle Ages, lived in the cities and not on their fiefs. All these people—for the most part Jews, Christians, and Zoroastrians—enjoyed the protection of the Arab ruling class. They had to pay taxes, but this was nothing new, as they had always been required to do so when conquered by others in the past. Over time, increasing numbers of them embraced Islam, and, as *mawāli* or "new Muslims," in accordance with Arab custom, had to join an Arab tribe. Considerable dissatisfaction arose among these new Muslims, particularly in Iran, since they felt at a disadvantage in comparison with the Arab ruling class.

The Abbāsids, who could trace their ancestry back to an uncle of Muhammed, skillfully exploited this situation to their own advantage. During their reign, which began in 750, the Iranian element predominated in the Caliphate. The eastward shift in the center of power was outwardly reflected in the foundation of a new metropolis, Baghdad, not far from Ctesiphon, the old royal seat of the Sassanid rulers. The second Abbāsid Caliph, al-Mansūr, founded it in 762. Certain institutions and offices typical of the Sassanid Empire were now further developed, and the state apparatus, the administration, court ceremonies and jurisdiction underwent a process of stabilization. Translations provided access to Greek and Indian works on science, medicine, mathematics and philosophy. Stimulated by the cultural values of the various peoples within the Islamic world—Spaniards, North Africans, Egyptians, Syrians, Byzantines, Greeks and Persians —a flourishing civilization developed, whose unifying link was Islam and whose language was Arabic. The cities became wealthy centers of culture, science and art, as well as of trade, production and especially banking and finance. The dominant form of society was Oriental feudalism, whose characteristic feature was the States' position as the supreme landowner, acting through its representative, the Caliph. The broad upper and middle strata of the towns were based on trade and commerce, and did not emerge as a class with definite political aims, even though they were sometimes very active in the political sense. Islamic legislation made no distinction between urban and rural populations.

The Abbāsids ruled until 1258, but local dynasties began to emerge in individual parts of their territory only a hundred years into their reign. An independent Muslim empire came into being in Spain, under the Umayyads, as early as 756 A.D.. Independent dynasties subsequently appeared in Morocco, Tunisia and Egypt. In the tenth century, when local Iranian princes held power, there was a revival of the Persian language, and with it an Iranian cultural renaissance in which the literature of the new Persian language flourished. Up till then, even writers of Iranian origin had used Arabic. At about the same time, a new ethnic element, the Turks, gained significance within the Caliphate. Their power was ultimately consolidated in the dynasty of the Seljūqs, who captured Baghdad in 1055. The sovereignty of the Caliphs was recognized by local courts, apart from the Umayyads in Spain and the Fatimids in Egypt, and at first their existence did not have an adverse effect upon cultural developments in the Caliphate. Rather, patronage of the arts increased.

The wave of Mongolian conquests that swept over Baghdad in 1258 put an end to the Caliphate of the Abbāsids. In the following centuries, various centers of power emerged in the Islamic world. The Mamlūks in Egypt maintained the traditions of Arab-Islamic culture, there and in Palestine and Syria, until their realm was incorporated into the Sultanate of the Ottoman Turks in 1516-17. The Turks had conquered Constantinople by 1453 and subsequently advanced across southeastern Europe as far as Vienna. In Iran, art and culture flourished once more under the Safavids (1502-1722). In 1526, Bābur, a descendant of Timūr the Lame, established the Mogul Empire in India. Southern Russia and present-day Central Asia was ruled by the Khans of the Golden Horde and the Chagatay.

In the fifteenth century, the Muslims were driven from the Iberian Peninsula; their domination of Sicily had ended even before that. Merchants and traders, however, brought Islam to Southeast Asia and Africa. With the progressive decline in the power of the Islamic world from the end of the eighteenth century on, its individual centers increasingly fell within the spheres of influence of the European colonial powers, which took control of some of them during the nineteenth century. In the first Balkan war (1912-13), those Balkan countries which were still under Turkish domination regained their independence. It was only after the First and Second World

Wars that national states emerged in the Islamic territories, most of them designating Islam as the state religion in their constitutions. The former Muslim regions in Central Asia were Soviet republics for several decades and followed a different pattern of social and ideologocal development.

In this examination of the position of women in Islam, it should be borne in mind that Islam served as a unifying link between disparate ethnic elements and cultural traditions. In spite of this all-encompassing religion, then, a variety of opinions was possible, and differing viewpoints may thus be found. A saying attributed to Umar, the second Caliph, is frequently quoted: "Take refuge in God from the evils caused by women, and beware (even) of the most pious of them!" [53, 158][2] The theologian who quotes these words in his eleventh-century treatise on statecraft says, a few pages further on, that the prosperity and population of the world may depend on women but that "it is a fact that all the trials, misfortunes and woes which befall men come from women." [53, 172]

The Spanish-Arab mystic Ibn-al-Arabī (1165-1240) may be quoted as evidence of a contrary view, however: "Whoever knows the worth of women and the mystery reposing in them will not refrain from loving them; indeed, love for them is part of the perfection of a man who knows God, for it is a legacy of the Prophet and a Divine love." [137, 480] And the Spanish-Arab philosopher Averroës (Ibn Rushd, 1126-1198), influenced by Plato, courageously and harshly attacks the attitude of his Muslim contemporaries toward the female sex: "In these (our) states, however, the ability of women is not known, because they are merely used for procreation. They are therefore placed at the service of their husbands and relegated to the business of procreation, child-rearing and breast-feeding. But this denies them their (other) activities. Because women in these states are considered unfit for any of the human virtues, they often tend to resemble plants. One of the reasons for the poverty of these states is that they are a burden to the men." [140, 190]

---

[2] Numbers in square brackets [ ] designate sources. The first figure is the number in the Bibliography; the second indicates the page. Roman numerals refer to the volume.

Differing attitudes toward women are also reflected in the popular literature of Islamic countries. In Princess' Arūs al-Arā'is, the "bride of brides," the epitome of irresistible beauty and seduction is linked with unfathomable, murderous evil and corruption. [188, 7ff.] By contrast, the merchant's wife Marhūma in the Turkish *Book of Parrots* (she appears as Marjūma in other sources) is the personification of true marital love who defies even the worst trials and tribulations. And everyone knows how the Vizier's beautiful daughter Shahrāzād astutely and patiently conquers her royal spouse's misogyny, born of adverse experience, with her fascinating narrative talent, in the early recensions of the *Arabian Nights*. In the later, Egyptian, version she is spared from execution because she is a good mother and a faithful wife unlike the disloyal wives of the prologue.

These various attitudes were determined by local, ethnic, religious and social factors. Thus Arab women originally had a freer position than those in Sassanid Persia, for instance, and the Turks never restricted the freedom of their women to the extent practiced by other peoples of the Near East. Admittedly, a mere suggestion is all one can give of these differences, partly due to limitations of space but also because of the lack of research to date. A word or two should also be said about the validity of our sources, which mainly reflect the urban society that characterized Islamic culture. Relatively little information is given about the situation of the Bedouins and the peasants. Within the urban and court society, the sources primarily mention the Court circles, the upper strata and their slaves. The Muslim aristocracy considered all other strata of the population, without distinction, as *āmma,* a "great mass" or even "mob," and looked down on them with contempt.

Around 800, a Vizier of the illustrious Iranian Barmakid family divided Islamic society into four "classes:" "(1) rulers, who owe their leading position to merit; (2) Viziers, who are characterized by sagacity and intelligence; (3) persons of high rank, who owe their position to wealth; and (4) the middle class, who are associated with the first three by education. The remainder are dirty scum, a muddy brook, low animals. Each of them only thinks of eating and sleeping." [115, 144]

Thus political rank, wealth and eventually education were the factors which determined one's status. Not even the numerous merchants and craftsmen are included, apart from those who were extremely rich. This is a standpoint that differs totally from the Islamic ideal of social equality of all Muslims.

The best documented sources regarding women deal with the wives of the Prophet, that is, with their relationship with Muhammed, as he was held to be the "fine example" for every good Muslim in all subsequent periods. In what the Arabs call *adab* literature (i.e. the medieval Arab form of belles-lettres), there are charming anecdotes about high-ranking ladies, poetesses, singers, and educated female slaves of the Court circles. Many of these tales, which are partly amusing and partly didactic in character, may be inventions from a later period, but they illustrate how the authors imagined an above-average woman to be—always, of course, from a male viewpoint. In any event, these little tales would have had no effect had they not reflected reality at least to some extent. Since they often provide us with a glimpse, as if through a gap in a curtain, of "intimate life" at that time, several of the tales will be referred to occasionally in the pages that follow.

We have no specific data about most of the women with whom we are concerned here, since a woman had to keep within the protected zone of the harem. In very few cases is the date of birth known, as there were neither registry offices nor birth registers in the Islamic countries until a few decades ago. Variations as to the year of death are also frequent. The sources are mostly full of praise concerning the physical, intellectual and ethical qualities of the women, especially princesses and ladies of society, with the criteria for beauty, wisdom and virtuousness being based, of course, on the time and setting in question.

Women from the common people are to be found in popular tales such as the *Arabian Nights* . The mother of Alā ad-Dīn (Aladdin), known for his magic lamp, says: "I toil away, day and night, spinning cotton to earn a few loaves of bread" [164, II, 656], and although she is atypical, living alone without any family ties or support, we can conclude that this kind of toil was probably the fate of many of the women of the urban proletariat. Only the imagination of the narrator, aided by magical devices, allows such women to escape from their daily toil.

Social utopia is also found in fairy tales. But the one found in the story of Prince Ahmed and the beautiful fairy Perī Bānū a dream of female emancipation, which, even centuries later, has by no means been realized everywhere, is probably the dream of the translator Richard Burton, whose wife Isabel married him against the will of her puritanical family. In the fairy world of Perī Bānū girls are at complete liberty to choose a partner for themselves and do not have to accept the man selected by their parents. This is why marriages there are happy, unlike those in the human world. Girls in the fairy tale world can reveal their feelings to the man they love without having to wait until he courts them. Incidentally, the cosmographic literature of the Muslims contains islands inhabited and ruled exclusively by women.

As relatively little may be assumed to have changed over the centuries in such markedly conservative ways of life, conclusions may be drawn from sociological works of recent decades, such as those about the Bedouin and fellah women of certain districts, about living conditions in the past. Finally, reports by European travelers, from the sixteenth century on, contain information about customs and living conditions, although their accuracy and credibility are variable.

Even more so than literature perhaps, the art of the Islamic countries was a product of Court circles, and its function was to satisfy their predilection for pomp and luxury. It is well known that Islam, like Judaism and early Christianity, is characterized by a hostility toward images. The Koran forbids practicing Muslims to worship idols, but only the literature based on sayings and actions of the Prophet hadīth, written down from the eighth century onward, expressly prohibits the depiction of man and beast. There it is stated that on the Day of Judgment, whoever makes such pictures will be required to breathe life into what he has created. [82, II, 55] This means that the artist has usurped a power of creation belonging to Allah alone. Thus there are no decorative figures in mosques or in copies of the Koran. The state of perfection attained in calligraphy and in geometrical and plant ornamentation, found in the sacral structures of Islam and in manuscripts of the Koran, is probably due to the constraints imposed by this attitude toward sacral art on the one hand and by the persistent desire for ornamentation on the other. Arabic writing, which was adopted by the Persians and the Turks, is, by reason of its flowing elegance, exceptionally well suited to such artistry.

Other than those of the earliest period of Islam, hardly any tableaux or large statues have survived. In secular buildings, however, the ban on pictorial representations of man and beast was not taken so seriously. In harem rooms and baths of Umayyad palaces in the Syrian desert, murals have survived, and statues have also been found in one of the palaces. In the generously-proportioned figures of

Mural from a Caliph's palace in Samarra (ninth century). Female hunter.

women and in the depiction of rulers, riders, hunters and musicians, there are signs of the influence of Late Antiquity. In contrast, the Sassanid tradition predominates in the murals of the Caliph's palace at Samarra. Traces of mural paintings have also been found in other regions of the Islamic world.

From about the eleventh century onward, paintings started to appear in books. To begin with, scientific texts and above all translations of Greek or Syrian works into Arabic were illustrated they were followed, in the thirteenth century, by illustrations of belletristic literature. The miniatures from the Baghdad of the second half of the thirteenth century, which appear in manuscripts of the *Maqāmāt* "assemblies," of al-Harīrī, the polished narratives of an educated vagabond's adventures, achieve a considerable degree of verisimilitude.

From the middle of the thirteenth century, the Mongols began contributing elements of Far Eastern origin, which survived in the miniature paintings of Iran. Subjects for the bookmaker's art in Iran were initially provided by the *Shāh-nāmeh*, the Iranian "national epic," and later by the romantic epics of the poet Nizāmī, his imitators, and Jāmī, who will be discussed later.

There were also other poetic works, mostly of a mystical character. From time to time, historical texts were decorated with miniature paintings; from the fifteenth century on, this was also the case with legends of the Prophet. (Fig. 2)

Schools of painting emerged at the various courts and certain motifs were repeatedly depicted. The painter was regarded far less highly in the Islamic Middle Ages than the calligrapher or the gilder. This is also why so few miniaturists are known to us by name. Only from the sixteenth century on artists signed their miniatures. It was the calligrapher who determined the position and layout of a miniature painting, by arranging the text on the page or by leaving a blank page.

Iranian miniatures of the Middle Ages are charmingly characterized by brilliant colors, by the total lack of perspective in their naïvely sensual presentation, by dreamy, romantic landscapes, and often by boyishly delicate human figures. But precisely because certain subjects were taken up time and time again and because so much was copied, they only have limited value as documentary evidence.

From the twelfth century on, figures are suddenly found on metal and ceramic products. Since Islam prohibits the use of vessels of pure gold or silver—a proscription that was subsequently disregarded —silver was inlaid in a highly artistic manner on vessels of copper or brass, while ceramic products were coated with lustrous gold. These decorations were greatly influenced by the miniature paintings of the period, as was the depiction of figures woven in fabrics and later in carpets. From the mid-sixteenth century, portraits of individuals appeared in Iranian painting, possibly because the Courts no longer patronized artists on the same scale as before, and the latter were now dependent on less wealthy clients who could only afford to collect single pages, not entire manuscripts as rulers did in the past.

Turkish miniature painting (Fig. 17) was more realistic than many of the Iranian paintings, and often contained elements of humor as well. In Mogul paintings, Persian and Indian influences are apparent in the obvious attempt to apply perspective and three-dimensional representation. A notable degree of realism can also be observed in most cases, everyday scenes being depicted, not just life at Court and in the towns.

From the beginning of the nineteenth century, the influence of European art becomes increasingly evident in the art of the Islamic countries. It is at this point that large statues and oil paintings make their appearance.

After this brief overview, we can now turn to the position of women in a sphere that has been aptly described by a German orientalist as "the most decisive expression of Islamic thought" and as "the essential nucleus of Islam in general" [146, 1], this being Islamic law. On Islamic territory, it applied and in some respects still applies only to Muslims; members of other religions were subject to their own jurisdiction. Jews and Christians were, however, free to consult a Muslim *qādī* if they wished to do so.

Woman in Islamic Law, in the Koran and in Tradition

Islamic law, as described here in its broad outlines and as it applies to women, is still in force at the present time, although—in most countries—in a modified form, one which takes modern social conditions into account. Turkey, which was massively secularized under Kemal Atatürk, introduced Swiss civil law in 1926, though not without encountering some difficulties in the course of time.

In the context of divorce, the Koran says that ". . . they (women) have the same right as is exercised over them, though the men have a rank above them." (2: 228) In each religion, every age has its own interpretation of the Holy Scriptures; this is true for Islam as well. Thus liberal Moslems now take the superiority of man over woman to refer only to his greater physical strength and to the responsibility he has toward women. A non-Muslim is inclined to interpret the statement in a way which takes into account the era in which the Koran was written and the circumstances of Muhammed's life; even the first Islamic historians relate the revelations to circumstances in the life of the Prophet.

We would therefore say that the Koran retains the view, prevalent in Antiquity and in the Ancient Orient, that men are essentially superior to women. This is even clearer in another verse from the Koran: "The men are overseers over the women by reason of what Allah hath bestowed in bounty upon one more than another, and of the property which they have contributed. Upright women are therefore submissive, guarding what is hidden in return for Allah's guarding (them); those on whose part ye fear refractoriness, admonish, avoid in bed,

and beat if they then obey you, seek no (further) way against them."
(4:34/38) The economic superiority of men is thus clearly one basis
for the superior status they have enjoyed, not only in the Arabian
Peninsula of the seventh century but in many other countries of the
world, down to the present day. Further, the sexual abstinence recommended here as punishment for an obstinate wife (nāshiza) is proof of
the importance attached to sexuality and sexual fulfillment for women
as well as men in Islam. In a polygynic society however, man can
look for sexual satisfaction with one of his other wives or his slaves.

The Koran is not the only source of Muslim law. Soon after the
death of Muhammed, it was noticed that the prescriptions in the
Koran were not sufficient for the shaping of a life which would be
pleasing to God. And so his followers began by collecting narratives
(hadīth, in Arabic) of what Muhammed did, said or merely tacitly
approved of in certain situations. The aim was to shape one's own life
according to *Sunna* or "custom" the "fine example" of the Prophet, in
other words. This even included such details as Muhammed's pro-
nouncement that it was better to eat and drink with one's right hand,
since the left was used by the Devil. From the eighth century on,
these *hadīths,* which the orientalists call prophetic "traditions" were
recorded in great compendia. Six of these compendia became canonical, particularly those of Bukhārī (d. 870) and of Muslim (d. 875).

If the *hadīths,* such as those which reflect attitudes toward
women, are examined closely, it soon becomes apparent that they
contain a very wide range of views, some of which are contradictory.
In one place, Muhammed is reported to have said: "I have left behind
no temptation more harmful to my community than that which
women represent for men." [82, V, 200] In another, the following saying is also attributed to him: "The whole world is delightful, but the
most delightful thing in it is a virtuous woman." [82, II, 168]

In the traditions, there are anecdotes referring to towns that had
not even been founded or captured during Muhammed's lifetime and
to factions that emerged only after his death. It may therefore be
assumed that this literature does indeed include the *Sunna* of the
Prophet, but reflects to a greater extent the various trends and opinions within the Muslim community in the first two centuries after

Muhammed. The representatives of different views and factions wanted to stabilize a social structure made up of the most diverse elements. They hoped to arrive at a standard of general validity by attributing to the Prophet Muhammed values and modes of behavior which they considered religiously and ethically appropriate. As proof of the authenticity of such traditions, the *isnād* or "chain of authorities" was produced, i.e. the names of those who claimed to have heard this tradition one from the other. Consequently, the ultimate authority always had to be one of Muhammed's companions or one of the members of his family.

Since the Muslims realized, at a fairly early stage, that not everything said to have originated with Muhammed could, in actual fact, have been said by him personally, the successive narrators were the subject of criticism. Just as the collection of traditions became an independent branch of knowledge, with its representatives traveling among the Islamic countries to hear traditions from authorities in the various regions, so another branch of knowledge developed, concerned with the collection and investigation of the biographies of those who handed down these traditions. This was called "the Science of the Men," although a fairly large number of the traditions are attributed to women, to Ā'isha, Muhammed's favorite wife, for example. The last of six volumes in the collection of traditions of Ahmed Ibn Hanbal contains merely traditions attributed to a female authority.

The Koran and the *Sunna* are thus the two principal sources of Islamic law, at least for the Sunnites. The Shī'ites accept only those traditions which go back to Muhammed's cousin and son-in-law Alī and his descendants. Nevertheless, Shī'ite law differs but little from Sunnite law in most cases, since the content of the traditions considered correct by both groups is often identical only the sources are different.

It soon became apparent that passages in the Koran and in the traditions allowed for different interpretations. Another authority was needed, and this was found in the *ijmā'*, the "unanimous consensus, the concurrent opinion of all Muslim scholars alive at the same time in a certain period" [92, 46] on a given problem. This consensus was not established by any sort of commission, such as a council or synod, but had to emerge by itself. In the course of Islamic history, institutions and even doctrinal opinions which did not exist in early Islam have been sanctioned by *ijmā'*: the Caliphate, which only appeared after Muhammed's death, of course; the veneration of saints; and the doctrine of the Prophet's infallibility and freedom from sin, which conflicts with the message of the Koran. The validity of the *ijmā'* is justified by the well-known tradition: "My community shall never agree upon an error."

The fourth and final source of Islamic law is analogies (qiyās, in Arabic); in fact, this is a method of reasoning by. In those cases which are neither to be found in the Koran nor in the *Sunna* nor in the *ijmā'*, an independent decision was made on the analogy of examples contained in the sources. However, there were differences of opinion as to the extent to which analogies could be used. In the course of time, four different schools of law—the Hanafī, Mālikī, Shāfi'ī, and Hanbalī—developed in Sunnite Islam, and these acknowledged each other as alternatives. They are to be found in various regions of the Islamic world, but they do not vary very much in their dogmas.

Since Islamic law deals with every aspect of life from a religious perspective, it also includes moral judgments. There are "Recommended," "Indifferent," and "Reprehensible" categories, as well as "Mandatory" and "Forbidden." This provides ample scope for differences of opinion. However, the application of the category in question is agreed to depend upon the circumstances leading up to the act. These categories have not applied in penal law.

In addition to provisions concerning family law and penal law, Islamic law *(sharī'a)* also contains prescriptions concerning the religious duties of Muslims. The role of women in Muslim observance is examined here.

A number of verses in the Koran are addressed both to men and women. *Sūra* 33:35 reads as follow:

The self-surrendering men and the self-surrendering women, the believing men and the believing women, the obedient men and the obedient women, the truthful men and the truthful

women, the enduring men and the enduring women, the sub-
missive men and the submissive women, the almsgiving men
and the almsgiving women, the fasting men and the fasting
women, the continent men and the continent women, the
Allah-remembering men and the Allah-remembering women -
for them Allah has prepared forgiveness and a mighty
reward.

Contrary to the belief that was widespread in Christendom for centuries, the Islam does not assert that women have no soul. They have the same claim to a place in Paradise as men (see 40:8). However, the misogynistic elements among the pious of the first few centuries, whose numbers evidently increased after contact with Christian asceticism in particular, circulated a tradition that was frequently quoted in later years. Muhammed is reported to have said: "I stood at the gates of Paradise, most of those who entered there were poor, I stood at the gates of Hell, most of those who went in there were women". [82, V, 209f.] This is also explained: "Those who tell secrets when they confide in someone, who are too obstinate when they request something and are ungrateful when they receive it." [82, V, 137]

Still, the Koran does not regard Eve as the seducer of Adam, as she is presented in the Old Testament—that is, as responsible for Man's expulsion from Paradise and for his arduous existence on Earth —but considers that Satan led both of them astray. (2: 34; 7: 19ff.)

The religious duties imposed by Islam on the faithful apply to women just as much as to men, apart from the few restrictions concerning special physiological features of women. Like the sick, menstruating women are required to make up for corresponding fast days later and are likewise freed from prayer and from certain rituals of pilgrimage. This is tied in with concepts concerning the religious uncleanliness of a menstruating woman, a view widely held by many peoples in earlier times. From these few restrictions, the misogynists among the Muslims developed a body of arguments that they claimed established the inferiority of women in the religious sphere. In the same way, they asserted that women were intellectually inferior, pointing out that their testimony was considered to have half the value of a man's. [24, 6, 6] A woman should make a pilgrimage only if accompanied by her husband or a male relative. Opinions are divided as to whether and how long an unaccompanied woman should travel; they vary between not at all and two to three days.

Apart from the obligatory prayers at the mosque on Friday, the Islamic day of rest, Muslims can say their prayers just as well at home as in the mosque. A large number of traditions indicate that in the first centuries of Islam, women took full advantage of their right to pray in the mosque. There are, however, traditions calling on them not to adorn or perfume themselves for their prayers in the mosque. One recommendation that was regularly observed by women entering the mosque for prayer was that they should pray separately from men and place themselves in a row behind them. This is similar to the practice in Orthodox synagogues where, down to the present day, women have their own gallery; likewise, in some village churches of Germany, symbols on the pews indicate that men and women used to sit separately. The purpose of these arrangements was certainly to prevent men and women from being distracted by each other in an unseemly manner in a House of God.

But even at a relatively early period, efforts must have been made to prevent women from attending prayers in a mosque, since traditions warn Muslims against their doing so. With the social degradation of women that accompanied the economic and political decline of the Islamic countries, they were increasingly deprived of the right to pray in a mosque. A woman of any self-respect was not even expected to leave the house once she was married, unless she was obliged to. An example of this is to be found in the trilogy of the well-known Egyptian novelist Naguib Mahfouz (b. 1911), set in Cairo in the first half of the twentieth century. Amīna, the wife of a middle-class merchant, has never left the house since her marriage except in a closed carriage to visit her mother. Encouraged by her sons, the representatives of a new generation, she once satisfies her greatest wish during the First World War while her husband is away and visits the Hosayn Mosque, situated not far from her house. When her husband learns of this, he repudiates her, the mother of his five children, the wife who had shown him obedient affection for many years and who had never failed to meet his every wish. Even in the 1960s, a sociologist reported that women in small towns in Morocco did not enter the mosques, mostly because they were not familiar with the prayer ritual. Those familiar with it were afraid that people might say they only entered the mosque to meet their lovers. They only dared to visit a mosque in the large towns where nobody knew them. [106]

In a few Islamic countries, however, women were allowed to participate in prayers at the mosque on major religious festivals. The Turkish authoress Halidé Edib tells in her memoirs of how, as a child in the 1880s, she accompanied her nurse to a mosque in Istanbul for ceremonial prayer at the end of the month of fasting. She also relates how a sensitive Muslim sees Islamic prayer, the outward ritual of which appears so strange to a non-Muslim:

> *The Imam stood in front of the mihrab, his back to the people, and began the prayer. It is wonderful to pray led by an Imam. He chants aloud the verses you usually repeat to yourself in solitary prayer. You bow, you kneel, your forehead touches the ground. Each movement is a vast and complicated rhythm, the rising and falling controlled by the invisible voices of the several muezzins. There is a beautiful minor chant. The refrain is taken up again and again by the muezzins. There is a continual rhythmic thud and rustle as the thousands fall and rise. The rest belongs to eternal silence.* [39, 72]

Only in large harems, however (that is, before an exclusively female congregation) have women performed the office of the *imām*, the prayer leader.

Still, it should be noted here that women played a considerable role in the religious life of the Islamic countries, especially in mysticism. But this is a subject that will be examined later.

Now to family law. It is taken for granted that a distinction must be drawn between Islamic law per sé and the law that was actually applied in the Islamic countries. "Tell me, what did we ever do that was permitted by law?" to quote the protest of a prince of Mosul in the eleventh century, when he was criticized for being married to two sisters at the same time. [14, 17f.] Expressed as this may be in particularly crass terms, a great deal of literature on legal loopholes exists, showing that ways and means were always being sought to lessen or circumvent the application of the sometimes strict prescriptions. It was certainly not just pettifoggers who indulged in this but also celebrated jurists, famous for their skill in interpreting rules in a pragmatic manner.

One of the punishments laid down in the Koran, flagellation for drinking wine or other alcoholic beverages, was seldom, if ever, applied. At any rate, lyrics in Arabic in praise of wine have existed since the second Islamic century. Persian poets such as Umar Khayyām and Hāfiz lauded wine-drinking as a form of opposition to Orthodox Islam.

In any case, it was probably always true that people mainly felt bound by the provisions in Islamic law concerning the family. As already noted, the Koran explicitly stresses the superiority of men over women, and in actual fact women are legally at a disadvantage in some respects. Down to the present time, according to the Koran (2: 282) the evidence of two women is considered equivalent to that of one man in certain cases of law in Islamic countries, where it is impossible to adduce one male witness. Nevertheless, Islamic law led to an improvement in the position of women in comparison with the pre-Islamic period, especially as regards the laws of marriage and succession. In the pre-Islamic period there was no question of a woman being an heir, since property had to stay within the tribe. Under Islamic law, she inherits half of what male members of the family receive.

Marriage is recommended to the faithful in Islam both in the Koran (24:32) and in the *Sunna,* but it is not a sacrament as it is in the Catholic Church. It still has a certain sacral character according to the Koran, which speaks of a "firm compact" (4: 25/21) between husband and wife. The same expression is used in the Holy Scriptures of the Muslims for the alliance of Allah with Muhammed and with the prophets of the other "book" religions. In Islam, marriage is based on a civil law contract which, in the first centuries, according to the pre-scription in the Koran and just as in Roman law, did not have to be in written form. The parties to the contract are the bridegroom and the bride's guardian *(wālī),* i.e. her closest male relative, usually her father or brother or, if need be, even the judge himself. Two free male witnesses, or one male and two female witnesses, must be pre-sent. The *Sunna* recommends that the bride should not be married without her consent. However, silence is sufficient indication of agreement in the case of a virginal bride, since she is considered to be too shy or timid to speak for herself. When the girl is a minor, her guardian can also force her into marriage, but she has the right to annul this as soon as she is of age. The Mālikī, Shāfiʿī and Hanbalī even permit an adult woman to be forced by her guardian to contract marriage. On the other hand, the Hanafī allow an adult woman to ar-range her own marriage, on condition that she chooses a man of her own rank and fixes an adequate dowry.

According to a large number of traditions, Muhammed recom-mended that anyone wishing to marry a girl or woman should see her first. However, the content of some of these traditions indicates that this was certainly not or no longer customary at the time they appeared or were handed down, and resistance was encountered. In one tradition, for example, a man attempting to look at a girl is reproached by the narrator as follows: "You, a companion of the Prophet, will do this?!" The other replies that Muhammed had recom-mended it. [82, IV, 225] All of the traditions end with the appearance of the girl being pleasing to the narrator and with his marrying her. Clearly, this was a way for the narrator to reinforce his argument.

An important part of the marriage contract is the fixing of the dowry *(mahr* or *sadāq,* in Arabic). To begin with, the *mahr* was not a purchase price, as has often been said, but a kind of compensation the bridegroom had to give the parents of the bride for the loss to the tribe of the sons the woman would bear. The evidence for this is that the *mahr* was not paid when the girl married her cousin on her father's side; that is, when she remained in the tribe. This is still true among Bedouins today. The *sadāq* was the wedding gift the girl received. As early as the time of Muhammed, a distinction was no longer made between these two terms. The *mahr* or the *sadāq* was given to the bride, and it symbolized the status that she had. In Europe, for centuries, it was customary for parents to give their daughter a dowry when she got married. Not seldom, this led to the bride's being considered an unavoidable addition to property one could only acquire by marriage. If, in the Islamic Orient even today, the man is required to give the woman a dowry upon marriage, the European form of "marriage for money" is certainly excluded. The Islamic custom provides an opportunity for the parents of the bride to deny an unwelcome suitor their daughter, by making excessively high demands.

The *mahr* was, and mostly still is, used for the purchase of furnishings for the household and of clothing for the wife. In earlier times it even consisted of such articles. The various schools of law quote different minimum and maximum figures for the dowry; but marriage contracts that have survived indicate that the top limit could be greatly exceeded. The origin and rank of the bride, her age or rather her youth, her beauty—in short, whether or not she was a desirable match—determined the size of the dowry.

In the early Muslim community, it was obviously recommended to give a suitor the chance to marry by fixing a dowry appropriate to his circumstances. Thus one tradition tells of a man who wanted to marry but possessed nothing he could give to the woman as dowry. Muhammed decided that he should have her for the sections of the Koran he knew by heart. [24, 67, 14] Incidentally, this woman had offered herself in marriage to the Prophet himself, and it is said that she was not the only one to do so. This is proof of the magnetism Muhammed must have had for those around him. It is also evidence of a self-confidence on the part of women in Ancient Arabia that is totally lacking not only among Muslim women of later centuries. There are reports of other women who were married to Muhammed but who, when he came to them in the bridal chamber, said: "I take refuge from you in God." At this, so it goes, he had them sent back to their families without delay. [87, VIII, 100ff.] This, too, shows that Arab women at the time of Muhammed were assertive enough to make no secret of their desires or disinclination.

It was often agreed in the marriage contract that a part of the dowry was to be paid only in the event of divorce, so as to protect the wife from hasty action by her husband. Payment in installments was also possible if a fairly large down-payment was made at the time of the wedding.

Islam allows a man to have more than one wife at a time. Opinions differ as to whether polygyny was prevalent on the Arabian Peninsula before the time of Muhammed. Recent European research [158, 62, 81; 176, 274ff.] indicates that there is no unequivocal evidence of this, at least as far as Mecca and Medina are concerned. Admittedly, early Islamic historians tell of a man having several wives, but they also list the various husbands of many women. These early historians assume that for the women it was a question of marriages contracted one after the other, as was true in later periods. However, this could equally well have been the case for men. It is a fact that there were polygynous marriages in other countries of the Middle East, such as Iran, in the pre-Islamic period. It is just as certain that very loose sexual mores were the rule in pre-Islamic Arabia. It was actually through Islam that the institution of marriage contracts was first introduced to the Arabian Peninsula.

The verse in the Koran from which the right of man to a polygynous marriage has been derived for centuries reads as follows: "If ye fear that ye may not act with equity in regard to the orphans, marry such of the women as seem good to you, double or treble or fourfold —but if ye fear that ye may not be fair, then one (only) or what your right hands possess; that is more likely to secure that ye be not partial . . . " (4:3) Modern Muslims often interpret this verse as essentially an exhortation in favor of monogamy, since at another point the Koran states that a man who is married to several wives at the same time cannot be equally just to all of them. (4:128/129) Still, the first part of the verse might suggest that Muhammed was concerned here with the maintenance of the widows and especially the daughters of men killed in battle during the early years of Islam. Muhammed, himself an orphan, often regarded himself as the advocate of the weak and underprivileged. Consequently, at a time when marriage represented the only way for a woman to be provided for, the Koran recommends marriage to widows and female orphans. This assumption is supported by the fact that the verse quoted probably dates from the time immediately after the battle of the Muslims against the Meccans at Ukhud in which many Muslims lost their lives. Muhammed himself set an example for his community and married two widows of slain Muslims. Indeed, in most of his marriages, if not in all of them, he is said to have had the solidarity of his community in mind.

Islamic law requires a man to provide each of his wives with a household of her own. Thus polygyny was usually the privilege of the prosperous who, in addition to their wives, could also select any number of concubines from among their slaves.

As impediments to marriage, Islamic law lists situations and conditions similar to those that preclude marriage in many other societies; an excessively close blood relationship, for example, or a relationship by marriage (4: 26ff.) or by foster-relationship. Furthermore, the law prescribes that a man may not be married to two sisters at the same time. A Muslim woman may not marry a non-Muslim, but a Muslim man is permitted to marry a Jewish or a Christian woman. The man should not be of a lower rank than the woman, but the converse is permissible (except for the Shī'ites).

After the death of her husband, a free woman must observe a period of mourning of four months and ten days. After a divorce, she must wait three months before remarrying. Men, however, are permitted to remarry immediately. (2:234, 228) The waiting period for the woman was introduced by Muhammed in order to determine whether the woman was expecting a child, so that the paternity could be established without any doubt. If the woman was pregnant, she could only re-marry after the birth of the child.

As in the pre-Islamic time, extreme youth was no bar to marriage, at least not in medieval Islam. Muhammed himself married his favorite wife Ā'isha, the daughter of Abu Bakr, one of his closest associates and future first caliph, when she was six years old. When she came to him, she was nine and still played with dolls, according to historical reports. It was later laid down that a mentally healthy Muslim became marriageable at puberty, but there is a difference of opinion as regards age.

The duties of the man in marriage include providing his wife or wives with shelter, food and clothing. If she is accustomed to being waited on, he must provide her with a female servant. At least according to the law, the wife cannot be required to contribute to the upkeep of the household by doing work or by a financial contribution. However, among the poor, she would certainly have been obliged to do so. In Islamic marriage, there is no joint ownership of property. The wife can therefore freely dispose of her own property and in this respect is in a substantially more favorable position than European women have enjoyed for centuries. According to early traditions, the duties of the wife include feeling responsible for her husband's household and for those belonging to it.

Traditions of later periods, it is true, give the husband the highest possible authority not only over the wife's possessions, but also over her sexual behavior toward him, over her decision to fulfill her religious duties and even over her merely leaving the house. [see 120, IV, 411f.] They thus contradict the *shari'a* but doubtless reflect the customs of later centuries.

The Koran has this to say about the relations between husband and wife in marriage: "Amongst His signs is that He hath created for you of your own species spouses that ye may dwell with them, and hath set love and mercy between you." (30: 20) Here, as in later traditions in which women are defined as mothers, sisters, and daughters, their roles are defined from a man's point of view, women are seen in their family relations and in their sociability with men. We have similar anthropological patterns in Judaism and Christianity. But it is to be emphasized that the Koran and the greater part of the traditions define these relations as based on love.

One of the few marriage deeds that has survived, dating from thirteenth-century Egypt, contains the recommendation that the husband should "make his relations with her (his wife) pleasant" and that she is under the same obligation toward him. [35, 170] Traditions urge the man to treat his wife well, as in the following, which refers to the concept prevalent in the Ancient Orient that woman was created from one of the ribs of man: "Treat the women well, for woman was created from a rib, and the most curved part of the rib is the top part. Should you try to bend it straight, you will destroy it, but if you leave it as it is, it remains curved. So treat the women well!" [24, 60, 1] A modern woman would certainly object to this lofty attitude of male superiority, but it should be recalled, for instance, that as late as the seventeenth century, there were arguments in central Germany as to whether women were human beings at all. [74]

The ideal image of a good Muslim wife is to be found in a tradition that relates how Muhammed answered the question of what the best wife should be: "She who pleases him when he looks at her, obeys him when he commands, and does not oppose him in things which he rejects for her and for himself." [82, II, 25] She should thus be pretty and submissive, although later chapters will show that intelligent women were often prepared to accept anything but this ideal of submission to the will of a man.

The famous theologian, mystic and religious reformer al-Ghazālī (1058-1111), in the part of his *Revival of the Religious Sciences* which deals with marriage, defines the advantages of marriage:

1. Offspring (that is the origin, and for this marriage was instituted)
2. The overcoming of carnal desire (to be protected from the devil)
3. The organization of the household (to spare the heart the organization of household affairs, the cooking, sweeping, spreading the carpets for sleeping, cleansing the vessels, caring for livelihood)
4. The increase of the kinsfolk (gaining more strength by the mixing of the families to protect oneself against evil and to gain welfare/security by helpers)
5. The endeavor of the soul to care for them (the women) or to bear them.

What is notable here is the completely male-oriented, thoroughly patriarchal standpoint of this famous theologian. He was born in Khorasan, near the modern Meshhed, was later a professor at the Nizamiyya, an Islamic High-school in Baghdad, and one of the most outstanding figures in the town. In his opinion, a woman in her role as housewife and spouse is a man's helper to religion, a helper on his way to God and to paradise, because she protects him against carnal desire and spares him tiresome work like the household affairs mentioned above. Men, by comparison, are the intellectual guides for women on their way to religion and paradise. Al-Ghazālī, who quotes a large number of traditions confirming different standpoints towards women and marriage, sees women from an ambivalent perspective. On one hand, he states that "in intimacy with women there is a rest, which does away with sorrow and refreshes the heart, and for the souls of the pious men relaxations by permissible actions are necessary." On the other hand, concerning the fifth point listed above, he explains that it consists in "patience towards womens' characters, in enduring the trouble and insults from them, in the effort to encourage them and to guide them in the right way to religion." The famous theologian seems to have been somewhat absentminded when he wrote this part of his voluminous and well-known religious work—which was and is regarded as the pious Muslim's guide to a life pleasing to God—because there is a certain disorder in the points and their explanations. When he speaks about the evils of marriage (he gives three disadvantages and five advantages) and mentions as the first and strongest one "the difficulties of providing for the family's legitimate keep in these times of disturbances of living," one gets a glimpse into the social circumstances of the time. This chapter of Al-Ghazālī's book is a rather dry and rational debate of the reasons that speak for and against marriage. It is the debate of a man, who, as a religious reformer, is famous for assigning equal importance to heart and intellect, but of whose personal life, especially his own relations to women, we know practically nothing. But in speaking about the sexual life in marriage he stresses women's right to sexual fulfilment and admonishes men to try to avoid premature climax.

The Arabic word zinā' that is often translated by the word "adultery" really means something more than that, namely any sexual relations between a woman and a man who are not bound to each other by a legal marriage, and, as long as slavery existed, intimate relations between a man and a slave who did not belong to him. All this is punishable in Islam for man and woman alike.

In *Sura* 24: 2, it is stated: "The fornicatress and the fornicator—scourge each of them with a hundred stripes; let no pity affect you in regard to them in the religion of Allah, if ye have come to believe in Allah and the Last Day." A number of the faithful should be present as witnesses to this punishment. At a relatively early stage, it became the custom, deriving from Jewish penal law, to stone the adulterous pair and not to flog them. The application of such a harsh punishment was greatly restricted, however, by the demand specified at another place in the Koran (4: 19) that four witnesses must be able to testify to the adultery. Since they were required to have witnessed the act itself, it must have been difficult in most cases to find the necessary witnesses. A man who accuses a woman of infidelity and cannot provide four witnesses of this is to receive eighty strokes of the lash for slander. To avoid this punishment, however, he can repeat his allegation four times, calling on Allah to witness the truth of it. His wife can defend herself by likewise swearing four times that her husband has lied. After this fourfold oath, the two of them must call on Allah to curse them should they not have told the truth. (24: 6-9)

It was an episode that took place in Muhammed's own family that led to this severe punishment for libel. Muhammed usually drew lots before he set out on a military expedition to determine which of his wives should accompany him. Thus it happened that he took his wife Ā'isha along on one of his campaigns against a Bedouin tribe; she was thirteen years of age at the time and accompanied the train in a closed litter on the back of a camel. One evening, while the people were preparing to set off again, Ā'isha went away from the others to answer a call of nature. On the way back, she later said, she noticed that she had lost her necklace and retraced her steps. When she at last returned to the camp, she found that Muhammed and his band had already departed. At that time, Ā'isha was a slight little person—she herself said it was a result of the Muslims' frugal diet—and the men who placed her litter on the camel did not even realize that she was not in it. Ā'isha wrapped herself in her robe and lay down in the desert sand, hoping that the others would return when they noticed she was missing. A young man then appeared, one of the followers of Muhammed,

Calligraphic illuminated page with the Basmala

who for some reason had also been left behind by the others. Ā'isha did not yet wear a veil, so he recognized her immediately and tried to talk to her. But she gave him no answer, she subsequently said. He placed her on his camel and led the animal along. When they finally caught up with the others on the following morning, her absence had not yet been noticed. But now the storm broke. All those to whom the young woman was a thorn in the flesh because she was so greatly favored by Muhammed, as well as those who bore ill will toward him, contributed to the gossip about her. As Ā'isha later said, she was the last to hear of all this. She only noticed that Muhammed was not so friendly to her as hitherto. She fell ill and with Muhammed's permission returned to her parents to be looked after. Muhammed, deeply wounded and confused, asked others for their advice. A variety of opinions was expressed. The harshest was that of his cousin Alī, who may have been goaded by his wife, Fātima, Muhammed's daughter, who maybe resented the privileged position of her youthful stepmother. "There are women enough," he said, "you could make another her successor"—a remark for which Ā'isha never forgave him, as future events would show. But in the end, Muhammed decided in favor of Ā'isha. He visited her at her parents' house to urge her to show remorse, but she wept and refused since this would have been an admission of guilt. It was then revealed to Muhammed that all the rumors were "slander" and that those who had spread them were "liars," and it was this revelation which led to the provisions described above. Some of those whose words had been especially harsh received eighty strokes of the lash. The wise Ā'isha subsequently remarked that hitherto she had considered herself too slight and insignificant for Allah to have revealed a verse of the Koran on her account, one which was then recited in the mosque and used in prayer; she had only hoped that God would reveal her innocence to Muhammed in a dream. [84, 736ff.]

A large group of the Shī'a also recognized another form of marriage, which was still common in the early years of Islam until it was prohibited by Caliph Umar, a man of strict morality. This was the *mut'a,* which is generally translated as "temporary marriage" or "marriage of sexual pleasure." A Shī'ite was allowed to contract a "marriage" for a certain period of time. This usually happened when a man was traveling, since it was not customary for a wife to accompany her husband. The sole purpose of such a "marriage" was to enable a man to satisfy his sexual desires in a legal manner but without founding a household or producing children. Nevertheless, when a child resulted from such a union, it enjoyed equal rights with children from other marriages under the law of succession.

All other forms of "marriage" practiced in Arabia up to the time of Muhammed were done away with by Muhammed. These included, for instance, the custom whereby a man whose wife had remained childless would send her to another, preferably to one of high social rank, for a short time, so that she might conceive, or the group marriage of several men with one woman, or a form of marriage in which a son inherited his stepmother from his dead father or his sister-in-law from his deceased brother, so that they would be looked after.

In Islam, like in Christianity, the death of one of the two spouses in a marriage signifies the end of that marriage. However, a marriage might also be dissolved by *talāq*, the repudiation of the wife by the husband. Islamic law permits every man in a healthy mental state to do this without having to give any reason for it and without consulting a judge. However, there are traditions which describe the *talāq* as the act most hateful to God among all acts permitted by law.

The form of the *talāq* that emerged as customary, until the law was modified in many Islamic countries in recent decades, was as follows: The man pronounces the formula of repudiation—variations in the choice of words exist—twice, either in immediate succession or with a month inbetween. At that point, he can still take it back. Only after the third time is the divorce valid. It is laid down in the Koran that after the divorce the husband must provide for a wife who is suckling a child until it is weaned this can extend to a period of two years. (2: 233)

If the man desires to remarry the woman, even though he has repudiated her three times, there is a provision for this which may seem odd at first sight. The original idea behind it, however, was doubtless to protect the wife from a hasty step the husband might take. According to this provision, a wife who has been repudiated must first marry another and be repudiated by him in turn before she can go back to her first husband. (2: 230) This led some men, usually those who were not believed to possess excessive virility, to make themselves available (in return for a fee) for fictitious marriages, after which they would quickly repudiate the women who could then remarry their original husbands. In a pleasant little story, the Egyptian author Mahmūd Taymūr (1894-1973) presents such a "good sheikh," to whom men entrust their divorced wives in the belief that he is too unworldly to touch them. In the end, however, he falls in love with one of these women and does not wish to give her back.

There is only a limited number of ways in which a wife can free herself from her husband. The *khul'*, or redemption, was adopted from heathen practice and consists in the wife's purchasing her freedom from her husband by the payment of a certain sum–frequently equivalent to the dowry. But the wife or her guardian can also have a clause included in her marriage contract specifying that she can oblige her husband to pronounce the *talāq* under certain conditions: if he beats her, for example, or wishes to marry a second wife. Nevertheless, the extent to which a woman can take really advantage of this possibility depends, to a very great degree, firstly on her self-confidence and secondly on the social position of divorced women in general. In Muslim India, for instance, this type of marriage contract was widespread in the 1950s, but in Egypt, as I was informed in the spring of 1977 by several sources, including a deputy of the Minister of Justice, only a few women had the courage to have a marriage contract prepared in this form. In certain instances, such as when she can prove that her husband is not able to provide for her, is impotent or is suffering from a mental disorder, an adult woman can demand that a judge dissolve the marriage.

The provisions determining whether children are regarded as legitimate, apart from those actually born during a marriage—according to Hanafite law, every child born within two years after the dissolution of the marriage is legitimate—are to be explained by the medical knowledge, or rather lack of medical knowledge, of the time. The mother has the right of custody for girls until they are of age or until they marry and for boys until puberty or the age of seven years. However, the father is the legal guardian of the children; only when they are poor he is obliged by law to maintain them. Thus the mother usually returns to her family, which maintains her, with the children she has to look after.

One of the numerous anecdotes of classical Arab literature tells of how a mother fought before a judge for her son, who was claimed by the father, the child probably having reached the age of seven years.

She said: "This is my son. My womb was a vessel for him, my lap a courtyard to play for him, my breasts were milksprings for him. When he awakes I care for him with delight, I protect him when he sleeps at night. For several years I have done this, and now, when he is fully weaned, his limbs are well formed and his character has proved to be fine, his father wants to take this son of mine." The judge then said to the husband: "You have heard the words of your wife, what do you have to answer them with?" The man replied: "She has spoken the truth, but I carried him in me before she gave birth to him, and I placed him in her before she put him in the world. I will teach him knowledge and wise wisdom." The judge turned to the woman: "What is your answer to this, woman?" She replied: "He is right in what he says. But he carried him when he was weak and light, while I was burdened with his weight. He put him in me yearningly, while I put him to the world with agony." Her words were pleasing to the judge, and he ordered the man: "Give her her son, for she has more right to him than you." [19, 6ff]

If this little story is to be believed, judges were sometimes led by the well-chosen words of a clever woman to turn a blind eye to legal regulations and to show more humanity than was provided for by the law.

In Islamic law, slaves occupied a special position in a certain sense. Like Judaism and Christianity, Islam did not do away with slavery, which existed as an institution throughout the Ancient Orient. It did attempt, however, to improve the living conditions of the slaves.

In the Koran the emancipation of slaves is recommended as a meritorious act (2: 177), and traditions refer to slaves as the "brothers" of Muslims and advise the latter to treat them well and to provide for their maintenance. Only those captured as infidels in war or born into slavery could be slaves in Islam. For a debtor, say, to sell his children or others or even himself into slavery was prohibited by law, but it probably happened on occasion. Incidentally, the slave trade between Christian and Islamic countries of the Mediterranean area was a flourishing and profitable business for centuries.

In law, slaves were regarded as objects or things. Good-looking and well-educated female slaves often served as valuable gifts with which to obtain the favor of high-ranking persons. In fact, under certain conditions, both male and female slaves could rise to very influential positions and achieve great prosperity. There were, for instance, slave dynasties, such as the Mamlūks in Egypt. Clever and adroit slaves were often employed in shops and in trade. There was no industrial slavery.

Basically, slaves had no legal power, but they had certain rights as persons. With the consent of their master, they were allowed to marry up to two female slaves, or up to four among the Mālikī. Still, a slave owner could force his slaves to marry. A female slave could marry a free Muslim; the children of such marriages were slaves. But she could not marry her own master unless he first set her free. In this case, her children were also free. Slaves could be used as concubines by their masters, but only by them; slaves could not be forced into prostitution, as had obviously often been the case in pre-Islamic Arabia. A free Muslim woman clearly did not have the right to concubinage with one of her slaves. According to the Mālikī, the female slave had the right to share the nights of her master with his free wife on an equal basis, but other schools of law allowed her only one night in every three.

In other respects, too, certain conditions and responsibilities which Islamic family law imposed upon free persons were restricted as far as slaves were concerned. The punishment for immorality (zinā') and for slander in connection with immorality, for example, was only half of that fixed for a freeman. The period a widowed or divorced female slave was required to wait before remarrying was shorter than for a free person. A slave could repudiate his wife but could take her back only after one *talāq* had been pronounced. The owner of a female slave who was married, regardless of whether her husband was free or a slave, did not have the right to make her his concubine. Nor was this allowed when a female slave was owned by several men. The owner of a female slave who had borne her master a child was no longer entitled to sell her, give her away, or use her as a pledge after the birth of the child, and she became free on her master's death. In law, the children of legal concubines had exactly the same status as the children of free wives. As will subsequently be seen, this provision was of great importance in the further development of Muslim society.

Since the mid-nineteenth century, starting with the more progressive Islamic countries, decrees were issued for the restriction of slavery. Most Islamic countries officially ended slavery in the constitutions adopted after the First World War. In conservative countries of the Arabian Peninsula, such as Saudi Arabia and Bahrain, slavery was ended only recently.

It is thus evident that the Sharī'a draws social distinctions between men and women and between free persons and slaves. However, all free women are equal before the law, whatever social stratum they belong to.

In the 33rd *Sūra* of the Koran, dating from the time spent by Muhammed as the respected head of the Islamic community in Medina, there are special provisions concerning the position within the young Muslim community to be held by the wives of the Prophet, by then nine. The same *Sūra* emphasizes Muhammed's right to special provisions unlike all other Muslims, who were permitted to have four legal wives at most. It is unlikely that those around the Prophet would have criticized the special privileges he claimed for himself. They probably considered it self-evident that an exceptional personality like Muhammed should enjoy special rights. In the same 33rd *Sūra*, the additional name of "Mother of the Faithful" is given to the wives of Muhammed, and they are forbidden to marry again after his death. Much has been written and said about the wearing of the veil by women in Islam. Basically, there is no binding prescription for this in Islamic law, but there are suggestions, as in the 33rd *Sūra*, which says: *"O prophet, say to thy wives, and thy daughters, and the womenfolks of the believers, that they let down some (part) of their mantles over them; that is more suitable for their being recognized and not insulted."* (33: 59)

A verse from another *Sūra*, which is quoted as evidence of the exhortation to women to veil themselves, reads:

Tell the believing women to cast down their eyes and guard their private parts and not show their ornaments, except so far as they (normally) appear, and let them throw their scarves over their bosoms and not show their ornaments except to their husbands or their fathers or the fathers of their husbands, or their sons or the sons of their husbands, or

69

their brothers or the sons of their brothers, or the sons of
their sisters, or their womenfolk, or those in their possession
(i.e. slaves) . . . (24: 31)

In neither of these two passages is there any specific mention of veiling the face, only of a certain more general covering. The second of the two verses quoted seems to assume that certain parts of the body were visible anyway. Opponents of veiling, such as the free-thinker Jāhiz in the ninth century [49, 57 ff.], have also pointed out that while on a pilgrimage, one of the "pillars" of Islamic faith—in the state of *ihrām* (ritual consecration), as it is called—men and women are required to uncover face and hands.

It is known that noble ladies of the trading city of Mecca wore veils even before Islam. In one tale, set in the market place of the Ancient Arabian city of Ukaz, a group of jaunty youths struck up a conversation with a young girl from another tribe. The young lady was veiled and wore a gown with a train. Full of admiration, they bade her to reveal her face, but this favor she refused them. One of the youths then approached her from behind and, without her noticing it, fastened her train to the neck of her robe–the others probably distracting her attention by talking to her. When she stood up, she unwittingly revealed her naked back to the rowdy throng. The layabouts hooted with laughter and mocked her: "She refused to let us look at her face, now we can see her back." This demeaning treatment of a young woman caused a bloody feud. [104, 15ff.] Incidentally, the story also indicates that women of that time, even though they were veiled, could converse freely with men.

The veil already existed in countries that were conquered by the Muslims, such as Persia. In the Ancient Near East, among the Assyrians and Babylonians, the veil was a symbol of class distinctions. It was the right of free women to wear it. In contrast, the slave who did this was liable to be punished. An early Arabian historian explains *Sūra* 3: 59 in this way; Muhammed's wives had been bothered by his opponents in Medina when they left the house at night to relieve themselves, because they took unveiled women for slaves [87, VIII, 126ff.]

The custom of wearing the veil spread quickly, at least in the upper tiers of society. In the countryside, among the Bedouins and wherever women had to perform heavy physical toil, the veil was more of a nuisance, and the custom of wearing it has never been strictly observed. The veiling of female slaves was likewise not taken seriously, and the Koran permits women "past child-bearing" a less strict covering. (24: 60)

If we wish to use miniatures as documentary evidence, we must conclude that even high-ranking ladies did not always strictly adhere to the wearing of veils, not only in the urban society of thirteenth-century Iraq (Fig. 13), but also that of fifteenth-century Iran (Fig. 3). We often find examples of distinguished ladies without veils meeting with freemen who were not related to them, at least in their own gardens and palaces, but not only there. Admittedly, these miniatures are illustrations to literary texts, but one may assume that the painters were inspired by their environment. Moreover, reports by European travellers confirm these observations, for fifteenth-century Iran in any case. [64, 171f.] When visiting the mosque (Fig. 12) and also when female aristocrats mixed with the people, the hair and the lower part of the face were certainly always covered. But when ladies of noble houses appear without veils on Indian miniatures of the Mughal period, we know that these ladies did not sit for the portraits themselves; one of their female slaves did it for them.

At times, certain men, such as social revolutionaries who appeared in the garb of a prophet, also wore veils. One such was the leader of the Zanj insurrection by black slaves who were used for the drainage of swamps in Southern Iraq in the second half of the ninth century. In most later miniatures, the Prophet Muhammed is shown with a veil over his face, but it is not like the veil worn by women, as the eyes were covered. (Fig. 7)

Closely connected with the veil is the exclusion of women from public life. This is based on a verse in the Koran which clearly refers to the wives of the Prophet: ". . . When ye ask them (i.e. the wives of the Prophet) for any article, ask them from behind a curtain; that is purer for your hearts and for theirs." (33: 53; see also 33: 55). It is reported in an Arab historical work dating from the ninth century that this revelation originated at the marriage of Muhammed to the beautiful Zaynab Bint Jahsh, former wife of his adopted son Zayd Ibn Hāritha. Muhammed had once seen Zaynab in her undergarments as he was about to enter Zayd's house and had coveted her from then on. Zayd, who was very much attached to his adoptive father, wanted to divorce her immediately so that Muhammed could marry her, but Muhammed did not want to accept Zayd's offer. But Zaynab had been married with Zayd against her will and now displayed a clear lack of affection for him. In the end, her marriage with Muhammed took place. Toward the end of the wedding feast, the guests showed no signs of departing. Muhammed impatiently left the room several times and went out into the courtyard, hoping that he would finally be left alone with his new bride. But this was not the case. It was now that the verse quoted above was revealed to him. [87, VIII, 74ff.] This shows that Zaynab's attractiveness for her guests—at the time, she was in her mid- or even late thirties—was considered to have been very great.

In Sassanid Persia, it was the custom for high-ranking persons to be hidden by a curtain from the sight of ordinary mortals. We do not know whether Muhammed was aware of this. However, even the first Umayyad Caliph Mu'āwiya was often separated from his subjects by a curtain, especially when he was not in full control of his senses, on account of an excessively high alcohol consumption. In later times, some of the Islamic dynasties, such as the Fātimids in Egypt, evolved their own ceremonial in connection with this. Thus, originally the veil and the curtain were symbols of honor and rank.

The restriction of women to the domestic area, which grew out of the use of the veil and curtain, and their exclusion from public life, which was paralleled by increasing limitations on their opportunities for education, proved to have unfavorable consequences for the social position of women and for the development of the whole of society in the Islamic countries in the course of later centuries.

Life in Family and Society

In most cases, the birth of a girl caused a mother less joy than that of a boy. Even before anything was said to her or the child shown to her, she could guess that she had given birth to a daughter from the fact that the women attending her at the birth did not rejoice aloud and praise Allah as soon as the child arrived, but kept their voices low as they whispered to one another. [78, 255] This applied to all levels of society, from the Bedouins and peasants to the lower, middle and upper classes in the towns and even to Court circles. The wealthy did not consider the arrival of a baby girl an occasion for an elaborate feast of joy, as was customary at the birth of a son. The reason for this was essentially a practical one; existence was an uncertain matter in those times, and a son could contribute to the maintenance of the family. Among the Bedouins, he could even help in defending against enemies, whereas a girl could not. Furthermore, when a girl married, she left her own family to live with that of her husband and, added to its strength with the sons she bore. Among the Bedouins of pre-Islamic Arabia, it even happened that baby girls were buried alive in the sand of the desert immediately after their birth. This was strictly forbidden by the Koran, which also censured fathers for scowling at the birth of a daughter and being resentful of their fate. (16: 58f.) Yet it explains the reason for this cruel custom: fear as a result of poverty, or more precisely, dire need.

The child's name was chosen by the parents. In most of the Islamic countries even today, the standard names for girls include names from the family of the Prophet, such as that of his mother Āmina, of his wives Khadīja, Ā'isha and Zaynab, and of his daughters

Fātima, Umm Kulthūm and Ruqayya. Just like everywhere else, the chosen names were and are subject to fashion, family traditions, and local or social factors. Either directly after the birth or, in many places, seven days later, a teacher of religion would come to the parents' dwelling and whisper the name, the call to prayer and the Islamic creed in the child's ear. With this, the child was received into the community of the faithful and, according to superstitious beliefs, protected from being harmed by evil spirits.

The *Sunna* further stipulated that a child's hair should be shorn on the seventh day and a sacrificial animal be slaughtered in his honor. Here, too, the lesser esteem in which girls were held becomes evident. For a boy child two wethers were slaughtered, for a girl child only one; or the offering was even omitted. The meat of the sacrificial animal was given to the poor. The faithful were also asked to weigh the shorn hair of the child and to offer its weight in silver or gold as alms. This custom clearly originated from Ancient Arabic paganism but was approved of by Muhammed. There is a whole series of little poems in classical Arabic literature which reveal the various feelings aroused by the birth of a girl. An Arab poetess indicates how a daughter was regarded in the family:

> *How can I help it that she is a girl?*
> *She washes my hair and is a credit to me,*
> *She brings me the veil that has fallen down,*
> *And when she is bigger and is eight,*
> *She will look splendid in a Yemenite gown.*
> *I will marry you to Marwān or Mu'āwiya,*
> *Noble men, for a high dowry certainly.*
> [174, 221]

Concern about the future of a little girl could also give rise to such pessimistic verses as these:

> *Is Wasnā not like a pearl,*
> *At least in her soft little gown of silk.*
> *But her loveliest gown is a spotless shroud*

In which she is wrapped on the bier
And when she is hurriedly buried,
Our heart leaps and jumps with joy.
[174, 223]

This concern in an environment which is basically well-disposed toward children could also be expressed in another way:

If I had no little daughters,
Small and tender like downy chicks,
The Earth would offer me space enough
To look for my livelihood
Yet our children are for us
like our hearts wandering over the Earth:
If but a gentle breeze touches one of them,
We find no peace from pain.
[174, 224]

The Arab poet Bashshār Ibn Burd (d. 784) mourns the death of a daughter in the following poem:

O my little daughter, whom I did not want,
You were hardly five when Death took you away.
Then I had loved you so tenderly,
That sorrow seemed to break my heart.
Yes, you were better than a son,
Who's to drink at dawn and pays whores at night.
[Ibid.]

It would seem that even at that time the education of sons was not without its problems. Traditions of a rather late time recommend different kinds of education and socialization for boys and girls, and thus inform us about the prevalent customs, at least in the court society: "A son has a claim against his father to learn writing, swimming and throwing javelins." In the upper and middle strata of the towns population boys should be taught the Sūrat al-Mā'ida, the fifth *Sūra,* which contains several religious prescriptions concerning the prayer ceremonies, concerning different foods, concerning the forbiddance of drinking alcohol, of games of chance, and of venerating idols. It also concerns the relations between the Muslims and adherents of the other "book religions," the Christians and the Jews, but which allow a Muslim to marry a Christian or a Jewish woman. Concerning girls, one of these rather late traditions states: "Don't teach women writing, teach them spinning and the Sūrat an-Nūr." This is the twenty-fourth *Sūra*, which contains prescriptions concerning the punishment for zinā', fornication or adultery, and prescriptions for modest relations between men and women, especially for womens' modest behavior and clothing. [174, 109]

The little girl grew up in the women's quarters of the house or in the women's part of the tent. The Arabic name for the former is *harīm*, while the Persian-Indian designation is *zenāneh*. The term *harīm* has come to us, via Turkish, in the form "harem," and is associated with a great deal of fantasy about voluptuous extravagance and sensual pleasures. In fact, the Arabic word *harīm* designated a holy and inviolable place, since, in the Arab view, it was through his female relatives that the honor of a man could be most profoundly violated. The harem, the part of the house where the female members of the family and household lived, was normally out of bounds to all males except the master of the house, his sons, and perhaps a physician. At the same time, *harīm* also referred to the women who dwelt in this area; that is, a man's wife or wives, his mother, sisters, daughters and daughters-in-law. In the palaces of the great men of the country, the Caliphs, Sultans, Emirs and Viziers, the harem usually consisted of a sizable number of persons-not only the wives of the master of the house but also their numerous female servants, his concubine's the children of all these women and eunuchs to attend and watch over them.

Relatively little is known about the education of girls in Islamic countries before the beginning of modern times (in the nineteenth century). It was certainly dependent to a large extent on their social position. It is probable that the majority of them were prepared for their future role as housewives from early childhood; that is, they were familiarized with domestic activities, including needlework, and practiced them from an early age. At any rate, this is what sociologists report about the Bedouins in Central Arabia [134] and small Moroccan towns in the second half of the twentieth century [106], whose markedly conservative way of life has probably changed little in the course of the centuries.

Girls from patrician families, with a tradition of erudition, were certainly also instructed in the fundamentals of the Islamic sciences. They were sometimes given the same thorough education as their brothers, who had private teachers, but the girls were entrusted to female teachers only. It must have been exceptional for anyone to give his daughters the same education as his sons, since otherwise it would not have been given special mention in the texts. Nevertheless, Arab biographical literature name works of a whole series of women who were outstanding in the science of traditions, especially up to the tenth century but in later periods as well.

Until the beginning of the twentieth century, the educational establishment for the majority of children from the lower strata of the urban population was the Koran school, which was almost always reserved for boys. For a small charge, the children learned to recite the Koran by heart, to read and write, and to grasp the basic concepts of arithmetic. If one is to believe the romantic epic of the Persian Nizāmī, which narrates the famous love story of Laylā and Majnūn in poetic form, there must also have been some mixed Koran schools, since it was in the Koran school that Laylā and Majnūn fell in love with each other. (Fig. 14)

Daughters of royal families may well have had the same upbringing as Qudiya Fakān in an Arab novel of chivalry inserted in the *Arabian Nights*. Together with her cousin, she learns to ride, "to strike with the sword, and to thrust with the lance." Another princess in a tale of Persian origin from this famous collection says of herself: "None shall have me for a wife unless he overcomes me with horse and lance in a contest of arms in an open field." Women such as this also appear in the *Shāhunāmeh*, the Persian national epic. Miniatures illustrating other works of Persian literature also depict women on horseback swinging a sword or a club. However, such figures were not at all typical of women in Islam. Exceptions in most civilizations, amazons have left their mark as such on literature.

The advice that the Persian Kay Kā'us gave his son in the eleventh century clearly indicates that not all princesses were like those in different tales from the *Arabian Nights;* indeed, these tales may have only been dreams in literary form. Kay Kā'us, a prince of the Ziyārid dynasty, which at that time ruled the southern bank of the Caspian Sea, wrote his *Qābūsnāmeh* when he was 63 years old as a guide for his son and successor. He has this to say about the upbringing and treatment of a daughter: "Entrust her to chaste and virtuous nurses, and, when she is older, give her to a woman teacher so that she learns to pray and fast and to perform her religious duties, which are prescribed by the law of religion. But do not teach her to write! When she is grown up, try to hand her over to a husband as quickly as possible; for a daughter, it would be better if she did not even live, but once she is there, she should either lie in the grave or be married." What now follows indicates that he was motivated by concern for the girl who, unlike a son, was helpless without the support of a man. He thus advises his son: "As long as she dwells within your house, have compassion for her, since daughters are the captives of their parents," and he tells him to take good care of her. As a dynast entirely dedicated to patriarchal family relations, he also urges his son to find the girl, if she is still a virgin, a good-looking husband who is equally innocent so that the young woman will feel bound to her spouse and cause him no scandal. His son-in-law should not only be of pure religion, honest, and a good master of the house but also of lower rank and dignity, so that the young man might look up to his father-in-law and not expect the opposite. [94, 98 ff.] Thus, in a Persian ruling family of that time, reputation, rank and solidarity were important.

In many Islamic countries, the preparation of little girls for marriage included circumcision, in which either the prepuce of the clitoris or the entire organ, and sometimes even parts of the inner labia of the vulva were removed. In modern terms, this is mutilation; the girl was, at the least, greatly affected in her sexual sensations.

In the traditions, there is usually no express reference to the circumcision of girls but only to that of boys. Thus the circumcision of girls is obligatory only in the Shāfi'ite school; in the Mālikite school it is merely regarded as customary. The circumcision of boys and girls probably dates from pre-Islamic times, and was simply continued under Islam. Even today, however, it is so firmly established as a popular custom in some countries, such as Egypt and the Sudan, where the Shāfi'ite law is predominant that a law prohibiting circumcision of girls, dating from April, 1959, has not put an end to it, not even in such big cities as Cairo. Even now, the Bedouins of Central Arabia consider that an uncircumcised girl is unworthy of being married. During the Umayyad period, at a drinking party given by Caliph Hishām Ibn Abdal-Malik, the son of a Byzantine woman was abused as the "son of a woman with a clitoris." The man responded as follows, however: "Are you boasting with that which was cut off from the clitoris of your mother." [34, 80ff.] Nevertheless, the circumcision of a girl was not celebrated as was that of a boy.

Most little girls covered their face with a veil at a very early age —eight or nine years old, and even earlier in noble families. Their feeling of modesty developed in such a way that, as several European travelers noted with astonishment, a Muslim woman would prefer to let a physician examine her body than to unveil her face in front of him.

Marriages were arranged for little girls at an early age, in most cases when they were only ten to twelve years old. One of the reasons for this was certainly the requirement that a young bride had to be a virgin; marriage is of course recommended by Islam. The unhappy figure of the old maid, so often the subject of compassionate laughter or even scorn in Europe, was practically unknown in Islamic countries of the past. On the other hand the early marriage of a girl, which neither allowed her the opportunity to mature intellectually nor further education in most cases, was also certainly one of the reasons for the increasing degradation of women in the Islamic world. From the early period of Islam it has been repeatedly passed down that a woman or a girl received the proposal of a suitor personally. [164, IV, 412 ff.; 50, 231] On such occasions there were also refusals.

As was also the custom in Europe not so long ago, marriage was not something decided upon by two young people who loved each other but was—and often still is—a matter arranged for the most part by the two families concerned.

Since women were always veiled if they appeared in public at all, it was not possible for a man to see his future bride or become acquainted with her beforehand. Only when he married his cousin—and this is still a common occurrence in all Islamic countries—was he already acquainted with his bride before the ceremony. With the close feelings of family solidarity existing among members of the extended Near Eastern family, such marriages were always recommended indeed, a young man even had priority over any other possible suitors if he wished to marry his cousin on his father's side. If this was not possible, a man who wanted to marry had to resort to the agency of his female relatives or to the services of a professional marriage-maker.

The female marriage brokers often endeavored to exploit their position and dupe their male clients. Thus, in a work of eleventh-century Arabic literature, it is reported that a man of Baghdad had long sought a beautiful wife. Finally, a matchmaker promised him one who looked like a "bouquet of narcissi." After the wedding, the bridegroom discovered that the vaunted bride was an ugly old woman. The matchmaker, when accused of trickery by the man, became indignant at this reproach and justified the comparison by saying, "Her complexion is yellow, her hair is white, and her legs are dark in color." [18, XLVI] A similar deceit is reported from Cairo in the 1930s. [105, 33 ff.]

Consequently, it was better for the young man to rely on his mother or on other female relatives to make enquiries in the neighborhood about families with daughters of marriageable age. They arranged a visit, took a look at the young girl, and maybe also had the chance to exchange a few words with her. The duration of the visit was a possible indication of whether the visitors had received a favorable impression or not.

The mother of the young girl certainly gave her some advice beforehand, perhaps in words like the following: "My little daughter, here is your aunt who has come here to have a look at you. Conceal nothing from her that she would like to know about your appearance and your character, and speak freely to her about the things she will

Turkish bridal procession of the seventeenth century with the bride heavily veiled and pages leading the way.

discuss with you!"

One matchmaker, an honest woman, came to the following conclusion: "If the veil is lifted, the suitor is not cheated". [78, 110] If the young girl pleased the visitor or visitors, they paid a second visit to her family to describe the financial situation of the bridegroom and to describe his appearance. When the matter was in the hands of a professional agent, she usually lauded the bridegroom in extravagant words. Truthfulness was rarely one of her strong points.

The representatives of the bride and groom then negotiated over the bride money. Once a settlement agreeable to both sides was reached, both recited the opening *Sura* of the Koran and fixed the day on which the marriage contract was to be drawn up.

On that day, the bridegroom brought the agreed dowry to the bride's house and handed it over to her legal representative. Until the early years of the twentieth century, the conclusion of the contract was often only a verbal affair, and here, too, the first *Sura* of the Koran was recited. In most cases, a religious teacher was present and made a short speech. A few refreshments were taken, and it was decided when the *laylat ad-dukhla* (literally "the night of entrance," the wedding night) should take place, this being the night on which the bride was to be taken to the house of the bridegroom to become not only his wife but also a member of his family. This interval of time could vary; sometimes it was eight to ten days, while in other cases it could be several months. The "engagement period" was used by the bride's family to buy her everything she needed—clothing, domestic utensils, bed linen and carpets—with the dowry and with their own money. Depending on his social status, gifts such as fruit, sweets or a scarf were sent by the bridegroom to the bride and she also occasionally sent small presents to him. However, he was not yet permitted to see her. Only after 1910 could the strict customs be circumvented to some extent; the bride could send her future husband a photograph of herself as a substitute for a real meeting.

The actual wedding customs varied according to the social stratum to which the bridal pair belonged and also according to the region in which they lived. They did not remain the same for all time either. They were simple in the early days of Islam. The bride was combed, ornamented, and dressed in a particularly attractive gown for her special day. The house of the bridegroom was prepared for the festivities and for the wedding night.

Ā'isha wore a gown of striped red cloth from Bahrein for her marriage to Muhammed: subsequently, every woman of Medina who wished to marry borrowed this gown from her. This was probably because the gown was not only elegant but was believed by the brides to be especially lucky.

At the wedding of Muhammed's daughter Fātima to his cousin Alī, Ā'isha and one of Muhammed's other wives strewed soft sand on the ground, filled two cushions with palm fiber and prepared figs, dates and fresh water. In this instance, the marriage took place at the bride's house, but it was customary for the bride to be escorted to the house of the bridegroom. Young girls accompanied her and sang something like this: *Ataynākum ataynākum fa-hiyānā wa-haiykum,* "We are coming to you, we are coming to you; god give us a long life and give it to you." A wedding feast was obligatory by tradition at every Islamic marriage. However, it was held separately for men and women. At Muhammed's wedding to the beautiful Jewess Safiyya, *qays* was served, a dish consisting of dates, cottage cheese and fat it probably included flour from roasted barley as well. Bread and meat were also offered on such occasions. Safiyya received particular praise for offering her guests a drink which she herself had prepared from soaked dates.

For the wedding night, the *shari'a* recommends the following prayer for the bridegroom "O God, I beg Thee for the goodness in her and for her good inclinations which Thou hast created and I take refuge in Thee from the wickedness in her and from the wicked inclinations which Thou hast created." It was customary for the husband to spend seven nights with his wife if she were a virgin. If she had been a widow or divorced, this "honeymoon" was shortened to three days.

In later times, and especially at the Courts and among the upper strata of the towns, marriages were elaborately celebrated. One of the most magnificent and extravagant weddings reported by Muslim historians was that of the later Caliph al-Ma'mūn, a son of Hārūn ar-Rāshid, to Būrān, a daughter of the Vizier al-Hasan Ibn Sahl. The Vizier, obviously a man of extreme wealth, entertained the leading figures of the realm, including the top military commanders and the relatives of the Caliph, for nineteen days on his country estate near the town of Wasit, arranging all kinds of pleasures for them during this time. The grandmother of the bride arranged for a shower of pearls the size of hazelnuts to pour over the bridegroom. Zubayda, the mother of al-Ma'mūn, presented the young Būrān with a gown embroidered with precious pearls, the symbol of purity and wealth. The Vizier distributed gifts and garments of honor and even organized a kind of lottery. He had little balls of musk and amber—that is, expensive perfumes—thrown among the crowd, each of these balls bearing the name of an estate, a female slave or a steed. Whoever received one of these little balls was given what was named on it. The bridal chamber was lit by candles of precious, sweet-smelling amber, each of which is said to have weighed eighty pounds. It is related that this wedding cost fifty million silver dirham, a sum which, by all accounts, does not seem to have been exaggerated at all.

The report of another wedding tells of the gigantic quantities of food consumed on such occasions. When a daughter of the Mamlūk Sultan an-Nāsir Muhammed Ibn Qalāwūn was married in Egypt to the Emir Kausūn, the celebrations lasted seven days; five thousand sheep, one hundred cattle, fifty mares and innumerable birds were slaughtered for the occasion. Eleven thousand loaves of sugar were used for making confections and sherbets. The Emirs sent 311 hundredweight of wax candles to illuminate the wedding feast. The bridegroom received gifts worth fifty thousand dinar from the other Emirs. A magnificent fireworks display, held on the night of the wedding, cost eighty thousand dirham, and the artists who performed during the festivities were given the noteworthy sum of ten thousand gold dinar. The princess was presented with a tent on which there were a hundred thousand *mithqāl* of gold, equivalent to 468 kilograins. The Sultan treated eleven daughters in this manner. [4, 154]

In 1830s Cairo, weddings of the urban middle class usually began on Monday and lasted until Thursday night, which was the wedding night. A particularly pleasant high point in most wedding celebrations was the bathing of the bride. If her parents' house did not have a bath of its own, a public bath was rented for a day or half a day on Wednesday. Often preceded by musicians, the bride was brought to the bath by her female relatives and friends. She was then washed, massaged, combed and perfumed. Entertainment by female vocalists was frequently provided while this was going on. Food and refreshments were then taken together, before the bride, well wrapped, was discreetly brought back to her parents' house. The "henna night" was the next item on the program. The hands and feet of the bride were dyed with henna, the edges of her eyelids were blackened with *kohl* (sulfur antimonide), and she was dressed and ornamented for the wedding. In many regions it was usual for the bride to appear in seven costly gowns, one after the other. She might also wear a bridal crown, which was similar to a myrtle garland this was customary in Egypt from the fifteenth century on. She was then seated on a kind of throne or high chair, and had to listen, with modestly lowered eyes, while her guests sang, danced and made music.

On the following day, the Thursday, more closely wrapped than usual, she was solemnly brought to the bridegroom's house by the light of candles and to the sound of music. Here she was usually welcomed by her mother-in-law and taken to the bridal chamber. In the meantime, accompanied by his friends, the bridegroom had also paid a visit to a public or private bath and held a feast. When the bride arrived at the groom's house, yet another meal was served, the sexes again dining separately. [99, I, 175 ff.]

The Italian Pietro della Valle describes bridal processions in Turkey at the beginning of the seventeenth century in slightly different words:

> *I also saw their wedding ceremonies at which the bride was entirely covered, and, if she were only of middle-class rank, went on foot, carrying a sack on her back like a monk; if, on the other hand, she was of higher standing, she was led on horseback and covered as if by a bed-curtain whose ends were carried by the many persons around her . . . every bride, whatever her rank, has a fairly tall torch carried in front of her, this being decorated with flowers, painted paper, gold foil and other leaf and flower arrangements, or even with gold, silver and precious stones, depending on the wealth of the bride.* [173, I, 43b]

Wherever weddings were held, they were always one of the principal family celebrations in Islam, and this is still the case. If a divorcee or a widow remarried, though, the festivities were far less elaborate.

When the bridegroom finally entered the bridal chamber, he was permitted, usually in return for a gift, to raise the veil of his bride and, if she was not his cousin, to see her for the first time. If he subsequently discovered that she was not a virgin as promised, he could immediately repudiate her. Since this was regarded as a great disgrace, brides who were no longer virgins but had been lauded as such used every kind of subterfuge to fool their bridegroom. For instance, they showed a cloth spattered with the blood of a freshly killed dove or, shortly before the arrival of the bridegroom, they made a small cut at the critical spot. Even today, girls prefer to submit to a minor operation rather than admit the truth to a bridegroom holding conventional views on the matter.

It was the custom for centuries in many areas, as it still is today in rural localities, to show the token of virginity to the guests. The women greeted this with shrill cries of joy. After the wedding night, the bride and groom took separate baths, and sometimes another festive banquet was provided.

It was now that the young woman's life in her husband's family began, and she had to adapt to their ways and customs. Many parents probably gave their daughters advice of the kind given by an Arab woman in the pre-Islamic period to her daughter who was about to be married: "My little daughter, you are now leaving the house from which you originate, the nest from which you came. You are going to a man who is unknown to you, a husband to whom you are not yet accustomed. Therefore be a maidservant to him so that he will be a manservant to you. Observe ten things towards him that are especially precious to you!" There then follows a list, in rhymed prose, of the qualities of an exemplary wife: she should humbly submit to him, listen to and obey him, pay attention to when he wishes to eat and sleep, watch over his property and take care of his family; she should not oppose him, nor betray any of his secrets. "Don't be merry when he is in pain and don't be sad when he wants to laugh again!" [78, 83ff.] were the final words of the mother concerned about the welfare of her daughter.

If the young wife took note of such wise advice, if she was adaptable and her husband was good to her, then her feelings, after a period of married life, were probably similar to those of the women in Arab literature who lauded their husbands in rhymed prose in the following manner, thus providing a picture of the ideal husband not only of that time: "A husband is power in times of adversity, is assistance in times of prosperity, if I am content he inclines to me, when I am angry he cares for me." Another wife praises her husband as follows: "When he takes me with love for me it is enough, his embracement is medicine for me, his kisses are honey-sweet, his hug is eternity, neither from near or from far he is boring me." The third woman says this: "When I feel cold he is a sheltering gown, he soothes me when I lay down. The fate of my lust is transparent, and when he loves me again, it is excellent." And the fourth asserts: "A husband is happi-

ness not to describe a delight without ending and compensation."
[78, 124]

Still, much bitter experience of life was probably reflected in the custom, known from later periods, which required a virginal bride to be sad and silent during the wedding festivities, and even to weep. Marriage meant a far more drastic change for a young girl than for a man. She had to leave her own family, become the wife of a man who, in most cases, was totally unknown to her, and fit into a new community, his family. Rural marriage-songs from Palestine express this in the following way: "She goes from her father's to her husband's house, she goes from the house of joy to misery, from her own people to strangers." [61, II, 143] Various ethnologists and travelers report that the young wife, who continued to bear the name of her father (this is still the custom, at least in Arab countries) was more closely attached to her parents than to her husband and his family. It is only with the transformation in our time of the the Near Eastern family structure that this, too, is changing.

As wives for their sons, wise mothers liked to choose very young girls or slaves who had grown up like daughters in their own house, since they considered them to be more adaptable. The mother-in-law was often glad when a young woman joined the household, since she no longer had to do all the housework by herself, or, in the case of the fellahin, to work in the fields. Among the fellahin, mothers who had several daughters-in-law in their house were regarded as "ladies" with female servants, since the young women now had to grind the corn, fetch water, do the washing, collect wood, and so on.

It was a matter of great importance for a young wife to have children of her own—especially sons—as rapidly as possible, so that she could assume the respected status of a mother. Already the Koran orders that a man respect his relatives (4: 1), and traditions state that the Prophet forbade a man to disobey his mother. Just as a husband had the greatest right to his wife, so a mother had the greatest claim over the man to whom she had given birth. A well-known Islamic tradition asserts: "Paradise is at the mothers' feet."

A woman's failure to bear children was one of the main reasons for a man to take a second wife, since it is said, even in the Koran, that those who see not only their wives but also their children as a joy to behold will partake of Paradise. (25: 74f.) According to the views of medieval Islam, and under the conditions of life then prevailing, children were not simply a source of joy but also a kind of insurance against the misfortunes and poverty of old age; for peasants and Bedouins, this still holds true. Thus an astute but childless wife would herself advise her husband to marry this or that woman, mostly one of lower social standing, and then treat the latter's children as her own, while the second wife was sometimes relegated to the status of a maidservant.

The Arabic word for second wife, *darra,* is derived from a stem which also means "harm" or "disadvantage," and this is also how many women have regarded the institution of polygyny. Male "logic" has produced such sayings as: "If your wife desires to surpass you, marry a second one to restrain her," or as this one from Palestine: "Subdue a woman with another woman and do not strike her with the stick!" [61, II, 209] For their part, women expressed their feelings in such sayings as: "The co-wife is bitter, even if she be honey in a jar." [61, II, 186]

Popular humor and popular wisdom are reflected in stories like this one, related in two versions coming from different regions. A man had two wives, one old and one young. The old wife, who did not wish him to appear too young, pulled out all his dark hairs (alternatively, the hairs of his beard). The young wife, who naturally wanted the opposite, pulled out his gray hairs. When he washed himself he discovered, to his horror, that he was completely bald (alternatively, beardless).

Muslim theologians of the present day often assert that Islam, with its institution of polygyny, is kinder to women than Christianity, since the legitimate second or third wife of a man is in a better position than an unlawful mistress. This may have been economically true in earlier times, but it takes absolutely no account of the psychological situation of wives. As early traditions relate, there was jealousy even among the wives of the Prophet. [24, 67, 107] A Muslim woman, who suffered a great deal as a child from the polygynous marriage of her father and who separated from the husband she had married for love when he proposed taking a second wife, has this to say: "The nature and consequences of the suffering of a wife who lawfully shares a husband with a second and equal partner in the same house differs both in degree and in kind from that of the woman who shares him with a temporary mistress." [39, 144ff.] This woman was the Turkish authoress Halidé Edib, and she adds that in the first case other people—children, other relatives or servants—are also often involved.

The normal life of a Muslim woman in the harem varied, of course, according to her social position. The Bedouin and fellah women had to perform heavy physical labor, as they still do today. Of the fellahin, it is told that a second wife was not unwelcome, but only for this reason.

One tradition gives an idea of the harsh conditions of life suffered by the early female followers of Islam in Medina. Asmā, daughter of the future Caliph Abu Bakr and elder sister of Ā'isha, relates the following: "Az-Zubayr married me. But he had no possessions and no slaves, only his horse and a camel for carrying water. I fed and watered his horse and sewed skins to make water-bags. I kneaded dough, but I was not good at baking bread. My neighbors from the Ansār baked bread for me; they were good women. I also always used to carry home the date-pits (presumably for feeding the animals) from the plot of land which Muhammed had given to Zubayr. This plot of land was two-thirds of a parasang (almost four kilometers) away." She says that Abu Bakr subsequently sent her a manservant who looked after the horse for her. Her relief is evident in her words: "It was as if he had freed me." [24, 67, 107] It is said of Muhammed's daughter Fātima that grinding corn gave her blisters on her hands; it was one of the hardest tasks performed by women with the primitive domestic utensils then available, and this continued to be true even later.

In later times, the wife of a member of the urban upper or middle classes had to perform a greater or lesser part of the domestic work, depending on the financial situation of her family, and to supervise the children and the servants. In an illustrious work of Arab prose of the tenth century, a merchant praises his house-proud wife in the following words:

> *If you had seen her, even once—when she toils, with her apron around her—how she rushes and runs—in every corner, everywhere—how she turns and bends—flies from the oven to the pot—and back again immediately—how she fans the fire—and how she prepares the spices—crushes and powders them—while her pretty face—blackened by smoke—which leaves its mark on her smooth cheeks—The sight would enchant you—if you could see her at work—love for her rises from deep in my heart—since she honestly repays my love—Happiness is only granted to a man—when it gives him a wife of the same mind—a life together with her in harmony and peace.* [67, 53ff.]

This blissful husband stresses that the main reason the harmony in his marriage is so complete is that his wife is also his cousin.

A woman of the upper or middle classes could only leave the house when veiled and with the permission of her husband. Such

Woman crushing corn

occasions included visits to relatives or to the cemetery, as well as prayers at the mausoleum of a holy man, or, on the major dates of the religious calendar, in the mosque. One of the most popular relaxations for middle-class women who did not have a bath of their own at home was a visit to the public baths at the times reserved for women. It was here that the women displayed their finery and spent hours chatting with the neighbors, passing on the latest news of their families and being manicured, massaged, and so on.

Ultra-strict Muslims, like the Hanbalī of Baghdad in 934, often voiced their objections to women appearing on the streets at all. Caliph al-Hākim of Egypt, about 1000, famous for his cruelty and his excesses, pretended that he was restoring the original Islamic practice when he forbade women to leave the house and shoemakers to make shoes for them. Midwives and those who washed the bodies of the dead needed written permission to pursue their trade.

What was initially regarded as pious behavior subsequently became an upper-class custom that was followed with varying degrees of strictness in the different Islamic countries. Thus the French jeweler, Chardin, tells us that women in seventeenth-century Persia were more closely guarded than anywhere else in the world. By comparison, Turkish harems were open houses. Middle-class women only left the house to bathe, and were then covered from top to toe. Whenever a high-ranking lady actually showed herself in public, the men had to turn away, even though the noblewoman was being carried in a totally closed sedan chair [30, VI, 8], or eunuchs armed with sticks rode ahead to drive the people from the streets with loud calls. In contrast, the Italian nobleman Pietro della Valle says that around 1617, "Turkish females" came to the Constantinople bazaar "in droves" and even tried to flirt with "strangers" there. [173, I, 19a]

The English physician Russell says that women in eighteenth-century Aleppo left their houses fairly frequently, especially on Mondays and Thursdays. They also visited the gardens, where female slaves preceded them with carpets, pipes, food and coffee. Songs were sung in the shade of the trees. Men were only excluded from the gardens when several harems arranged to rent a park for an entire day so that they could have it to themselves. The sounds of merriment could then be heard from afar. Russell, who lived in Aleppo for twenty years, had this to say of the attitude of women toward the male sex: they "do not appear very desirous of a liberty which, in many instances, they regard as inconsistent with their notion of female honour and delicacy." [142, I, 257]

In Egypt, as late as 1910, noble women boasted that they never left their husband's house after crossing its threshold as a bride. In a country like Iraq, even in the capital Baghdad, it is noticeable still today that only about a quarter of the people in the streets are women, and that many men still walk a few steps ahead of their wives when they go out in public. This is accounted for by the perceived need to protect and to guide women. A young middle-class woman of Baghdad told the author that her mother, who was 45 years old, only left the house for an occasional visit to the cemetery or the *sūq* (the market), and then, of course, wrapped in her black *abāya*.

Thus, in many regions, the harem became a luxurious prison for upper-class women, at least in Western eyes. It was here that they idly passed their time, trying out beauty aids, scenting themselves, smoking water pipes *(nargīla)* and later cigarettes, drinking coffee, eating confectionery, playing cards or board games, being entertained by female singers and dancers, or cultivating the art of narrative. On hot summer days, they probably spent many hours chatting or doing needlework in the shady gardens of their houses, in most of which there was a fountain. However, they were always strictly segregated from any men who were not close relatives. The food, cosmetics and materials they needed were brought to them by female traders or servants. Russell, the physician mentioned above, was surprised that the ladies of the middle- and upper-class harems of Aleppo in the eighteenth century did not read, unlike the women of his own country, who passed their time by reading novels of a more or less sentimental nature. He reports that although they had learned to read and write as children, most of them soon forgot it again, "so that reading ought not to be reckoned a common female amusement, and is never a study." [142, I, 249] Since the standards of female education were low, superstition flourished, especially in polygynous households. Recipes for getting a husband, for acquiring supremacy in the household or for taking away the virginity of a new wife so as to make her unhappy were passed on from one generation to another. This, in turn, resorted to tricks of their own to upset the plans of their co-wife (or wives). [98, 101]

For centuries, the father was the undisputed head of the family. Not only his wife (or wives) and daughters but also his growing or grown-up sons had to submit to his will and, at times, to his moods. In general, it was customary for the wife and daughters to wait on him at mealtimes, but not to eat anything in his presence themselves. When the husband entered the harem, the women stood up; many men liked to behave in a particularly taciturn manner in their harems, in order to emphasize their authority. Amīna, from the trilogy of the Egyptian novelist Naguib Mahfouz, may be regarded as a typical example of a middle-class woman in the traditional Islamic society of a later period; every evening she waits up for her husband, who spends his leisure hours with women of a doubtful reputation, but never asks him where he was. When he comes home, she just illuminates the stairs for him and helps him change his clothes. She only dares to speak when he addresses her. And yet, for all her gentleness and humility, she is a mainstay for her children. Her sons as well as her daughters love and honor her, whereas the father, who is always strict at home, only has their respect. In her obedience and submission to the will of her husband, it is she who holds the family together, and she knows how to influence her husband in those matters that are important for her and her children.

A European traveler described a family of the Islamic Indian military aristocracy at the beginning of the twentieth century. The mother and daughter, who had traveled a great deal in Europe and had moved around freely, talked in a relaxed and easy manner as long as they were alone. When the father of the family appeared, however, they fell silent and did not say a word as long as he was present. They "became at once true Indian women silent before that superior being—the man." [32, 169]

In the next chapter, however, we shall see that there were women, particularly in the first centuries of Islam, who did not regard

93

this submission as their ideal.

The division of the community into male and female societies was most strictly observed at the Courts of the Caliphs, Sultans and Emirs. At the time of Hārūn ar-Rāshīd, large numbers of women already lived in harems, and a strict system of regulations was necessary to control communal life. Music and poetry were cultivated in the harems, political decisions taken, intrigues and plots hatched, and Viziers appointed and dismissed. Sensuous scenes, of the kind usually associated with the word "harem" in the West, certainly also took place. Such harems were found in the Near East long before Islam, of course. Their existence is noted in the Iran of the Akhaemenids (700-330 B.C.) it was essentially the Ancient Near East which provided the prototype for the harems of the Abbāsids and of the later dynasties.

A well-ordered hierarchy prevailed in the harem, but a ruler's entire administrative powers were often needed in order to preserve peace there. The friend and secretary of the Mughal Emperor Akbar, who reported in detail about his sovereign's period of government, lauded him in the following words:

> *Through order, the world becomes a meadow of truth and reality; that which is merely external receives a spiritual meaning through it. For this reason, the large number of women—a vexatious question, even for great statesmen—furnished his Majesty with an opportunity to display his wisdom, and to rise from the low level of worldly dependence to the eminence of perfect freedom. The imperial palace and household are therefore in the best possible order.* [6, 44]

Although there were more than five thousand women in the harem, he says, the Emperor had given each her own apartment. He had divided them into various sections and ensured that each performed her duties. The Emperor had appointed "chaste women" as supervisors of each section, and one performed the duties of a scribe. In this manner, everything was in order in the Imperial offices. The women were paid generous monthly stipends, ranging between 1,028 and 1,610 rupees for the senior ones, 20-51 for the attendants and 2-

40 for the lowest ranks of servants.

A diligent and intelligent female scribe belonged to the staff of the private audience chamber of the Palace and supervised every expenditure. When a woman wanted to buy something, she had to contact the book-keepers of the seraglio, who sent a memorandum to this scribe. The interior of the harem was guarded by serious and active women, the most trusted of whom were stationed before the apartments of Her Majesty. The eunuchs were positioned outside the harem and then, at a suitable distance from them, there was a guard of loyal Rajputs.

The harems of the potentates were so closely guarded that, as late as the nineteenth century, not even the wives of accredited diplomats were allowed to visit them. The women of the local aristocracy first had to apply to the eunuchs when they wished to enter the Imperial harem. Various travelers tell of uniformed female battalions who guarded the harems in Persia [30, VI, 12ff.] and India [108, II, 332]

In Court harems of the later period, women filled the same offices as those held by men in the parts of the palaces reserved for male courtiers. These included a female general of musketeers, female prayer leaders, female supervisors of the linen department, coffee stewardesses, treasurers, physicians, cooks, tailors and shoe-makers.

Describing the harem of the Mughal Emperor Aurangzēb (d. 1707), Manucci, a Venetian, says that on the days when the Emperor did not leave it, palace officials who worked outside the harem were given their instructions by ladies appointed for the purpose. "Every person employed in these offices," he says of these ladies, "is carefully selected they have much wit and judgment, and know all that is happening in the Empire. For the officials outside are required to send written reports into the *mahal* of all that the king ought to know." Eunuchs were responsible for communications between the two parts of the Palace. Public and private "news reporters" of the Empire had to summarize the most important news in a kind of newspaper once a week. These reports were usually read to the ruler by ladies of the harem at about nine o'clock in the evening so that he could know what was going on in his realm. In addition, "spies" had to send in weekly reports about other important matters, mainly concerning the doings of the princes, who were his potential rivals. [108, II, 331] Aurangzēb thus seems to have dealt with much of the business of government from within his harem, with the assistance of sagacious harem ladies. It may certainly be assumed that they also counseled him.

For centuries, the ladies of the princely harems were recruited from subjugated peoples and included Greeks, Armenians, Georgians, Circassians and Slavs. When they joined the harem, they were usually given an imposing name with a beautiful meaning. To begin with, Arabic names were preferred in the harems of Turkey, Persia and India, but Persian names subsequently predominated. Thus empresses and princesses at the Mughal Court in India in the second half of the seventeenth century had such names as Tāj Mahall, "Crown of the Palace"; Nūr Mahall, "Light of the Palace"; Nūr Jahān, "Light of the World"; Nūr un-Nisā Khānum, "Light of Women"; or Durr-e Durrān Begom, "Pearl of Pearls." Female slaves of the harem in this period had such names as Gul-andām, "Rose Figure"; Gul-ānār, "Pomegranate Blossom"; Banafseh, "Violet"; or Gul-rang, "Rose Color." [108, II, 333ff.]

Chardin reports that noble families in Persia considered it a privilege to give a daughter to the royal harem when this was demanded by the ruler. Not only were her close relatives then paid a kind of pension, but her family hoped she would be able to influence the monarch in their favor and assist their progress at Court.

The Queen Mother was in charge of the royal harem and was usually a very strict mistress. Just as all those whom she supervised had duties according to their rank and were under surveillance, they, in turn, checked up on those subordinate to them. Occasionally the ruler gave away some of the ladies of his harem; only those who were not of free origin and were not his favorites, of course. They were given an appropriate trousseau, and were a special honor for the recipient, usually a close friend, whose wife they then became. For the other ladies there was scarcely any chance of ever leaving the harem again, particularly if they had borne the ruler's children. Only the mother of the first-born son could consider herself fortunate; the mothers of subsequent sons, especially in Persia and Turkey during the late Middle Ages, had to live in constant fear of their lives and those of their children. If they were allowed to live, they were practically prisoners, especially when the ruler, on whom they depended, died and another acceded to the throne.

The Italian Pietro della Valle describes a particular pleasure of the ladies of the royal harem in seventeenth-century Persia. When men were present, they went hunting in an elevated cabin and fired guns from this perch. When there were no men present, "they ride on horseback and display their dexterity both with the sword and with arrows." [173, II, 142b] There are many miniature paintings that show ladies on horseback, hunting and playing polo. It will be noticed, as della Valle also noticed, that sidesaddles were not used the women straddled horses "like a horseman with one foot on this side and the other on that." [173, II, 12b]

Since the standard of education, at least among the higher-ranking ladies of the princely harems, was more advanced than that of middle-class women, they also engaged in reading. Manucci relates that the ladies in the harem of the Mughal Emperor Aurangzēb liked to read such illustrious works of Persian literature as Sa'dī's *Gulistān* and *Bustān*.

Links between the princely harem and the outside world were maintained by eunuchs. The exclusion of high-ranking women from public life necessitated the existence of such sexless beings, although the Koran and traditions prohibited the castration of man and beast. Castration had, however, been practiced in the Ancient Orient and in Byzantium; as in other areas of social life, the established practice proved more powerful than the later prohibition. The devout Muslim let the infidels do the castration and purchased his eunuchs from them. The privilege of guarding the harem's inner gate was mostly given to a guard made up of black eunuchs, while white eunuchs watched over the outer gate.

With the division into male and female societies, special trades for women became necessary. Mention has already been made of women who laid out the dead females and who served as midwives. In addition, an investigation of the situation of women in Egypt at the

Indian dancer

time of the Mamlūks brought to light the following female professions, which must also have existed in other Islamic countries: the bath attendant, matchmaker, trader supplying goods to the harem and often bringing the latest gossip as well, a kind of hairdresser who plaited the hair of young girls as part of their wedding preparations, and professional female mourners, who attended funerals and expressed the grief of those present with their loud cries and lamentations.

The most common trade for lower-class women was spinning, which was done at home. Miniatures often depict women either with a spindle under their arm or, in later periods, at the spinning wheel. Pietro della Valle has this to say of the fine embroidery done by Turkish women in the seventeenth century: ". . . the women are highly skilled in the working of linen and other materials, including silks of various colors; also in the embroidering of silver and gold on delicate and transparent cloth so that the same thing appears on one side as on the other; and they know how to make such a shading with this gold that nothing can be more beautiful than this." [173, I, 24b] In the *Arabian Nights,* there is mention of an unusual trade for a woman: as the daughter of a pigeon-post official in Baghdad, the astute Dalīla raised carrier pigeons and passed this trade on to her daughter, who was just as cunning as her mother.

Like many other things forbidden by religious law, one of the oldest professions in the world, prostitution was strictly prohibited by the Koran and *Sunna,* but was not unknown in Muslim society. Chardin records that in Isfahan, the illustrious metropolis of the Safavids, there were reputed to be fourteen thousand registered prostitutes in 1666. These women were also listed as taxpayers-"non olet" obviously being the rule almost everywhere. They lived together in special caravanserais, and were under the control of a female "superior"who "hired them out." Accompanied by one or two servants, they rode on horseback to those who had ordered them. [30, II, 211 ff.]

Olearius tells of a certain place in Qazvin which was frequented by numerous merchants and where, when night had fallen, "many *cahbeha* or immoral women, their faces concealed, stand in a long line and offer their shameful wares. Behind each of them is an old woman, known as the *dalal,* who carries the bed clothes, namely a cushion and a cotton-filled blanket, on her back and holds an unlit lamp in her hand. When a man wishes to come to an arrangement with them, the *delal* lights the lamp; and with this the man sees each *cahbeha's* face, and orders the one who pleases him most to follow him." [126, 483] Olearius also says—obviously to avoid offending the current morality—that he had not seen this for himself but had heard it from others.

The everyday life of female slaves varied according to the family they belonged to or the status they held in the harem. The most fortunate were certainly those who were married by the man who bought them or acquired them as booty in war. Of course, he had to set them free first. In *Sūra* 4: 3, the Koran recommends marriage with a slave, and *Sūra* 2: 221 even affirms that marriage with a Muslim slave is better than marriage with a beautiful pagan. In the traditions, it is reported in several places that a man who has a slave educated (well educated, that is) then sets her free and marries her shall receive a double reward. [24, 49, 16] On the other hand, there is a *hadīth,* presumably originated by race-conscious Arabs, which affirms that whoever sets a slave free and then marries her is like one who mounts his slaughter camel. [179, 141] During the reign of the Umayyads, when race-proud Arabs predominated, marriages of this kind were despised, even though the law approved of them. At that time, for instance, one free woman rejected a proposal of marriage from a man because his mother was a slave. [78, 262] The reign of the Abbāsids had a leveling influence in this respect, to such an extent indeed that only three of the Abbāsid Caliphs had mothers who were free Arabs. Slaves could consequently aspire to the most exalted ranks in society, and not a few in such a position attempted to exert an influence on politics as well. This shall be discussed further.

The bel-esprit Jāhiz (d. 869), who, like many writers, was not a pure-bred Arab himself, finds that most free men prefer slaves to free women, the reason being that a man can take a good look at a slave and get to know her before he buys her. In the case of a free woman, he has to rely on the judgment of other women. And women, in his view, have no eye for female beauty and know nothing of what men want from women or of the qualities in which men and women have to be compatible. Men are more perspicacious, he claims, when it is a question of women.

A few decades later, the *Unique Necklace,* an encyclopedic work of *adab* literature by the Andalusian Ibn Abd Rabbihi, says that one must be surprised at men who take it upon themselves to approach a free woman after they have gotten to know slaves. "A slave is bought with the eyes and is returned when she has faults. But a free woman is like a fetter on the neck of the man to whom she comes." [77, 129] Clearly this text reveals the prevailing opinion on women and reflects their degradation. Another verse in this work states that one should not despise a man because his mother was a Byzantine, a Negress or a Persian. Mothers, it is claimed, are only receptacles in which the seed is placed. Only the fathers are important when it comes to origins. [77, 128]

In medieval Islam, fantastic prices were paid for beautiful slaves who had a literary and artistic education. In an age when free Muslim women, like their free Greek sisters before them, were practically excluded from public life, such slaves celebrated one glorious triumph after another in the salons of the aristocracy. The slave traders used every trick of the trade to match their "merchandise" to the ideals of beauty current at the time, and there was so much of this merchandise from so many parts of the world that slave women could be classified by their suitability for different spheres of life, from domestic work to love and child-rearing to the fine arts and sciences. In a slave-buying guide of the first half of the eleventh century, a Christian physician describes the ideal female slave as a Berber, who is "exported" at the age of nine years, spends three years each in Medina and Mecca, and then, at fifteen, comes to the Land of the Two Rivers to be educated in the fine arts. When she is then sold at the age of twenty-five, she combines the wit of the woman of Medina with the mildness of the inhabitant of Mecca and the education of Mesopotamia—a piquant blend of wisdom and femininity that was greatly appreciated at that time.

Slaves of this kind were well aware of their value. In certain circumstances, they could insist that the slave dealer sell them only to men who met with their approval. Indeed, they were even able to lend financial assistance to the men who bought them, since they were allowed to possess assets of their own. Their worth was consequently lauded to an interested public in many fine words, perhaps something like these: "You merchants, you men of money! Who will begin the bidding for this slave/the Mistress of the Moon/the Pearl of High Profit/her name is Zumurrud, "Emerald," the embroiderer of curtains, /the object of desire/the bliss of him who yearns for love?" [164, II, 210]

In spite of their great value and the esteem in which they were held, these slaves were exposed to the moods and whims of their owners until they were set free. Thus, in 1009, in a fit of religious mania, the Fātimid Caliph al-Hākim had all of his favorite concubines put in crates, having decided to abandon sensual pleasure; the crates were then weighed down with stones, nailed up and cast into the Nile. In the *Arabian Nights,* a beautiful slave is made to work in the kitchen as she will not yield to the ugly son of the woman who owns her. The jewelry and silken garments which her former owner, a wealthy man, gave her are taken away.

Kitchen work and domestic tasks were the domain of the less attractive and less well-educated slaves, and these were often the black ones. Black slaves were usually regarded less highly than white ones, even though many men, including some of high rank, prized them as sexual partners. From the eleventh century on, the sons of black mothers were also able to attain high positions.

It was precisely because of the uncertainty of their fate that slaves needed their natural wit and shrewdness to defend themselves; they were rewarded by the recognition given to such gifts in the Arab world of the Middle Ages. "How much is given to the slaves depends on the bad qualities of the free women," said a pert and cynical slave to her master when he, on her couch, complained about his wife's bad character. [78, 193] This was obviously at a time when free women were more highly regarded than slaves. A son abused one of his father's slaves with the words, "You whore!" to which she sarcastically replied, "If I were that, then I would have borne your father a son like you." [78, 228]

The anecdotes that have been passed down indicate that female slaves often had enough self-assurance to express themselves freely, rather than flattering their owners all the time.

We will now take a look at some women who stand out by virtue of their artistic talents, political ambitions, or lifestyle.

Women in Islamic History

The Koran assigns women a social position subordinate to men. Religious tradition required them to subject themselves to the will of men. This culminated in the saying, allegedly from the Prophet: "If it is proper for a human being to kneel in adoration to another human being, then this is only for a woman to kneel to a man." [120, VI, 411] Still, despite attempts from a very early stage to keep women out of public life, there were always women who, by virtue of a strong personality or special gifts, were outstanding members of the society of their time and played a role in the cultural life and history of Islamic countries.

Women even had a hand, whether directly or indirectly, in the rise of Islam. Among the first was Khadīja Bint Khuwaylid, Muhammed's first wife. She had been widowed twice before she married Muhammed, and had also had children. By fitting out caravans for Syria and by engaging in trade, she increased further the considerable fortune she had inherited. At the time, this was not unusual for a woman in Mecca. She appointed Muhammed, who was then 25 years old and, as an orphan, not very well off, leader of one of these caravans. Since he performed this task to her satisfaction and, it may be supposed, made a pleasing impression on her, she, at the age of forty, proposed marriage to him through the agency of another woman—another procedure that was not unusual in those days. For Muhammed, who had lost his mother at an early age, marriage to the respected and prosperous Khadīja represented material security. Definite references to this are found in *Sūra* 93: 6, "Did He not find thee an orphan and give (thee) shelter?" and in verse 8 of the same

Sura, "Did He not find thee poor, and enrich (thee)?" Khadīja bore him seven children, though of these only four daughters survived. It was she, too, who gave him moral support when he experienced the first revelations which initially had an overwhelming and terrifying effect on him. She prayed in secret with her husband, and became the first follower of Islam at a time when the people around Muhammed considered him a liar and a dreamer.

Western critics like to censure the Prophet for his sensuality, since he subsequently maintained a larger harem than that accorded to his followers by the Koran; but while Khadīja was alive, she remained his only wife. Khadīja was probably able to insist on this, by virtue of her position. Even decades later, Muhammed's child-wife Ā'isha was still jealous of the memory of the "toothless old woman," as she called her angrily, for whom, she said, Allah had given the Prophet a better replacement. But Muhammed chided her: "He has not given me a better one. She believed in me when no one else did. She considered me to be truthful when the people called me a liar. She helped me with her fortune when the people had left me nothing. Allah gave me children from her while he gave me none from other women." [82, VI, 117ff.]

It was only after Khadīja died at the age of 65 that Muhammed turned to other women. As mentioned above, most, if not all, of the Prophet's marriages were partly inspired by his desire to keep the young community together. Thus his favorite wife, Ā'isha, on whom the discussion will now focus, was the daughter of one of his first followers, the future Caliph Abu Bakr, for whom he felt a special affection. Ā'isha was proud, not only to be the cause of revelations, as we have already seen, but also because she was the only wife with whom Muhammed obviously felt so relaxed that he received revelations in her presence. Despite, or perhaps because of her special position, she was particularly jealous, and after Muhammed's death, boasted of her other advantages over her "co-wives." Not only was she the only virgin among the wives of the Prophet, but he shared a washing bowl with her, prayed in her presence and had requested to be tended to by her during the last days of his life. He died in her lap, and was buried under the floor of her living room. At the time, Ā'isha was a young, blooming woman of eighteen.

Mention should be made here of an event that took place in Muhammed's harem, and that was the cause of a revelation. It shows that, at times, even Muhammed's wives were not subservient. Arab history relates that after the Muslims had emigrated to Medina, the future Caliph Omar said: "We, the men of the Qoraysh tribe, had supremacy over the women. But after we arrived at Medina, we came to people who were governed by their women; our women then began to acquire the customs of the inhabitants of Medina." He then tells the following story: "My wife was angry with me and began to quarrel with me, but I forbade her to do so. She objected: 'Why do you deny me the right to quarrel with you? The wives of the Prophet also quarrel with him, and today one of them even left him and did not come back until nightfall.'" [87, VIII, 131] At this, he hurried in consternation to his daughter Hafsa, one of the wives of Muhammed, and urged her to do no wrong to the Prophet, since otherwise the fury of Allah might strike her. He also said that she should not be misled by Ā'isha, since the latter had a special position. He informed Abū Bakr, who immediately put Ā'isha straight. If she wanted worldly goods, she should ask him for them, not Muhammed, who could not afford them. The two men then went to the proud Umm Salama, another wife of Muhammed from the respected tribe of the Makhzrūm. Here they met with a cool reception. Umm Salama said to them: "What business is it of yours what goes on here? The Envoy of Allah stands over us, and if he had wanted to forbid us anything he would already have done so. Who should we ask then, if not him? Does anybody interfere in your family affairs? We did not ask you to do so." [87, VIII, 129] The two left, having achieved nothing. The other wives of Muhammed thanked Umm Salama for her courage, adding that they had not dared to say anything like that to Umar and Abū Bakr. Muhammed withdrew from his wives for 29 days, and was greatly troubled. However, he succeeded in restoring order in his harem. He received the revelation of *Sūra* 33: 28ff, which confronts his wives with the following alternatives; to choose the worldly life with all its goods and then be sent away by Muhammed, or to decide in favor of Allah, his Prophet and the life to come, and be rewarded in Paradise. Ā'isha was the first to be persuaded by this, then Hafsa and finally his other wives, one after the other. This story shows that Muhammed did not attempt to convince his wives by insisting on male superiority and giving them no choice; instead, aware of his status as Prophet, he won them over with diplomacy and kindness.

After Muhammed's death in 632, Ā'isha and the other widows lived together as the "Mothers of the Faithful." When, after a reign of two years, Abu Bakr, the first Caliph, found himself on the point of death, he also entrusted himself to the care of Ā'isha who was obviously his favorite child. When he died, he was buried (as was his successor, Khalif Umar) next to Muhammed under the floor of Ā'isha's room. It is said that at his death, Ā'isha addressed the faithful in moving words of resounding rhymed prose. It is related in literature that Hafsa did the same for her father Umar, just as Fātima is said to have delivered the funeral oration for Muhammed. [78, 10ff.; 40ff.; 23ff.]

Ā'isha now became a respected authority on what Muhammed had done or said in certain situations; that is, on his *Sunna.* She was much in demand: women asked her for advice on questions of clothing and cosmetics in relation to religious law; even respected men consulted her on questions of religion and the way life was to be led, since she, of all his wives who were still alive, had been closest to the Prophet. Subsequently, over two thousand traditions were attributed to her, though little more than two hundred of these have been included in the collections of Bukhāri and of Muslim, which are regarded as canonical.

Besides having a good knowledge of Ancient Arabic poetry and genealogy, Ā'isha is also reported to have laid down the fundamental rules of Arab-Islamic ethics. She is said to have affirmed that noble qualities of character were "honesty of speech, reliability, truthfulness and steadfastness in misfortune, the provision of protection for friend and neighbor, and readiness to give aid in the ups and downs of life, to feed the needy, to treat slaves with kindness and to revere one's parents." [78, 21 ff.]

Nor was Ā'isha afraid to tell the third Caliph Uthmān what she thought of his personnel policy: he liked to give leading positions to members of his own tribe. Following the murder of Uthmān in 656, she once more found herself the center of public attention under sensational circumstances. Responding to the call for vengeance for the murdered Caliph, she joined forces with two early followers of Muhammed, Talha and Ubaydallāh, adversaries of the newly elected Caliph Alī. The three of them went to Iraq with their followers, hoping to find further support there. A battle took place not far from Basra in 656, which came to be known as the Battle of the Camel, after the camel on which Ā'isha was seated in a litter and from which she urged on the combatants. Although Ā'isha employed all her eloquence and strategic skill, the battle was lost for her and her followers, after Alī, perceiving the role that Ā'isha was playing, cut the pasterns of her camel. Talha and Ubaydallāh were killed.

Ā'isha's litter was covered with so many arrows that it looked like a hedgehog, but she had not been injured. Alī allowed her to return to Mecca with an appropriate retinue, after she declared publicly that there had never been any dispute between them, apart from those that occur from time to time between people related by marriage, and Alī confirmed her statement. It is said that she later deeply regretted this period of her life, since much blood had been spilled in vain. The childless Ā'isha is even thought to have said that rather than bear the Prophet ten sons who were as brave as her bravest followers in the battle, she would have preferred not to have gone to war. As late as the 1940s, a well-known Egyptian author pointed to the Battle of the Camel as an example of why women should stay at home and not interfere in public affairs. [12]

Ā'isha died in 678, at the age of sixty-four. In the subsequent historiography of Islam, she was depicted as a devout ascetic whose principal wish was to live as a true believer.

Of the other women in the family of the Prophet, special mention should be made of his youngest daughter Fātima, although she did not play the same role as Ā'isha in the early Islamic community. Early Islamic historiography emphasizes how hard and austere her life was. The bed on which she slept with her husband, Muhammed's cousin and the future Caliph Alī, was the woolly side of a sheepskin, the inner side of which they used during the day to hold the fodder of the camel which brought them water. Their pillow was a cushion of tanned leather, filled with palm fibers. Incidentally, Muhammed forbade his cousin to take a second wife, saying that what caused pain to his daughter grieved him as well.

There seems to have been some rivalry between Ā'isha and Fātima. Fātima, it is said, was sent to Muhammed by his other wives to protest the preferential position enjoyed by Ā'isha. The Prophet is said to have replied that Fātima, as his daughter, must also like what pleased him. It may be assumed that Fātima was especially close to Muhammed, since she was the only one of his children whose offspring did not die prematurely. He could see his life continued in Hasan and Husayn, her sons and his grandsons.

As the mother of the Prophet's grandsons, she was of particular importance in later Islamic history, especially for the Shī'ites. Fātima was practically deified by some branches of the Shī'a, the Nusayris for example, and was given the additional name of "the Brilliant One," because she was the mother of those who, according to the Shī'ites, had the right to supreme power after Ali. Immediately after Muhammed's death, she and her husband Ali had called on the faithful to pay homage to Alī and not to Abu Bakr. Only after Fātima's death at the age of twenty-eight, a few months after the death of Muhammed, did Alī swear an oath of allegiance to Abu Bakr. The gnostic circles of the Shī'a believe that she will play an important role at the end of Time, ensuring, through implacable vengeance, that justice will prevail once more. An entire dynasty, the Fātimids, initially ruling in North Africa from 909 and then in Egypt and Syria up to 1171 AD, took their name from the daughter of Muhammed, their founder reinforced his claim to power with the assertion that he was a descendant of Fātima.

Women have consistently been prominent in Islamic religion, especially where Islamic mysticism is concerned. Illustrious Islamic mystics, who were not well disposed toward women in general, still spoke favorably of pious women, as illustrated by the following quotation: "An irresponsible woman is worse than a hundred irresponsible men. But a devout woman will receive the same reward as a hundred devout men." [10, 64] Women, it was believed, were exposed to greater temptations than men, and possessed a lesser degree of resistance. Another sage said: "When a woman walks on the path of God like a man, she cannot be described as a woman" [16, I, 59]: that is, she loses the negative female characteristics she was thought to be born with.

The first name to acquire fame in Islamic mysticism was that of a woman's. Rābi'a al-Adawiyya was a freed slave born at Basra in 714 or 717. Through her asceticism and boundless love for God, in comparison with whom everything in the world was insignificant, she achieved fame and became an example to later mystics. Popular belief associated her life with the kinds of miracles that are attributed to saintly figures in other religions. Once, it is told, her sumpter mule collapsed and died in the middle of the desert while she was on a pilgrimage to Mecca. Other travelers in the caravan offered her their assistance, but she replied that she had not set out on her journey to rely on them. As soon as she was alone, she prayed: "O God, is this how the weak, a woman, a stranger or a sick man are treated? You summon me to Your house and then You allow my mule to die halfway into the journey, leaving me alone in the desert." Scarcely had she ended her prayer when the mule moved and stood up. She loaded her baggage on it and continued her journey. [16, I, 61]

An illustrious figure was Fātima of Nishapur (d. 849), who discussed important questions with the most famous mystics of her time, and clearly guided her husband in religious and practical matters. In the course of her long discussions with the mystic Bāyazīd Bistāmī, she behaved in a relaxed manner and raised her veil, with the result that her husband became jealous. When, one day, Bāyazīd noticed that she had dyed the tips of her fingers with henna and asked her why she did so, she resolutely replied: "If you have discovered that I have dyed my fingers, then you have looked at me with eyes other than those of intellectual friendship. The familiarity between us must now come to an end! [10, 64]

Nafīsa, the great-granddaughter of Hasan, grandson of the Prophet, is revered today in Egypt as a saint. She was born in Mecca in 762-3, grew up in Medina, and subsequently went to Egypt with her husband (other reports say it was her brother). Her knowledge of theological matters made her so famous that even her illustrious contemporary, the jurist ash-Shāfi'i, paid her a visit to hear her relate traditions. She was famed not only for her thirty pilgrimages, but also for her strict asceticism and charity to the poor. When people complained to her about the injustice of the Egyptian governor of that time, she is said to have stood in his path and handed him a note in which she accused him of tyranny and called on him to be more just. She died in Cairo in 823-4 and, at the request of the local population, was buried there. Her mausoleum came to fame, says a later biographer, as a place where prayers were heard by God.

Many women combined devoutness in life with learnedness in religion. One such was Shuhda Bint al-Ibarī, known as Fakhr an-Nisā, "the Pride of Women," who died in Baghdad in 1178, at over ninety years of age. Like Zaynab Bint ash-Sha'rī, who was over a hundred years old when she died in Nishapur in 1218-9, she heard the most illustrious teachers of her time. Even when they were advanced in years, both women had a large number of pupils, some of whom became respected scholars.

A woman by the name of Fātima Bint Ahmed Ibn Yahyā became prominent in the field of religious law, which she discussed with her father. It is reported that her husband, an *imām*, consulted her when baffled by legal problems which he wanted to explain to his pupils. She gave him the appropriate explanations, and he passed them on to his pupils. When they were still unable to understand, they said: "That does not come from you yourself but from (her) behind the curtain." [93, IV, 31ff.]

There are no monasteries in Islam like those that played such a great part in the religious and cultural life of medieval Europe; already at a relatively early stage, however, there did exist convents for women who sought the mystical approach to the worship of God, or who wanted to lead a devout life. In Mamlūk Egypt, a *shaykhah*, or female sheikh, preached and led prayers. Female saints were and are known throughout the Islamic world. These saints also have shrines to which women come who seek refuge and comfort in times of distress.

It was probably in India that the cult of female saints flourished most. A whole series of miniatures from the Mogul period depicts female hermits surrounded by young people of both sexes. One of the saints from Mogul India who came to fame was the eldest daughter of Emperor Shah Jahān, named Jahān-ārā, whose book about her initiation as a mystic bears witness to the profundity of her faith and mystical understanding. Sidqī, a Turkish woman who died in 1703, was a poet and a mystic. Wealthy women were known for their donations to Sūfī sheikhs (mystics) and for the material support given to orders of Dervishes.

The early historians mention only one woman, Umm Waraqa Bint Abdallāh, who acted as the prayer leader of a mixed community, that of her clan, so numerous that it had its own muezzin. Muhammed himself is said to have instructed her to serve as prayer leader. She was also one of the few women who handed down the Koran before it was put in final written form. In addition, she had such a great desire to be known as a martyr that she bade Muhammed to allow her to take part in the Battle of Badr so that she could tend the wounded. From that time on, Muhammed is said to have called her "the female Martyr." [87, VIII, 335]

Another report from this early Islamic period tells of Umm Umāra, a woman who not only acted as a nurse, but also fought in some of the Muslims' battles. With her husband and two sons, she took part in one battle with the intention of tending the wounded and bringing them water. But then she fought boldly with the others, her garments tied around her waist. She lost a hand in battle, and was wounded several more times. [87, VIII, 301 ff.]

In the first decades of Islam, it was not unusual for women like Ā'isha to take part in battles, encouraging the combatants with passionate declamations in rhymed prose from their camel-borne litters. In the battle at Siffin in 657 between Caliph Ali and his adversary, the future Caliph Mu'āwiya, there were several women on Ali's side who gave vocal support to his warriors. Even afterwards, Mu'āwiya must still have regarded them as exceptional characters. He ordered them to come to him, so that he could talk to them and ask what had led them to act as they had at that time. All of the women claimed not to remember the passionate words with which they had encouraged the combatants. But Mu'āwiya remembered them and quoted the words they had used. When Mu'āwiya asked Zarqā the reason for her behavior, she replied laconically: "O Commander of the Faithful, there happened worse things than that." Whoever ponders on it sees more; and now the fat is in the fire." When the Caliph told her to ask for something for herself, she sagaciously replied that she had sworn never to request anything from a prince against whom she had fought, but that a mighty person like hers could be anyhow generous. And in this way, she received an opulent fief. [78, 50ff.]

In another battle which took place in the first century of Islam, the Muslim women used a trick to help their men. They turned their veils into banners and moved up behind the men with "standards" flying. The enemy, assuming that Muslim reinforcements were arriving, decided they would be no match for them, and retreated.

Female trickery, sometimes for a good cause but more often for a bad one, is a popular theme in the literature of Islamic countries. Old women in particular have a reputation for great cunning; for a person who has absolutely no power and no resources at her disposal, this can actually be a matter of life or death. According to a saying in Morocco, "What the devil does in a year an old woman achieves in an hour." [183, 68] And in the *Arabian Nights* story about "Tricky Dal'la" we read "Baghdad is full of women who trick men." [164, IV, 731] Anyone who wants to accuse women of trickery can refer to the Koran, whose Joseph *Sūra* says of Potiphar's wife, who tears Joseph's shirt from his back, "It is some of your guile, verily your guile is mighty." (12: 28)

The first century of Islam was characterized not only by women who were bold and courageous, but also by proud, beautiful women who played such an important role in the social life of their time that romances were woven around them in the literary tradition.

Sukayna was the granddaughter of Caliph Alī, daughter of his son Husayn, who was killed in battle at Kerbela and whom the Shī'ites still revere as a martyr. Sukayna was not part of the religious opposition to the worldly rule of the Umayyads, which was gathering in Mecca and Medina, the holy cities of Islam. Rather, she incarnated a high-spirited society which, untroubled by political wrangles

(Damascus, the residence of the Caliphs, was far away) wanted to enjoy its wealth and indulge in luxury. Music and poetry flourished in the Hijāz, a subject that will be examined later.

The attitude of these circles toward Islam is evident in a remark attributed to Sukayna. Asked why she was always so merry while her sister Fātima was always so solemn, she replied that she had been named after her pre-Islamic great-grandmother, her sister after her Islamic grandmother. Sukayna was famous not only for her beauty, humor and practical jokes but also for her astuteness and wit. She once assembled poets around her, had them declaim their latest works and then judged and rewarded them according to the way they described their beloved or their relationship in the poems. She was known for her elegance as well. She wore her magnificent hair in a special style that became fashionable and was named after her. When men began to imitate her, however, the pious Caliph Umar Ibn Abd al-Azīz had them whipped and their heads shorn.

Sukayna must also have been bold and courageous. When she had an abscess removed below her eye—with no anesthetic, of course —she endured the operation without moving and without a sigh of pain. She was left with a scar that was considered especially attractive. She was married at least four times, but sources disagree as to the sequence and names of her husbands. We know, at least, that they also came from respected families. The sources devote special attention to her marriage with Zayd Ibn Amr, grandson of Caliph Uthmān. She married him on the condition that he would never repudiate her on his initiative, nor touch another woman, nor refuse her anything she wished, allow her to live where she wanted and not contradict her in anything; otherwise he would have to repudiate her at her wish. The two often quarreled. When, because he was angry with her, he went to one of his estates where he had numerous female slaves at his disposal and remained there for seven months, she went to the Governor of Medina and lodged a complaint. The father had Zayd brought to Medina and ordered one of his subordinates to judge between them. Sukayna provoked the judge to such an extent that he threatened her: "If you were not a woman, I would have you whipped." A violent altercation broke out between the two, and when one of those present urged her to be reasonable, she abused him as well. Supposedly, the judge grew nervous because his wife was sitting in a niche and could hear everything Sukayna uttered in her rage. Zayd, who does not seem to have had much courage, "kept as close as possible to the raised seat of the judge as if he wanted to crawl into it out if fear." Sukayna cried: "Take a good look at me! From now on you will no longer see my face." The Governor of Medina, who had waited in the building for the meeting to end and then received a report of it, "laughed till his sides split." [5b, XVI, 155ff.]

Sukayna's rival in beauty and elegance was the capricious Ā'isha Bint Talha, a granddaughter on her mother's side of first Caliph Abū Bakr. For a time, they were both married to the same man, Mus'ab Ibn az-Zubayr, who was as handsome, chivalrous and generous as he was hard and unyielding. It is said of Ā'isha that she never veiled her face. Her husband Mus'ab did not approve of this, and he urged her to observe the customs. But she countered this by saying: "God, the Almighty, has honored me with beauty. I want the people to see this and understand what rank I enjoy before them. I will not veil myself. Nobody can reproach me with a fault." [5b, XI, 176]

She, too, was married a number of times, and it is said that she liked to annoy her husbands by lauding, in the most fulsome terms, the virtues of a deceased husband over those of the one she was married to at the time. Mus'ab is said to have admired her for her beauty, her nonchalance, her attractive figure—her large proportions at the rear are singled out for special praise—her willpower and her virtue. But it took verbal and physical abuse to make her obedient. One day, he spread precious pearls across her lap as she slept. This awakened the spoiled woman, who only grumbled, "I would have preferred to sleep." [5b, XI, 181] Mus'ab's secretary once promised to help him force her to give in. Mus'ab encouraged him, saying: "Do as you please, for she is the best of all the earthly things I possess." One night, in her presence, the secretary had two black slaves dig a grave in her house and told her that Mus'ab had ordered him to bury her alive in it. She was so alarmed by this that he was able to make her promise to be more obliging to her husband in the future. [5b, XI, 181 ff.]

Ā'isha Bint Talha's next husband bribed her maidservant so that he could really spend the wedding night with his new wife. When this husband died, she rejected all subsequent suitors and never married again.

Incidentally, she was so highly respected that while she was on a pilgrimage, the Governor of Mecca agreed to delay the hour of prayer so that she could complete the circumambulation of the Ka'ba. She could not, or would not, prevent his dismissal following this episode. Her beauty was sung in many verses. It is also reported that in her knowledge of Ancient Arabic history and its battles, Arabic poetry and astronomy, she was the equal of learned men from the ruling house of the Umayyads.

It is apparent that in the early days of Islam, women from noble families, especially when they had property of their own, not only had the same *de facto* rights as their husbands, but were sometimes able to demonstrate their superiority as well. It is related that Umm Salama, who had been married to two well-respected men from the ruling Umayyad family, one day happened to notice the young Abu l-Abbās as-Saffāh, later to become the first Abbāsid Caliph. His handsome appearance attracted her, and she sent a maidservant to him with a proposal of marriage and at the same time, money for the dowry. On their wedding night, she wore so many jewels that he could not touch her. And even when she removed them and changed her clothes, he was unable to demonstrate his prowess as a husband; she had to console him by telling him that this had happened to other men occasionally, too. He then swore that he would never take a second wife or a concubine. She bore him two children; until he became Caliph, he decided nothing before obtaining her advice and approval.

It is said that one of the authors at his Court one day expressed his regret that as-Saffāh had restricted himself to one woman. "O Commander of the Faithful," he argued, "if you saw a tall, white-skinned maiden or a brown-skinned one with dark lips or a yellow one with round hips, yea, those that have come to Kufa or Basra and are sweet-tongued, slight in stature, with a small waist and with curly locks around their temples, with dark eyes, firm breasts, dressed in beautiful garments and wearing fine jewels, you would see something wonderful." The Caliph liked the sound of this and bade him to repeat his words. When his wife Umm Salama subsequently saw him sitting there lost in thought, she soon discovered what had been said to him. Seething with anger, she sent some men to see the man of letters, Khālid Ibn Safwān, with instructions to give him a good beating. Khālid allowed the men to enter, in the belief that the Caliph wished to reward him for his good advice, but he was bitterly disappointed. Several days passed before he was well enough to leave the house. When, still groaning with pain, he then came to the Caliph who had sent for him, he noticed a slight movement in the curtain in front of a door and guessed that Umm Salama was behind it. The Caliph wanted to hear his words once more, but Khālid told him that the Arabs derive the word *darra,* meaning "co-wife," from a root that also means "damage" or "misfortune." "None of those who had more than one wife was happy . . . three wives are like three stones on which a pot is simmering, and four wives are the worst thing that can happen to a man, they make him gray, old and sick." The Caliph constantly interrupted him, saying: "You certainly didn't say that." Nevertheless, Khālid also told the Caliph that virgins were like young men, only without testicles, and that he had married a wise lady from a noble family and should not search for other women. At this, peals of laughter came from behind the curtain, followed by words of approval. Khālid did indeed receive a rich reward eventually, but it was from the Caliph's wife. [112, VI, 110-18]

Arwā (Umm Mūsā), wife of Caliph al-Mansūr, successor to as-Saffāh on the throne, traced her ancestry back to the South Arabian kings of the Himyarits. She also demanded written agreement from her husband that he would never take either a second wife or a concubine while she was alive. The Caliph subsequently regretted this declaration and wished to have it annulled. But his wife appealed to the supreme judge of Egypt, who was brought to Iraq solely for this purpose. His verdict was in favor of Arwā, since she was able to produce the marriage contract with the appropriate clause. When she died, in the tenth year of his reign, al-Mansūr established a large harem.

To his son by Arwā, the future Caliph al-Mahdī, who had a special weakness for women, al-Mansūr gave the fatherly advice that he should not consult them in his private affairs: but this obviously went unheeded. Al-Mahdī was very much influenced by his concubine and future wife Khayzurān, "Bamboo Stem." She was the mother of his two sons, Mūsā and Hārūn, and a daughter for whom al-Mahdī had such great affection that, clothed as a youth, she was allowed to accompany him on his travels. When she died, he publicly accepted the expressions of sympathy by his subjects. During the reign of al-Mahdī, Khayzurān, although she had to share her spouse with co-wives and concubines, became so addicted to her power that she did not wish to abandon it when her son Mūsā al-Hādī ascended the throne in 785. In the first four months of his Caliphat, people still gathered around her and sought her advice, and veritable "processions made a pilgrimage to her door," in the words of the historian Tabarī. [162, VIII, 205f.] This was too much for the young Caliph, who obviously attached more importance to getting his own way than his father had done. He, who until then had yielded to her every wish, used a pretext to refuse a request in harsh words; he also resisted her urgent pleas. He even said to her: "Women are not permitted by destiny to interfere in the affairs of government. You are to pray, to praise Allah, to withdraw from the world, and to devote yourself to the service of Allah. In addition, you must obey, as it is proper for women." He threatened her in the following words: "Beware, if you do not heed my words . . . If I hear that one of my chief people or servants is at your door, I will strike off his head and take his property. What are those processions which go to your door every day? Have you then no spindle to claim you, no copy of the Koran to call you to obedience, and no house to shelter you? Be careful not to come to me to bore or reproach me!" [112, VI, 269ff.] After this, the hatred between them became so great that each tried to have the other murdered. After Mūsā's premature death, which was not unconnected with Khayzurān, she made sure that her beloved son, Hārūn, son of Al-Mahdi, would succeed to the throne.

Khayzurān was one of the richest women of her time, and her annual income, at the peak of her power, amounted to 160 million silver dirham. It is said that in her palace she had eighteen thousand gowns of embroidered brocade. When, on one occasion, she demanded even more from Mūsā al-Hādī, he put a complete warehouse at her disposal. This love of pomp and luxury was a great stimulus for the textile industry, of course, but Khayzurān also invested her money in other undertakings. For example, she had a canal built to the Iraqi town of Anbar. She had a secretary of her own for her business transactions.

After Khayzurān's death in 789—she could have hardly been fifty years of age—another woman soon assumed a similar position of power in the Caliph's harem and in the country: Zubayda, cousin and wife of Caliph Hārūn ar-Rashīd, known to us principally from the *Arabian Nights*. In fact, her Islamic name was Amat al-Azīz, but since she was such a pretty and chubby child, her grandfather, Caliph al-Mansūr, called her Zubayda, "Butterflake" or "Marigold." In 781-2, during the Caliphate of al-Mahdī, she became the wife of Harūn ar-Rashīd and fascinated him to such a degree that he almost gave up his claim to the throne in order to devote himself to her. Although he later had very many beautiful and artistically gifted concubines, she obviously continued to enjoy a favored position, not only because of her royal origins, but for her personality as well.

Zubayda was famous for her generosity to poets. She had a hundred female slaves in her palace who all recited the Koran in sets of ten verses, so that it sounded like the buzzing of a swarm of bees. At a time of drought, she had an aqueduct twelve miles long built from a spring in the Hijāz to Mecca, across valleys and hills. The man entrusted with the work objected that it would be very expensive, but she ordered him: "Build it, even if every stroke of the mattock costs a dinar!" It is said that she spent 1.7 million dinar on this project. She also had houses, cisterns, and wells built in the Hijāz and along the frontier routes, and was active as a benefactress. [81, I, 337; 112, VIII, 297]

Islamic historiography, which likes to credit famous people with being the first to introduce things, affirms that Zubayda was the first to use vessels of gold and silver encrusted with jewels, the first to wear brocade gowns worth fifty thousand dinar each, and the first to recruit a palace guard of young men and girls to carry letters and bring messages. Finally, she is also said to have been the first to use candles of amber and to have worn sandals embroidered with jewels. She was thus considered responsible for the increasing pomp and splendor at the Caliph's Court.

Zubayda also tried to influence the succession to the throne. She wanted her beloved son Muhammed al-Amīn, who was not very competent, however, to be Hārūn's successor, and not al-Ma'mūn, his son by a Persian concubine. When Hārūn then decided to leave all the Arab areas of the Empire and the throne to al-Amīn and to give al-Ma'mūn the Persian areas under the sovereignty of his brother, Zubayda reproached him with being unjust, since he had not ensured the support of the generals and major figures of the Empire for Amīn. Hārūn then replied, "What business of yours (a woman) is the judgment of our actions and the experience of men?" [112, VI, 325 ff.] When discord subsequently arose between the two brothers, in the course of which al-Amīn was executed in 813, Zubayda went into mourning and wore gowns of haircloth. Like Ā'isha, Muhammed's favorite wife, she was urged to wreak vengeance, but she replied: "What interest have we women in this demand for a blood feud or in vaunting ourselves as heroes?" She sent al-Ma'mūn a poem in which she expressed her sorrow at the death of her son and her admiration for Ma'mūn, the new Caliph. He was so moved by this that he paid her his respect and also granted her a substantial apanage. Zubayda died in Baghdad in 831.

For centuries, there was a negative attitude in Islam towards the idea of a woman on the throne. It is true that the Koran mentions the legendary Queen of Sheba without any deprecating comments, but from about the eighth century on, *hadīths* such as these are found: "When men obey women, ruin is certain"; [82, V, 45] "A people which entrusts its affairs to a woman will have no success." [24, 92, 18] Nevertheless, in the course of Islamic history, there have always been women who influenced their leader husbands or sons in political affairs. But rarely indeed, and then only for a short time, did women themselves ascend to the throne. For the most part, these women were people of their time, just as ruthless, cruel, scheming and extravagant as their male counterparts. If they had not been so, they

The dinar of the Sultana Shajarat ad-Durr bears the place and date of minting (Cairo 648h), the name of the Caliph al-Musta'sim bi-llāh and the surname and title of the Sultana.

would probably have been unable to assert themselves.

In Egypt, there was a slave-sultana with the melodious name Shajarat ad-Durr, "Pearl Tree." She was initially the slave and later the wife of the last Ayyubid ruler al-Malik as-Sālih, after she had borne him a son who died at an early age. Her husband died shortly after the Crusaders of Louis IX landed at Damietta, his son and successor Tūrānshāh was murdered immediately afterwards. In this situation, she officially assumed the title of Sultan on May 2, 1250, and remained sovereign regent of Egypt until July 30 of the same year. A contemporary Arab historian described her as a "strong personality of great nobility . . . and an exemplary way of life," who had been "much loved" by the Sultan. [150, 43] A Syrian historian of the same period wrote of her: "She was a Turk, the most cunning woman of her age, unmatched in beauty among women and in determination among men." [150, 44] After her subjects had sworn the oath of allegiance to her, she carried on the business of government, signed the Sultan's decrees, and, as usual for an Islamic ruler, was mentioned in the Friday prayers as the sovereign. For the first time in an Islamic country, coins were minted bearing the name of a woman. Under Tūrānshāh, a crushing defeat had been inflicted on the Crusaders, and a few days after the Sultana came to power, Damietta was returned to the Muslims. But then, when the oath of allegiance to the Sultana was required from the Syrian viceroy, a dispute broke out in the course of which the Mamlūk Emirs decided that they could not leave the reins of State in the hands of a woman, and transferred power to Aybak, Supreme Commander of the armed forces. Shajarat ad-Durr afterwards became his wife. Arab historians generally present this dismissal as a tactical renunciation of the throne by the Sultana, in favor of her future husband. However, the struggle between Syria and Egypt, which had allegedly been caused by the presence of a woman on the throne, increased in intensity after this step. It is not known exactly when Shajarat ad-Durr married Aybak, but her Oriental contemporaries continue to describe her as the real regent who did what she wanted with the realm and issued orders which were obeyed. Of her relationship with her husband, a historian comments: "She dominated him, and he had nothing to say." [150, 79] There is also evidence that she continued to sign Sultan's decrees and to be addressed as Sultana. Finally, when she heard that Aybak intended to take a daughter of the Prince of Mosul as a co-wife, she had her husband murdered. Since she had taken no steps with respect to his successor, rioting broke out in the course of which the murderers were crucified. Shajarat ad-Durr's half-naked body was found in the moat of the citadel.

At almost the same time as Shajarat ad-Durr, who later became the subject of legends in the popular Baybars novel, Sultana Raziyya ruled as sovereign in Delhi; her regency lasted three years, six months, and six days, from 1236 to 1240. Raziyya also came from a Turkish slave dynasty.

A Persian historian, who had met her in person and who always showered praise on all the rulers of the dynasty, writes of her: "Sultān Raziyyat was a great sovereign, and sagacious, just, beneficent, the patron of the learned, a dispenser of justice, the cherisher of her subjects, and of warlike talent, and was endowed with all the admirable attributes and qualifications necessary for kings; but, as she did not attain the destiny, in her creation, of being computed among men, of what advantage were all these excellent qualifications unto her?"

[116, 637f.]   Her father recognized her abilities and named her as his successor, although he had several sons. This caused dissatisfaction, however, among his subjects. Since the ruler had sons he should have appointed one of these to succeed him. "Be pleased to remove this dffficulty from our minds," they said, "as this deed does not seem advisable to your humble servants." [116, 638f.]   But the Sultan was of the opinion that, unlike his daughter, none of his sons was capable of ruling his realm. When she ultimately ascended the throne, riots broke out, but she was able to suppress them. She won over most of her adversaries and gave them official positions. But then the equerry, an Abyssinian, became the subject of her special favor, and this provoked the envy of the other Court officials and Emirs. Finally, Sultana Raziyya put aside women's clothing—a remarkably early form of female emancipation in Islam—and dressed as a man. She wore a turban and appeared thus in public, naturally without a veil. Probably she believed that this would enhance her authority and that she would obtain firmer control of her empire. In 1239, rebellions again broke out among her liege-lords and Emirs led to her arrest. The governor, to whom she had been entrusted for safekeeping, married her and sent troops to Delhi to recapture the throne for her. But Raziyya's brother, who had taken over her position, mobilized his army against her and her husband. Her forces deserted her, and she and her husband were killed in 1240.

The twelfth volume of a famous biographical lexicon by an Arab scholar is devoted to women; in it is mentioned a princess by the name of Tandū of the dynasty of the Jalā'irids, who was the ruler of Southern Iraq and Khuzistan of the 15th century. This woman of exceptional beauty was married, so the author relates, to the Prince Shāhwalad Ibn Shāhzādeh as her second husband. Wanting to take power herself, she conspired against him, and he was murdered. His son by another wife, Mahmūd, succeeded him, but Tandū carried on intrigues against him as well and had him killed. She then reigned by herself from 1416-7 to 1419. She was mentioned in the Friday prayers, and coins were minted bearing her name. [144, 16] This energetic lady claimed, however, to be ruling for her son Uwais II, who was eleven years old at the time.

In the world of Islam, power-hungry mothers took over the business of state for their young or weak and incompetent sons on more than one occasion, despite public opinion that was becoming increasingly hostile toward women. This is reflected in the following remark alleged to have been made by the Prophet: "I know nothing of lower rank in knowledge and religion which overpowers intelligent people more than you (women)!" [54, 25]

There was, for instance, the mother of the Abbāsid Caliph al-Muqtadir who was herself a slave. When her son came to power in 908 at the age of 13, he was still so childlike and dependent that the government was *de facto* in her hands. This did not change very much even when the Caliph became older, but he also took advice from other ladies of his harem, which sheltered no less than four thousand women. Incidentally, in 918-9, his mother appointed her confidante, the castle bailiff Thaml "Drunkenness," (who was also a slave, judging by her name) as the principal arbitrator the criminal court, which met once a week. This resulted in general outrage. But this lady was able to exercise her office satisfactorily after recruiting male lawyers to help her. The twenty-five-year reign of al-Muqtadir, or rather that of his mother and his harem, was marked by riots and the increasing disintegration of his empire.

The mother of the Spanish Umayyad Caliph Hishām Ibn al-Hakam in Cordova, the beautiful Basque Subh, "Aurora," used her influence, even during the lifetime of her husband, to obtain a leading position both at Court and in the Empire for the ruthlessly ambitious upstart al-Mansūr (the Almansor of Christian chroniclers). He was able to exploit the good will of the lady (who was later accused of having been his mistress), and in combination with his own political abilities, to achieve a position of absolute power. At this time, the young Caliphs were allowed to grow up in total seclusion and concentrate on their theological studies.

In the eleventh century, Sayyida, a Būyid princess ruled in West Iran. The Qarakhānid Princess Terken Khātūn of Bukhara, wife of the Seljūq Malikshāh, governed in the name of their young sons. The latter even proposed marriage to her brother-in-law in order to guide political and military developments in the direction she wanted.

Mughal princess on the throne

The fact that the mothers of the Ottoman Sultans, at least in the period of the gradual decline of Turkish rule, possessed special political influence was certainly taken into account by their adversaries as well as by their political allies. The *Sultān Wālide* —the equivalent of "Queen Mother"—was usually a former slave, who had borne a successor to the ruling Sultan. She not only enjoyed the respect of her son, but was in charge of his harem, making the final decision in every matter concerning the ladies of the harem. It has already been noted in the previous chapter that mothers enjoyed a special position of respect in Islam. In a polygynous society, a man can have several wives, but everywhere he has only one mother. The *Sultān Wālide* was thus the First Lady of Turkey. One or two weeks after her son ascended the throne, she was fetched in a ceremonial procession and accompanied from the old to the new seraglio where her son resided. A special etiquette was designed for those who came into contact with her. It was only possible to speak to her after a request for an audience had first been submitted. Once permission was granted to appear before her, the applicant was allowed to speak and sit down only after she ordered him to do so.

When the Sultan was under age, and also when he was too weak or too addicted to the pleasures of his harem, real power was in the hands of the *Sultān Wālide,* who with energy and a greater or lesser degree of ability, directed the affairs of state, assisted by loyal Viziers. Thus Nūr Bānū (d. 1587, a Venetian of the Baffo family, under Murād III), Safiyya (d. 1609, under Mehmet III), Māh Peiker Kösem (d. 1651, under Murād IV) and Ibrāhīm I and Tarkhān Khadījeh (d. 1683, under Mehmet IV) played an active part in the policies pursued by their sons. Their opinion counted when it was a question of appointing or dismissing Viziers or other dignitaries of the Empire. Whoever had the ambition to advance at the Court endeavored to obtain their good will by presenting them with gifts. Tarkhān, for instance, concealed by a curtain, took part in and influenced the meetings of the *Dīwān* (council).

Incidentally, under Ibrāhīm I, a power struggle took place between the old and the new *Sultān Wālide,* between Kösem and Tarkhān. Each recruited followers and endeavored to assert her policy. Finally Kösem was being cruelly strangled with the cord of a curtain by the eunuchs of her rival.

Because of her large income, the *Sultān Wālide,* also possessed great economic influence. She had her own ships with which she carried on trade, and possessed estates whose tenants had to render military service. Her financial resources were so great that she could afford to erect mosques and other buildings as well as live in luxury.

Clever and energetic favorites of the Sultans also influenced their policies. The best-known of these was Khorrem, "Merry," (d. 1558), a slim slave girl who, by reason of her origin, was known to the scholars of the Renaissance as Roxolane, "the Russian", and is mentioned by this name in European descriptions of Ottoman history. Under Sulaymān I, the lawmaker, she achieved such power that he not only kept her in luxury and magnificence but also, to please her, married his other slaves to officials and officers of his Court. She was also an expert in the art of intrigue, and did not hesitate to have Viziers executed if they stood in her way. She was remembered by later generations for her pious endowments and public buildings: she built a mosque, a hospital, and a school.

The Sultan's sisters and daughters, who were married to Court officials, just like most of the wealthy women of the first centuries of Islam, usually had the principal command in their marriages. Whether it was really true, as reported by various European travelers, that their husbands on the wedding night had to climb on the marital bed at the foot end and gradually work their way up under the blanket—just as the concubines did with regard to the Sultan—can no longer be confirmed. However, a sixteenth-century Turkish Vizier, who boxed his wife's ears—she was a member of the Sultan's family—immediately lost his wife and his position.

Of the women who influenced regents, the one who must be especially noted is the Mughal Empress Nūr Jahān, wife of the Emperor Jahāngīr. She was born in Kandahar in 1577, and, four years after the death of her first husband, married Jahāngīr. She was thirty-four and he forty-two years of age. At the time they met, at the Spring Festival of 1611, she was lady-in-waiting of the widow of Emperor Akbar. He was immediately attracted to Nūr Jahān, and married her two months later. She soon became the actual ruler, since Jahāngīr's health had been undermined by asthma and addiction to alcohol. Her father and brother assisted the Empress, who was astute, educated, charming, and politically ambitious. It is reported by her husband's biographer that Jahāngīr repeatedly stated that he had handed over power to his wife, and that he was content with a flask of wine and a pound of meat. Jahāngīr's memoirs reflect his pride in his wife, who possessed the spirit of a man. During a hunt she shot four tigers from her litter on top of an elephant. Also apparent in his memoirs is Jahāngīr's gratitude for her ability and for the affection with which she tended his ruined health (better than any physician, in his opinion) and gradually eliminated his dependence on alcohol. The Englishman Thomas Roe, who stayed at the Mughal Court from 1615 to 1619 wrote in his diary about the Emperor Jahāngīr, "whose course is directed by a woman and is now, as it were, shutt up by her soe, that all justice or care of any thing or public affayrs either sleepes or depends on her, who is more unaccesable than any goddesse or mistery of heathen impietys." [139, 337] Nūr Jahān, he said, "fulfills the observation that in all actions of consequence in a court, especially in faction, a woman is not only alwayes an ingredient, but commonly a principall drug and of most vertue." [139, 325] It should be remembered here that the reign of Elizabeth I of England had come to an end little more than a decade previously. When Nūr Jahān was at the zenith of power, coins were minted bearing her name. She was a leader in fashion, and her gowns, veils, brocades, and also her sandalwood-colored carpets, were generally copied by those around her.

Shāh Jahān, a son-in-law of her brother, came to power in in 1627. Nūr Jahān, who had not supported his succession but that of her own son-in-law, then withdrew from politics. She received an appropriate pension and, until her death in 1645, devoted her time to erecting splendid tombs for her husband and father, and giving her money for worthy causes.

19

Ladies are preparing a picnic against a background of blossoming trees. A maid-servant, with full cheeks, is blowing on the fire to make it burn so that the food hanging over it in a large pot can be cooked. Pastry is being kneaded in the fore-ground, and a eunuch is in attendance. Further back, dancing and talking are going on. The ladies wear brightly colored gowns and attractive embroidered headcloths. Some have their gowns tied back and are revealing highly decorative trousers. (Iran, ca. 1575)

20

A young warrior on a black steed, accompanied by his retinue, fetches his bride. She is seated in a litter on a camel and is wearing the tāj-kulāh, *the crown-like headgear of princesses in Iran during the second half of the sixteenth century. She is followed by maidservants, while spectators have concealed themselves behind the hill.*

21

It is not only miniatures of Persian epics, such as this scene from a Shāh-nāmeh of about 1600, that show Court ladies taking part in the chase. European travelers of the seventeenth and eighteenth centuries in Iran also tell of this.

22

When death occurred, women expressed their grief with loud cries and much gesticulation. The painter of this Iranian miniature of about 1600 characterizes the sorrow of the women by the posture of their bodies and not by the expression of their faces. In the foreground are Koran readers, and the dead horse of one of the two slain heroes on an elephant.

23

This miniature conveys an impression of a harem during the Mughal period. A dancer is demonstrating her art in the garden in front of the house while one of the women watching is busy with her hair. A wet nurse is suckling a baby, and on the upper floor a maidservant is fanning a women in childbed. At the rear of the garden, four maidservants are preparing a meal. (India, seventeenth century)

The Mughal Emperor Akbar—in the center of the picture—is crossing a river with his harem. High-ranking Indian women of this period were not permitted to show themselves in public when they left the harem. They passed through the streets in closed litters on camels or on elephants, while the most exalted of them were carried in a carriage drawn by cows. The fish and the ducks in the river seem to be part of the magnificent imperial convoy which the artist has depicted like a Makimano caring for every beautiful detail.

24

25

This miniature shows a scene in Turkish bazaar around 1600. A veiled lady is offering a bracelet for sale, but otherwise business is the affair of men, as it still is today in many areas. The qualities of the merchandise are being extolled, and bargaining is in progress, accompanied by much gesticulation. Market supervisors are depicted with long swords on their shoulders.

26

A richly ornamented Mughal lady of the late seventeenth century, surrounded by maidservants, is seated on a carpet in the garden of the harem. The attractive profiles of the women with their black, almond-shaped eyes and curved eyebrows stand out beautifully against the green of the garden.

27

Gesticulating in lively fashion, a sheikh and an unveiled lady are engaged in discussion on this Iranian miniature from the end of the 17th century.

28

The wife of a goldsmith helping her husband to escape from a prison tower. In the background, the battlements of a town, on the left a landscape with blossoming shrubs and trees and a watercourse with birds. Female cunning for good as well as evil is a favorite theme of the literatures of the Muslim countries based on the 12th Sūra (12: 28).

29

A Turkish miniature from the end of the sixteenth century. Before the heavily veiled Muhammed, three women are kneeling who were of great importance to Islam. From right to left, they are Fātima, Ā'isha, Umm Salama. All three, like Muhammed, are depicted with a nimbus of flames, and wear a veil completely concealing the face. The maidservants, however, are not veiled.

30

A harp player entertaining a lady of high rank. She wears a precious diadem, secured by long ribbons, long and heavy earrings, and an anklet. The two of them are clothed in the brightly patterned gowns fashionable during the Seljūq *period at the end of the twelfth century.*

31

This Iranian princess of about 1540 is wearing the tāj-kulāh, a matching embroidered collar, long ear pendants, and strings of pearls around her face and neck.

32
"She plays the lute with such artistry that even the hardest rocks crack with joy"
[164, II, 600]

33

A troop of tumblers entertaining male spectators, including a high-ranking personage astride his horse. To a musical accompaniment, women perform acrobatics on a suspended beam, one of them even on stilts. Another performs a sword dance. In the background are splendid palaces of an Indian city of the Mughal period in the eighteenth century with great gates, towers, and minarets. Behind a river with boats upon it, other settlements can be seen between the hills.

Women in Islamic Culture

omen played a considerable role in the art of Islam, especially in poetry and music. They do not appear to have been active in the field of miniature painting. In an Arab source of the ninth century, it is reported that a daughter of the Abbāsid Caliph al-Mahdī painted a glass with a verse in golden letters [89, 187], but this was at a time when it was fashionable to decorate gowns, cloth, and headbands with golden verse or lettering.

Perfume of a dark color was sometimes used to write letters on the face, for instance the name of the beloved. The same source reports that women liked to do embroidery of the same kind. Female calligraphists from Spain are particularly well known; learned and artistic women were sometimes lauded for beautiful handwriting.

Arabic *adab* literature frequently mentions a popular and witty Court game, in which women, especially slaves, liked to take part: to answer verse with verse in intricate improvisation. Arabic poetry since pre-Islamic times has a complicated metrical system consisting of 16 metres, formed by different but regular sequences of long and short syllables. According to the rules each poem be it even rather long, must have a continuous rhyme. Consequently, the game was more difficult than might first appear to an outsider, who might easily regard the verses as off-the-cuff rhymes. In poetry games of this kind, the person giving the answer had to use the same meter and rhyme as the challenger.

In pre-Islamic and early Islamic time there were free Arab women who wrote elegies in praise of their brothers, father, or husband slain in battle. Al-Khansā, who expressed her profound sorrow at the death of her two brothers killed in tribal feuds in pre-Islamic times, was famous for her poetic laments of this kind. Islam, however, exercised no influence on the poetry of this woman; she was so dedicated to pre-Islamic traditions that both the second Caliph Umar and Ā'isha, Muhammed's favorite wife, are said to have criticized her for centering her laments on two men who had been killed as pagans. She is said to have replied to Umar that this was precisely the reason her grief was so profound, since the two were now suffering in the fires of Hell. Whether that was true or not, her imagery and the wealth of forms in her poetry was an inspiration to later poets.

The Arab poetess Laylā al-Akhyaliyya, of the seventh century, was famous for her funeral odes. The custom of the time was for poets to compete with each other in sarcasm and invective, and she exchanged such verses with Nābigha, another famous poet of the time. Poetic diatribes of this kind, in which blunt abuse, sometimes of a sexual nature, was not spared, were at times directed by Arab women against their husbands [78, 149ff.], hardly a sign of the modest submissiveness required by Islamic tradition.

The women of Islamic Spain, where a variety of ethnic and cultural elements had successfully synthesized, enjoyed a greater measure of freedom than women in the East of the Islamic empire. It was here that the art of Arabic poetry flourished among women as well as among men. In a monograph dealing with cultural history, an Arab author of the first half of the seventeenth century, in introductory remarks to discussion of Spanish women who wrote poetry, says: " . . . and so I will name a number of Spanish women who are very skillful in the art of words, so that it will be clear that this talent is almost a natural instinct among the Spaniards, even among the women and boys." [109, II, 536]

Only three of the most famous Spanish poetesses will be mentioned here. First Wallāda, daughter of a Caliph, who died unmarried in 1087-8 or 1091-2; she became famous for the frank love poems which she exchanged with her more illustrious fellow poet Ibn Zaydūn. One of her contemporaries, who was personally acquainted with Wallāda, extolled her qualities to her biographer, namely, presence of mind, purity of language, passionate feelings, and sagacity of speech. Another Arab author lauded her in descriptive language:

> *Her poetry and elegance were of the most perfect form,*
> *sophisticated presence of mind paired with passionately*
> *beautiful expression. She was beautiful to look upon and of a*
> *noble nature. It was pleasing to go to her and whoever left*
> *her felt himself refreshed and renewed. Her circle at*
> *Cordova was a rendezvous for the noble minds of the region,*
> *her court a race course for the proud stallions of poetry and*
> *prose. The learned were blinded by the radiance of her face,*
> *poets perished to partake of her sweetness. Although easy to*
> *approach and surrounded by many, she was of high rank, of*
> *noble heritage and virtuous nature. But her unconcern and*
> *poems of sensuous openness were a source of gossip.* [109,
> II, 565]

Verses that she embroidered on her sleeves—a fashion of the time—
are also evidence of her pride and candor. On the right sleeve were
the words:

> *By God I am fit for important things*
> *And go my way armed with pride.*

and on the left:

> *My lover I offer the curve of my cheek*
> *And my kiss, to whoever desires it.*
> [109, II, 563]

Nevertheless, according to the same author, Wallāda was famed for
her modesty and virtue. In this respect, however, attitudes of that
time seem to have been much more liberal in Spain than in the
Islamic East. We know that, in addition to Ibn Zaydūn, other men
desired her also, and that she exchanged love poems with them as
well. Ibn Zaydūn extolled a night he spent with her in the following
words: ". . . plucking the camomile blossoms of her lips and harvest-

ing the pomegranates of her breasts." [75, 22] After they spent a night together, she took leave of one of her lovers thus:

Thou brother of the Moon
Radiating brightness and sublime like him,
That I may see you again,
May God the Lord grant! . . .
The nights now seem long to me.
And I complain night after night,
That only those were so short,
Which I once spent with you.
[109, II, 564; 147, I, 290]

An Arab author praises her beauty and spirit, her wordiness, and her charm: "To gaze at her and to listen to her was such a complete pleasure that she stole hearts and restored to old men their youth." [109, II, 566]

Naz'hūn came from Granada. She lived in the eleventh century, and was famed for her kindness, her beauty, her talent for improvising poems, her knowledge of the art of poetry, and her memorable and apt turn of speech. She, too, was candid in her love poems. Thus she immortalized the joys of a night of love in which one could have seen "the morning sun lying in the arms of the moon" or "rather the white antelope of the tribe of Khuzayma in the embrace of a lion." [109, II, 637]

The most illustrious poetess of Islamic Spain was Hafsa Bint al-Hājj, who was born after 1135, died in 1190-1 and was famous for her long love affair with the poet Abu Ja'far Ibn Sa'īd. Nearly all her poems that have survived are passionate expressions of this love. Yet she was not so flippant as her predecessor, Wallāda. She once gave voice to jealousy of her beloved in the following words:

Jealousy fills me with pain,
Not only at my eyes, at you and me,
But at the time and place where you may be,
And if I locked up you in my eyes,

Until the Day of Judgment, it would not do.
[55, St. 13]

Hafsa lived in a stricter time than Wallāda; the Berber dynasties of the Almoravids and later the Almohads were puritanical in their views. Nevertheless, it can be inferred from her verses that she was free to visit her admirers. One of her poems begins: "Whether I visit you or you visit me, my heart always inclines to that which it desires." [109, II, 544] Poems written honoring oneself date back to pre-Islamic Arabia. When Hafsa once visited the house of Ibn Sa'īd without prior notice, she gave the maidservant who opened the door a note bearing a poem in which she lauded her beauty, which began: "A visitor with the (slim) neck of a gazelle has come . . ." and ended, "Do you think she may enter with your permission or do you believe it is better that she departs?" [109, II, 545]

Her love for Ibn Sa'īd was endangered when both the newly appointed Almohad Governor of the city and the future Caliph Abu Sa'īd Uthmān fell in love with her. For a long time, she endeavored to keep harmony between the love of the respected poet who was in aristocratic circles, and that of the representative of the State. The Governor, who was about seven years her junior, appears at first only to have admired her as a beautiful and witty woman. Soon he sent her with a deputation to his father, the Caliph, whose favor she quickly won with a poem. Subsequently, however, her long-standing admirer Ibn Sa'īd reproached her: "Why do you love this black man? (The Almohad was the son of a Negress.) I can buy you ten Negroes at the slave market who are more handsome than he!" [109, II, 546] This must have reached the ears of Abu Sa'īd. Ibn Sa'īd was later accused, not unjustly, of being involved in a plot. He was thrown into prison and executed in 1163. Hafsa mourned him in her poems, which bear witness to her profound feelings. She wore black, as a sign of grief, although, as she complains in a poem, she was rebuked for this. One of her poems to him reads:

He outshone me with a star's brilliant light,
But now I see the darkness of night.

I mourn his virtues full of pain
Far from the grace and joy
He brought me again and again.
[55, 18th stanza]

It was not long after the death of her beloved poet that she abandoned the writing of verse. She ended her life as a teacher of Almohad princesses at the Court of Marrakesh, and in this activity won such esteem that a later biographer described her as the greatest woman educator of her time.

Hafsa and Wallāda, the female poets of Arab Spain, are praised for their ability to express original feelings in a natural form, despite their close links with the traditions of Arabic poetry, and for their skill in the use of traditional poetic diction. The same is said of two Turkish poetesses, Mihrī Khātūn and Zaynab, who lived in the second half of the fifteenth century. They both came from families in which education was a tradition. Otherwise, little is known about their lives. To achieve a reputation in Arabic, Persian, or Turkish poetry, poets first had to learn by heart hundreds of verses written by predecessors; they had to be experts in the poetic tradition of their native tongue, its images, metaphors, and other poetic devices. Since this was not normally part of the education of a young girl—with the exception, of course, of educated slaves in the Golden Age of the Caliphate—one of Mihrī's biographers feels obliged to say something in favor of women by quoting an Arabic verse: "It is no disgrace to the sun that she is feminine, and no honor to the moon that he is masculine." [56, II, I29, n. 1] (The Arabic word for "sun" is feminine, and the word for "moon" is masculine in gender.) Mihrī herself protested against the discrimination experienced by women:

Since they cry that woman lacketh wit alway,
Needs must they excuse, whatever word she say.
Better for one female, if she worthy be,
Than a thousand males, if all unworthy they.
[56, II, 130]

148

Feelings of love inspired both Mihrī and Zaynab. Yet their relationships with men in Ottoman Turkey of that time were never other than platonic. A biographer lauds Mihrī who never married, for having remained a virgin until her death. Zaynab gave up writing poems when she married, obviously at the insistence of her husband.

Finally, mention must also be made of Gulbadan Begum, a sister of the Mughal Emperor Humāyūn, who, in her *Humāyūn-nāmeh*, wrote a fascinating report about the reign of her brother.

At least in the early centuries of Islam, women were particularly active in one branch of the arts: music. The attitude of Muslim religious scholars toward music was not at all positive. They regarded the beating of tambourines as permissible only at weddings, since such festivities should not take place in silence. It is related that Muhammed put his hands over his ears at the sound of a shepherd's flute; and on hearing a woman singing, he is said to have commented that the devil had blown in her nostrils.

One *hadīth* expressly forbids the training, sale, and purchase of female slaves as singers. But here, as in other spheres, devout Moslems were unable to make the pleasure-loving aristocracy and upper classes adhere to this tradition. In the first century of Islam, singing was an art, inspired by Persian and Byzantine influence, cultivated especially in the sensuous society of the Hijāz, in the cities of Mecca and Medina. It was not long, however, before the Hijāz met serious competition at the Court of the Umayyads in Damascus and, later, from the Abbasids in Baghdad. From the music-loving aristocracy comes a praise of singing to be found in Abu l-Faraj's *Book of Songs*. It was surely used as a weapon against the disapproving attitude of the religious scholars and is told in an apparently true anecdote.

Jamīla of Medina, the most famous singer in the seventh century, decided one day to give up singing. She had a natural gift, and had developed her talent after hearing a neighbor sing. She had also established a school of her own, and was a recognized authority on the art of singing. On the day she decided to stop, she invited men and women to come to her house, where she informed them that she had had a bad dream and feared for her soul. She asked those present

149

to comment on her decision, and opinions were divided. "An old man full of wisdom, experience, and knowledge of the law" then raised his voice. He encouraged her not to give up at a time when others, such as the Iraqi, were challenging the people of Medina in an art form they had inherited from them. He then began to praise singing, although, from what he said, it can be inferred that the ruling classes cultivated it not only for pleasure, but also as a kind of instrument of power for the maintenance of the social status quo:

> *"Singing is one of the greatest of pleasures and is more pleasant for the soul than any of the things which it desires. It stimulates the heart, strengthens understanding, brings joy to the soul, and provides wide scope for free opinion. Difficult tasks are made easier by it. Armies become victorious through it. Despots are so captivated by it that they despise themselves when they hear it . . . It heals the sick and those whose heart, understanding, and perception have withered away. It makes the rich richer and the poor more contented and satisfied when they hear it, so that they no longer demand possessions. He who retains it is a man of learning, and he who renounces it is ignorant. There is nothing more exalted and nothing more beautiful than song. Why is it considered right to abandon it, and why is use not made of it in Divine service?"* [5b, VIII, 224ff.]

Jamīla and all the others present were won over by this argument, so the narrator relates.

Men and women singers put music to the works of illustrious Arabic poets, but in most cases the singers were themselves poets and composers as well as performers. With very few exceptions, the women who cultivated music were slaves, whose talents were recognized as children and who were trained by the great artists of their time. Depending on their abilities and on their physical charms, too, they were traded at appropriate prices, and a few of them ascended the social ladder with such success that they became the wives of Caliphs. However, the fate of most singers probably took them to the wine taverns of the towns where, remaining nameless, they led an existence that did not differ much from that of prostitutes.

From the early Abbāsīd period, we know of only one singer of free origin, Ulayya, the beautiful and gifted half-sister of Hārūn ar-Rashīd, who had inherited her talent from her mother, also a singing girl (they were known as *qayna*) at the Abbāsid Court. With her poems, songs, and merry charm, Ulayya was always able to win over the Caliph, even once when he grumbled at her because she had made a slave the subject of her love songs. "There was nothing which gave her greater pleasure than reciting poems at the appropriate moment," says Abū l-Faraj. [5b, X, 163] With this talent for the popular art of impromptu composition of poems and songs, she was largely responsible for the happy atmosphere in the Caliph's harem. When she died around 825-6, it was the Caliph al-Ma'mūn who recited the prayer for the dead.

Most of the famous primadonnas were slaves. They played an important role at the Courts. There was no celebration by the Caliph or his senior officials that was not embellished by their art. However, since a great deal of money had been invested in their education, more than singing was expected of them. They were expected to use their artistic ability, education, wit, humor, knowledge of spicy anecdotes and bons mots to amuse and distract the great people of the Court, who were already glutted with a wide range of pleasures. They also had to be able to play such games as chess and trictrac. Some famous singers were also expert at preparing delicate dishes. They were consequently responsible for practically all kinds of sophisticated pleasures since, of course, they were frequently the concubines of their owner as well.

The later Caliph al-Mu'tamid refused to eat any food not prepared by the singer Shāriya. 'Arīb, probably the best known singer at the Court of the Abbāsids in the middle of the ninth century, once wrote the following lines to the Governor of Mosul, who, at her request for a share of his table, sent her bread, meat, and confectionery. "In the name of Allah, the Merciful, the Compassionate! O you stupid barbarian! Did you think that I belong to the Turks or wild soldiers that you have sent me bread, meat, and confectionery? May Allah protect

me from you!" To put him right, she then sent him some of the deli-
cacies of her kitchen on a plate covered with a gold-brocaded cloth,
these being pies of bread dough filled with fried partridge breast, veg-
etables, and palm blossom. [159, 77]

Famous entertainers, including singers, liked to compare their
ability with that of others. Much to the enjoyment of the spoiled
guests present, and often under the stimulus of wine, "competitions"
were held in the houses of patrons. Fadl, better known for her poetry
than her songs, had a real literary salon. Poets and men of letters met
at her house, not only because she was the "most poetically gifted
woman of her time" [5a, XVIII, 185] but also because they hoped to
win her protection at Court (she was still the Caliph's slave at the
time).

A passage in the "Book of Songs" deals with 'Arīb and Shāriya,
the two most famous singers of the period when, for a few decades,
Samarra was the capital of the Caliphat. "The inhabitants of Samarra
were divided into two parties: one group was for Shāriya and the
other for 'Arib; as a result, the members of one group did not mix with
those of the other group, and vice versa." [159, 84] The two rivals,
who were "deadly enemies," thus transmitted their feelings to the
entire metropolis.

Men and women singers usually accompanied themselves on the
lute, but we know from miniatures and the *adab* literature that there
were women who also played the tambourine, harp, oboe, and flute,
and also the *kānūn,* a string instrument resembling the harp.

Fewer in number than the singing girls were slaves educated in
various branches of formal knowledge. The most famous of these is
the slave girl Tawaddud, "Showing Winning Love," from a tale of the
Arabian Nights, which is probably of Greek origin and was wide
spread in Muslim Spain. She boasted that she was familiar with all the
then known sciences from grammar to poetry and music, religious
law, theology, mathematics, astronomy, philosophy, and medicine,
and she carried on discussions with scholars, in the presence of Hārūn
ar-Rashīd, to demonstrate her knowledge. She not only proved herself better than those who were supposed to test her, but also defeated
the trictrac player, and finally entertained everybody by playing the

lute and singing.

The principal purpose in educating such slaves was to cater to the spoiled tastes of sophisticated courtiers. The greatest ambition of the slaves, once they were educated, was to win the favor of the Caliph and find a place in his harem. One highly educated slave, whom Hārūn ar-Rashīd had had tested by the famous philologist al-Asma'ī, rewarded the scholar with a purse of one thousand dinar when, on his recommendation, she was selected for the immediate entourage of the Caliph. "Your daughter would like to share her good fortune with you," [2, 149] was the message she sent to him; her tact also shows that in this new position on the social ladder, she considered herself a step above the man of learning, to whom she expressed her thanks.

34

This mughal girl feeds a bird with a graceful movement of her hand. Her headgear resembles a turban, and her breasts shine through the close-fitting upper part of her costume. Over her narrow trousers, she wears a wide skirt of elegant, semi-transparent material, with lengthwise stripes, which reaches down to her feet.

"In love there is sweetness and bitterness"

Only he who feels real love,
Knows the joy and sorrow of life.
For in love there is sweetness and bitterness,
Only he who has tasted it, tells you the truth
(al-Kumayt, d. 743) [89, 67]

T he Lebanese writer Laylā Ba'labakkī was prosecuted at the beginning of the 1960s when, in a very delicately written story called "Spaceship of Tenderness to the Moon," she has a newly married woman speak openly of her tender and passionate mental and physical feelings toward her husband. And yet it was Lebanon in particular that had long enjoyed the reputation of being liberal in the erotic sphere. It was Lebanon, in the 1950s, that saw the publication of a rather frank book about the sex life of Arabs in the past [119] and a collection of love poems by Arab women of earlier centuries. In the latter work, the editor wanted to show that Arab women of the past spoke about their love for a man just as openly as men did about their feelings towards a woman. [143] However, in Islamic countries, not only in past decades but up to the present time, a distinction is clearly drawn between the rights of men and women to express opinions on sexual subjects. It is consequently not surprising that the publisher of the last-named book feels the need to argue strongly that a woman has just as much right to sexual expression and fulfillment as a man.

Indeed, *adab* works of classic and postclassic Arab literature speak openly of the sensual pleasure which, at least in the early centuries of Islam, both men and women expressed quite freely and frankly. There is a great deal of literature in Arabic on the subject of profane love, ranging from philosophical disputes on the nature of love, which are mostly influenced by Neoplatonism, to the pros and cons of certain states and manifestations of love, the whole spiced with anecdotes and verses intended to prove or reinforce with examples what is first described theoretically.

In addition, there is a vast sexological literature filled with recipes for mixtures to enhance men's potency and for cosmetics women can use to arouse men sexually. There are also works that classify women physiologically and psychologically as to suitability for the sex act. These works of medieval Arab medicine, whose authors were mostly renowned natural scientists, were also inspired by translations from the Greek.

From the Middle Ages till today Muslim books, letters, transcriptions of lectures, and contracts begin with the introductory formula of all Arabic literature and even that which, to our eyes consist of frivolous verses and anecdotes, that is, the *basmala:* "In the name of Allah, the Merciful, the Compassionate." For example, a small sexological treatise by the Egyptian as-Suyūtī, a respectable learned man of the fifteenth century, begins: "In the name of Allah, the Merciful, the Compassionate. Praise be to Allah who decorated the upper part of virgins with breasts and made the legs of women as platform for the privy parts of men, who raised up the spear-like penis of the man with which he thrusts into the vagina of the woman and not (like a real spear) into the breast (of an enemy)." [161, 1]

It would certainly be wrong to judge such works by today's standards of either morality or writing. Love poetry is known to have been written by pre-Islamic Bedouin poets of Arabia, but it was not an independent genre, appearing in what is known as the *nasīb*, the erotic introduction to the most widespread form of Arabic poetry, the *qasīda*. The actual purpose of the *qasīda* was to praise a patron or a tribe or even oneself, or to abuse an enemy. However, the *qasīda* also contained detailed descriptions of the environment of the Bedouins, including the animals which these nomads used for riding. The *nasīb* certainly shows that pre-Islamic poets were not always content to express merely platonic feelings. The ideal female they lauded was very different from the average Bedouin woman, whose appearance was marked by the harsh life the nomads led. The Arab poets of this and also later periods celebrated a voluptuous and white-skinned type of beauty; this will be discussed later.

In the period of the Umayyads, independent love poetry appeared for the first time, an example of which is that of Umar Ibn Abi Rabī'a, the Meccan Don Juan from the tribe of the Quraysh. In his numerous poems, he celebrated his amorous adventures with women from respected families, and there is no reason to doubt the truthfulness of his poems. It has already been noted that the aristocratic woman of Mecca at that time was self-assured and independent, as instanced by Ā'isha Bint Talha and Sukayna in an earlier chapter. It is also probably true, as we can infer from Umar's poems, that some of these adventures were initiated by the women themselves, that they arranged a rendezvous with the poet.

At about the same time, however, a love poetry of quite a different kind emerged, which at first was mainly cultivated in Medina. It is known as *Udhrite*, after the tribe in which this kind of love first and most frequently appeared. Heinrich Heine's verse from the "Romanzero" recalls this: *"Und mein Stamm sind jene Asra, welche sterben, wenn sie lieben,* (And my tribe are those Asra who die when they love.)" The religious basis of *Udhrite* love is the alleged saying of Muhammed, that is as famous as it is contested: "He who loves, hides his love, waits patiently and dies, dies as a martyr." [86, 194] This means that he shall go directly to Paradise.

The most important representative of *Udhrite* love of this period is the Bedouin poet Jamīl (c. 660-701), who loved Buthayna, of the same tribe, from childhood on, as she loved him; but her father married her to another man. Jamīl described the purity of his feelings and of the grief he had to bear on her account. In his poems, Buthayna became the "cruel one," who dominated him entirely. They both pined because of their unfulfilled love for each other and died of broken hearts.

From about the ninth century on, *Udhrite* love became the exalted ideal of Court society in Iraq, although its actual moral views were clearly quite different. It was at this time that moving love stories were told about tragic lovers, perhaps because people had had enough of the constantly increasing fickleness of erotic relationships. Whatever the reason, entire books were written about lovers who died of unfulfilled love for each other.

Kuthayyir (d. 732), a poet famous for his pure love for his cousin Azza, is reported to have once said to the Umayyad Caliph Abd al-Malik Ibn Marwān:

> *"One day I met Jamīl, who asked me, 'Will you go with me to Buthayna?' I agreed and went with him. When we drew near to the place where she was, he bade me, 'Go to her and tell her where I am.' I did so. She then approached with some women of her tribe. When the women saw Jamīl, they left them alone, and I went away also. The two of them, however, remained standing there, from nightfall until the gray of dawn. When they decided to take leave of each other, she bade him, 'Come closer to me, Jamīl!' He then approached her, and she whispered something secretly in his ear. At this, he fainted and fell senseless to the ground, and it was only the heat of the Sun (much later) that brought him back to his senses."* [89, 60 ff.]

The most famous lovers of this kind were Layla and Majnūn, who are probably better known throughout the Islamic New East than are Romeo and Juliet in Europe.

In some cases, genuine social reasons may have affected such relationships, since fairly often *Udhrite* couples were the result of a father's refusal to give his daughter to the man she loved and who loved her and asked for her hand, because he did not consider the suitor's social status to be good enough. She was then married to a more prosperous candidate, the lovers pined for each other, and eventually both died of broken hearts.

Poems and traditions appeared which declared that the upper part of a woman down to her navel was for the man she loved, and only the part below was the property of her husband. [86, 96f.] There are reports like this: The philologist al-Asma'ī (d. 828) once asked a Bedouin: "What does love mean to you?" The man replied: "To look at each other constantly, and to kiss each other repeatedly, this is already Paradise." To this al-Asma'i commented: "For us (townsmen) that is not love." The Bedouin then asked: "What then is love for you?" al-Asma'ī replied: "You straddle out her legs and go into her." "Oh," said the Bedouin, "you are not a lover, you just want a child." [89, 77].

The Court society of Iraq in the eighth century produced the classic voice of Court love, in the person of Abbās Ibn al-Ahnaf, one of the circle of poets gathered around the Caliph Hārūn ar-Rashīd. Fauz, a clearly fictitious name, was the person he celebrated, in his poems. Many suspect that in reality she was Ulayya, the lovely sister of Hārūn ar-Rashīd, to whom reference has already been made.

It may be assumed that some of Abbās' poems that have survived were commissioned by high-ranking ladies at the Court. The love celebrated here did not remain unfulfilled as with the *Udhrites,* but the brief hours of happiness are followed by long sorrow and hopeless laments and ultimately acceptance of a relentless fate. Practically nothing is learned about the intellectual and mental qualities of the lady, which might have given an indication of the ideal woman of that time. Nevertheless, this genre of Arab love poetry was a forerunner of the poetry of the troubadours of Provence.

From the ninth century on, books appeared on the theory of love, which initially corresponded to the ideal concepts of Court circles concerning a person of good breeding. One of the maxims in the *Book of the Flower* by the jurist Ibn Dāwūd (d. 909), a codification of what we have described as Court love, reads: "He who wishes to be well-bred and educated must be chaste," and, "It is not a sign of well-bred behavior when the beloved is treated in a contemptuous way by describing her."

In this literature, love is defined as unity of soul and character between two people, which causes a lover to consider that his beloved is beautiful, even when that is not at all the case in the eyes of others, or which causes him to look continually at the object of his affections and to feel sensual desire as well. This is also why the lover wishes to be united with the beloved in a kiss, since the breath of Man comes directly from his nature, and is thus in immediate contact with his soul. An embrace also enhances the spiritual nearness of lover and beloved. Seeking sensual pleasure for its own sake, a Muslim theologian of the fourteenth century affirms in a treatise on love, is to be condemned, since it is only followed by even greater pain or is an obstruction to finer pleasures, such as those that await the Faithful in Paradise. [86, 170] These pleasures, as we will see, are the highest intensification of those experienced on earth.

It is sometimes said that love makes one blind and deaf, but those who praise it affirm that it has ennobling qualities. "It gives the coward courage, makes the avaricious generous, conveys understanding to the ignorant, and lends eloquence to the tongues of the inhibited. The power of kings bows before it, the arbitrariness of the bold is shaken by it, it leads to decency." [86, 190] On being told that his son had fallen in love, a prominent man replied: "Thanks be to Allah, now he will become courteous and friendly, pleasant in his attitude and elegant in his movements, agreeable in his expression and serious in his messages, his nature will become freer for he will devote himself to the beautiful and avoid that which is ugly." [*Ibid.*] Wise people, it is said in the same source, consider that love is for the soul as a good meal is for the body; if one does not enjoy it, it is harmful, and when one has too much of it, it kills one. [86, 189]

An Arab anthology of early love stories collected in the fifteenth century contains the philosophical remark: "If women are snares of Satan, then they are also guides which lead to knowledge, since through love for them intelligent men will acquire knowledge of their Creator . . ." [11, 57]

While jurists, theologians, and philosophers argued about the nature of profane love, *adab* authors regretted, even at the beginning of the tenth century, the increasing decline in moral standards, although they admittedly took an idealized view of the early period. Thus, in his book about good morals, Ibn al-Washshā of Baghdad writes: "In the past when a man loved a woman, then he did not desert her until death, his heart concerned itself with no other, and he did not endeavor to find consolation elsewhere . . . and the woman behaved in like manner. When one of them died before the other, the latter killed himself or lived on in a spirit love for the other, remained true, and honored the memory of his partner." [89, 77] As to the happy-go-lucky poet who wrote:

I see a maiden and fall for her,
Then catch sight of another and love her,
I fall in love with eighty every day,
And to none can my heart truly stay,

Ibn al-Washshā wishes that Allah will show him the hatefulness of his words and declares: "Inconstancy is not a quality of educated people, and constant change is not the affair of the well-bred." [89, 79]

Even sharper is the commentary in an *adab* work of about 984 on a lascivious anecdote:

"In the past, when a man loved a girl, he exchanged letters
with her for the course of a year. After this, he was happy
enough to chew the mastic which she (first) had in her mouth,
and then, when they met each other, they talked to each other
and recited verses. Today, however, when a man loves a girl,
he has nothing else in mind but how to lift her legs as if he
wanted to make Abu Hurayra (a famous Early Islamic source
of hadīths from the Prophet) a witness to his coitus with her."
[163, 55]

But before we deal with these things in more detail, a brief résumé of the attitude of the Koran and *Sunna* to sexuality is necessary. The Koran exhorts Muslim men in a metaphorical manner thus: "Your women are a tilth for you, come then to your tilth as you wish, but send forward something for yourselves, and act piously towards Allah, and know that ye are going to meet Him. Give (thou) good tidings to the believers!" (2: 223) Thus the sexual relations between man and woman in marriage are treated here as something natural which had also to be viewed with reference to Allah and the Day of Judgment. In another *Sura*, the Believers—obviously men and women who are not married to each other—are urged to observe chastity. They are told here to "cast down their eyes" and to "guard their private parts." (24: 30/31) The first exhortation is a popular subject of the literature on worldly love.

With regard to the Prophet of Islam, early Arab historians—who certainly took account of their own interests as well—report that he took particular pleasure in three things in life: pleasant smells, women, and good food. [87, I, 2, 112] When it is affirmed in the same source that the archangel Gabriel, a messenger of Allah, had given Muhammed, through a certain dish, the potency of forty men [*Ibid.*], this merely shows that the Muslims of that time expected above average sexuality from a man who was supposed to be an example to them in every respect a concept of a founder of a religion that is totally different from the image of Jesus in Christianity.

The Muslim idea of Paradise also takes account of male wishful thinking; every Muslim man is promised the potency of eighty men. [*Ibid.*] A later source promises him every day a hundred buxom virgins whose virginity is continually renewed. [86, 270] They will be free from all the discomforts that plague earthly women, such as menstruation, and will also know no jealousy. Nor will they cause injury to their men, reproach them, or adorn themselves for any other.

The interests of women are considered here only in the answer that Muhammed is said to have given a woman, who asked what man she would belong to in Paradise when she had been married to several in succession on earth. He said that she would be able to choose and could take the one whose character had pleased her most. [86, 257] At any event, it is emphasized that there would be no bachelors in Paradise, and indeed a well-known saying affirms: "There are no monks in Islam"; that is, asceticism of any kind, including sexual, is not wanted. The great Muslim theologian al-Ghazālī (d. 1111) considers sexual abstinence permissible only for those without sexual desire. [54, 43f.]

Arabic has a comprehensive vocabulary for dealing with sex and, as for other aspects of life, has different designations for many nuances. The Arabic word *nikāh,* which even in the Koran is used exclusively to mean "marriage," originally meant coitus, and in classic

Arabic a woman who was married to a man was said to have been "under" him. This can, of course, also be interpreted figuratively.

To begin with, there was no trace of prudery in Arabic language, and the freethinker Jāhiz of the ninth century protests against the pious hypocrites among his contemporaries who preached it: "Many of the people who display their piety and ascetic way of life are disgusted and turn away when words such as vulva, penis or coitus are mentioned, but most of those who behave thus are men whose hypocrisy is greater than their knowledge, noble-mindedness, refinement, and dignity." [48, 434]

That sexuality and eroticism were not considered exclusively male attributes in the enjoyment of life can be proved in various ways. Jāhiz, who advocated a broad view of life, regards women as superior to men in matters of love: "Women are above men in many things. It is they who are wooed, wished for, loved, and desired, and it is they for whom sacrifices are made and who are protected." [48, 414]

The recommendation that consideration should be given to the woman in physical love is clearly made in a saying attributed to al-Hasan, grandson of the Prophet and one of the "much-married men": "Flirt with the women, and do not behave like a wild animal where the male suddenly descends upon the female. Flirting is to desire what thunder and lightning are to rain. The kiss is the herald of the game of love." [133, 159]

"The Blossoming Garden," by the Tunisian an-Nafzāwī, of about 1400, is probably the only book by an Arab on sensual love known to nonspecialists. It recommends that the man should prepare the woman for love and afterward should "not rise too quickly" [121, 81] in other words, he should respect her feelings. But the Egyptian as-Suyūtī, a man of many interests, to whose book reference has already been made, only gives instructions to the woman as to how she should behave toward the man.

Almost everything that we know of the frank remarks of women of that time, concerning their feelings toward their male partners, comes from reports by men. As we have already seen, it was only very much later that Arab women began to write love poetry, and this was in the West of the Islamic empire, which was more liberal than the East. Consequently, it can be assumed that some of the frivolous stories concerning the erotic behavior of women that are found in *adab* literature were related as "male jokes" in the evening conversations at Court, or among the aristocracy. It is true that women were usually present at such occasions, not free-born women, of course, and certainly not wives, but the educated entertainers, the singing girls. It is quite certain that not everything handed down here was solely male wishful thinking.

The literature that has survived credits not only pre-Islamic Arab women with frankness in sexual matters (it is said that it was a woman who taught the people of Mecca various forms of the love act hitherto unknown) [78, 215], but also women of the Arab aristocracy of the seventh century. Overhearing what was obviously a passionate love play between Ā'isha Bint Talha and her husband, a woman of Mecca once reprimanded the capricious Ā'isha with the words: "You, a free woman, behave in such a manner!" She replied: "We long for this kind of man with everything which excites them and of which we are capable." [5b, XI, 186]

The second Caliph Umar Ibn al-Khattāb is said once to have heard a woman lamenting on the roof of her house:

> *Long was the night for me, and black*
> *And, without my beloved to play with, I slept not,*
> *This bed would have shaken from our love,*
> *But for fear of Allah, the only God.*
> [86, 229]

At this, the Caliph, who could appreciate her feelings, is said to have enquired how long her husband had been away at war, and to have had him fetched back.

The following tale is related of the poet Umar Ibn Abi r-Rabī'a, the Don Juan of Mecca, in the "Book of Songs." Hind, daughter of al-Hārith of the tribe of the Murra, invited him to her house one day so that she and her companions could talk to him. She said to him: "Oh, oh, Umar, listen to this. If you could have seen me a few days ago. I was with my family, and I put my head under my gown and looked at my nakedness. It was just as if it filled a hand and was very desirable. At this I called out: 'Umar! Umar!'"... Umar replied: " I would have called out: 'At your service! At your service!'" [5b, I, 176] It was not unusual in poems for a woman to extol the charms of her vagina nor for a man to sing the praises of his penis.

However, as already indicated, an amorous adventure by a married woman was regarded as unchaste, and could result in grave consequences for one or both partners. The poet al-Waddāh is said to have paid a secret visit to the wife of the Umayyad Caliph Walīd I. A servant told the Caliph that the visitor had hidden in a chest shortly before the Caliph appeared on the scene. The Caliph asked his wife for the chest as a gift and had a deep hole dug in the floor of his palace. Before he had the chest lowered into it, he said to it: "We have heard something. If it is true, then we have wrapped you in a shroud and will bury you and the memory of you and will remove the traces of you until the end of time. But if it was only gossip, then we are burying only wood, and how worthless that is!" The narrator in the *Book of Songs* then closes with the words, "After that and up to the present time, no trace was ever seen of him." [5b, VI, 225]

In the centuries that followed, as a rule, only female slaves were still permitted to express openly their feelings for a man. A slave of a Caliph is said to have sent a poem to a female slave in which he said that he had dreamed he was lying hand in hand with her on a couch. It is said that she answered:

What you saw was good and what you beheld,
Despite the envious, once you will have.
I wish you would embrace me,
My swelling breasts resplendent under you.
I see you, enclosing my breasts and my body
Between my bracelet and my ankle-band.
[80, 219]

The narrator relates that the Caliph had them married to each other when he heard about it. From the reports of European travelers of a very much later date, however, from Turkey, for example, we know that such affairs often ended tragically with both lovers being thrown into the Bosporus.

The singing girls were actually trained to see their beauty and talents as a commodity and were known for their skill in marketing it. They were seldom honest when they told a man of their feelings for him. Jāhiz, the bel-esprit of the ninth century, has this to say about how a *qayna* (singing girl) attracted men:

"When an admirer looks at her, she glances discreetly at him, infatuates him with her smile, says words of love to him in the poems that she sings, is eager to return his approaches, drinks merrily, and demonstrates her desire that he should stay for a long time, her yearning for his speedy return, and her sadness at his departure. And if she notices then that her charm has trapped him and that he is ensnared, she even goes beyond that which she began with and makes him believe that her affection for him is even greater than that which he feels for her. She writes him letters in which she laments her passion and swears to him that the inkpot is filled with her tears and the paper wet with her saliva, that she worries about him day and night in her heart and in her mind, that she does not wish to have any other . . . that she does not have the intention of turning away from him and that she wants him for himself alone and not because of his money. She then places the letter in a sheet of parchment folded six times, seals it with saffron, and ties it with a piece of string." [48, 427]

At times, she trifles in this manner with several admirers simultaneously.

As a libertine, however, Jāhiz does not take a negative view of these cunning arts of seduction: "However, this should not be a criticism of her but, on the contrary, great praise. Is it not said in a tradition that 'The best of women are those who understand charm and seduction'?" [48, 429ff.] And he certainly recognizes, too, the reasons for the behavior of the singing girls:

166

"How can the singing slave be safe from temptation, and how can it be possible for her to remain chaste, since she acquires passion from her environment in the same way as she learns languages and customs and lives, from her birth to the hour of her death, in a milieu which discourages her from thinking of God, since it consists only of delectable entertainment and all kinds of diversions and vulgarities in the midst of depraved and shameless people from whom no serious word is to be heard, in whom one can have no confidence and who have neither religion nor honor." [48, 433]

On the other hand, Ibn al-Washshā, in his book on fine manners in Baghdad at the beginning of the tenth century, includes a chapter headed, "Damnation of the Singing Girls," which begins thus: "One must know that no virtuous and educated man, no person of good morals, can be afflicted by a greater tribulation than a passion for the singing girls, since their affection is treacherous, their love false, and their passion rapidly fades." [89, 92] He then describes, like Jāhiz, how they "angle" men of money and good family in order to take advantage of them. He does not, however, share Jāhiz' understanding of the reasons for their behavior.

The famous 'Arīb, to whom reference has already been made, may be taken as an example of the singers' loose morals, even among those who had attained a high position. She openly admitted that she had slept with eight Caliphs, but had felt no affection for any of them apart from al-Mu'tazz, who reminded her of a man she had once loved. It is therefore not surprising that she found ways to slip away at night from the Caliph's harem, which was presumably strongly guarded, to meet her current lover and then to return just as discreetly. The reports vary on the reaction of the Caliph who realized what was going on when, if not earlier, it became apparent that she was pregnant. [159, 149]

It once happened that a number of admirers paid a visit to 'Arīb. When they got up to leave, she begged them to stay a little longer since she wanted to serve them a dessert which one of her pupils, Bid'a, also a well-known singer, had prepared with her own hands from fresh almonds, and which would be accompanied with a song. The narrator continues: "I said: 'On one condition.' She asked: 'And what is that, by Allah?' I replied: 'Something which I have wanted to ask you for a long time, but I am ashamed to ask it in your presence.' She answered, 'You have my permission, and I will give you the answer before you ask the question since I already know it!' At this, I was astonished and challenged her: 'Then say it!' She went on: 'You wanted to ask me about the conditions which I demand (from a good lover).' I replied: 'Yes, that is what I wanted to ask.' She then answered, 'A hard penis and a pleasant smell, and if it is accompanied by an unusually good appearance and great handsomeness, then my lust increases, but if not, the two first conditions are something which I would not like to do without.'" [5a, XVIII, 185]

On another occasion, probably when she was older, one admirer asked another in her presence: "What about her desire now?" The other laughed, and she noticed it and wanted to know what they had spoken about. When they declined to tell her, she threatened to send all her singing girls away. They then told her, and she dryly commented: "So what? The desire is quite in order, but the instrument is inactive." [*Ibid.*]

Many anecdotes in *adab* literature are evidence of the frivolity of the singing girls. One story tells of a young man, who was obviously a little out of touch with the world and not very prosperous. He pursued a *qayna* with flattering words and high-flown letters, saying that he couldn't sleep at night, had no appetite and other "endless, meaningless twaddle," as the narrator puts it. One day, he sent a letter to the girl, writing that if she did not permit him to visit her, she should at least come to him in his dreams. "She was a woman of Baghdad and wanted only the world and its wealth," says the narrator: she sent a message to him that he should send her two dinar, then she would come herself and he would get more than her appearance in a dream. [18, 72 ff.]

Here, again, it would be wrong to make generalizations, since there were also singing girls who were famed for their faithfulness, for example Mahbūba's to Caliph al-Mutawakkil, or Farīda's to Caliph al-Wāthiq. It is even said that Bid‘a, ‘Arīb's pupil mentioned above, died a virgin. [159, 144]

To save herself from an insistent lover, a slave could only resort to her sharp tongue, a quality that was much respected. This is apparent from many anecdotes, including one concerning the poet Abu Nuwās of Baghdad (d. about 815), who was famous not only for his frivolous verses, mainly on the subject of boy lovers, but also for his excellent drinking and hunting songs. Once when he was visiting a friend, a white-skinned girl appeared, wearing a green gown. Abu Nuwās rubbed his eyes when he saw her and said: "I dreamt I was riding on a white mare with a green blanket, and she moved right merrily under me." The girl replied: "If you want to make your dream come true, order a white radish for the night." [177, 141] The following anecdote is more drastic. The well-known singer Ibrāhīm al-Mausilī (d. 804) is said to have once asked a singing girl in a verse to have sex with him, arguing that he was requesting something for which she did not even have to bare her back. She replied: "No, but I get a fat stomach from it." [133, 70]

The free-born woman, on the other hand, could rely on her family to protect her from male impertinence. This is demonstrated by an anecdote, which, at the same time, illustrates the early Islamic concept of a virtuous woman. It was told by a servant of Hajjāj Ibn Yūsuf, Governor of Iraq from 694 until his death in 714. Hajjāj had a nephew, who was the Emir in the Iraqi town of Wasit. A woman lived there who was considered more beautiful than any other at that time. He made propositions to her and sent her gifts, but she refused to yield to him and demanded that he ask her family for her hand. However, he did not wish to do this. So he told her that he would visit her one Friday night. She reported this to her mother, who did not believe it, but told the girl's four brothers about it. The brothers took up a position in the house opposite. When the nephew of Hajjāj arrived, he handed over his mount to his servant and ordered him to come back with it when he heard the muezzin calling the Believers to come to prayer at daybreak. He then entered the girl's house and found her lying on a bed. He lay down beside her and took hold of her, saying: "How much longer are you going to play cat and mouse?" She cried out that he should leave her alone. At this, her brothers

Scene from the Shāh-nāmeh.
Bahrām Gūr with his favorite slave-girl, the harpist Āzādeh, hunting.

rushed into the house, slew him with their swords, and wrapped the body in a leather blanket, the kind that was used at executions, and threw it into an alley in the town. The inhabitants of this alley subsequently discovered the body and took it to Hajjāj. He had his nephew's servant brought to him, and ordered him to tell what had happened, with the threat that otherwise he would be made a head shorter. He then ordered the appearance of the woman and her family, who confirmed what the servant had said and admitted the murder. Hajjāj praised the woman for what she had done and wished that there were more women like her. He had his nephew fed to the dogs and the servant cut in two. [123, 182 ff.] The end of the story shows that it was intended to have an educational effect, and that such an attitude on the part of a woman was considered exemplary, even though it was certainly not typical.

In his treatise on earthly love of the fourteenth century, the theologian Ibn Qayyim al-Jauziyya leaves no doubt about the woman's having exactly the same right to sexual satisfaction in marriage as that demanded from her by her husband. He quotes disputes about how often this must take place and how long a married woman can go without intercourse with her husband. Various authors even asserted that women have a stronger libido than men, an opinion adopted from Greek medicine. Ibn Qayyim considers the physical union, sanctioned by marriage, of two persons who love each other as the highest stage of fulfillment of their feelings for each other, and that this is enhanced by their humble love of God.

Others took a different view. The Ziyārid ruler Kay Kā'ūs of the eleventh century draws a clear distinction between marriage and eroticism. "A wife," he says, "must be chosen from a good family, and you must know whose daughter she is. For a wife is intended to be a housewife, not to give sensual pleasure. For sensual lust, a slave can be purchased at the bazaar without much effort or expense. But a wife must be fully mature and intelligent, a woman who has been trained by her mother and father to take charge of the household." [94, 93] In the Europe of the past, marriages in noble or royal families were arranged for dynastic or political reasons, and not much attention was paid to the possible feelings of the two partners.

Kay Kā'ūs considers it self-evident that a husband should have sexual intercourse with his wife, since one of the reasons for marriage is the procreation of children, but he should not do so too often, even when he loves his wife, so that she does not derive pleasure from it and make unreasonable demands. In this way, he says, the husband also preserves his freedom. [94, 94]

A tradition from a very early period affirms: "Whoever of you marries the most women is the best Muslim" referred, in fact, to the prophet Muhammed, who had more wives than his contemporaries. [87, I, 2, 95] The grandson of the Prophet, al-Hasan Ibn Alī, as already mentioned, is said to have been married to two hundred women in the course of his lifetime. The Persian poet Sa'dī (d. 1292) is said to have confirmed, "Take a new wife every year, my friend, since a used calendar is really not of much use." [166, 224]

It was easy for a husband to divorce his wife. A particularly crass example is told of al-Mughīra Ibn Shu'ba, who had twice served as Governor of Kufa in the seventh century. He was known for both his dubious morals and for his opportunism. One day, he saw his wife remove a fragment of food from her teeth. At this, he said to her: "You are repudiated, for if that remained from today's meal it is a sign of your gluttony, but if it was from yesterday's evening meal, your breath must smell." She replied: "No, may Allah soon replace you by another, it was from the toothpick." As if to justify her, the narrator closes by remarking that she remarried after this and bore the later Governor al-Hajjāj Ibn Yūsuf. [50, 136]

It was certainly such an attitude toward women that led to the saying, allegedly from the Prophet: "Women are only playthings, and a plaything should be pleasing to the one who plays with it." [133, 117] This saying is not found in the canonical collections of traditions.

It is to be assumed that most of the women in polygynous marriages, like the slaves in large harems, were physically frustrated. The following is told of the harem of Caliph Hārūn ar-Rashīd, but it could be equally true of any other large harem: Hārūn ar-Rashīd had two hundred female slaves and visited each of them in turn in the course of two hundred nights. One night, as he went up to the harem palace, he heard a slave singing thus: "This house is full of desirable women,

Layla and Majnūn have fainted with love.

172

but a single penis is just as incapable of satisfying two hundred harem ladies as a weak plaster-carrier of filling two hundred cracks." He had her brought to him and made her repeat her verse, at which he said: "Then we will visit you more often." But she replied provocatively: "I do not want that, if it happens as Abu Hukayma said in a poem: 'She came with her sack to fill it with corn, then she stood up and the sack was empty.' He answered: "No, we do not wish to leave the sack empty," stood up and had sex with her. He then said to her: "Beware, lest you have made me a weak plaster-carrier!" to which she replied, "I could not have eaten this bread with such a fierce hunger without making you that." [133, 157f.]

However, the ladies of the harem were also faced with competition from another quarter since, from the period of the Abbāsids, a custom became established that had been brought into Muslim countries from the Byzantine-Persian area. Tired of the multitude of women at their disposal, many men turned to pederasty, finding it more seductive than love for women. Perhaps the less prosperous were also driven to this by the exclusion of women from public life. A pious man remarked: "I fear more for a servant of God from a beardless young man than from seventy virgins." [123, 202]

Some men found pleasure in both sexes. In the eleventh century the Ziyārid Kay Kā'ūs advised his son to enjoy both sexes and thus avoid being satiated.

Zubayda, wife of the Caliph Hārūn ar-Rashīd, is said to have resorted to a particularly interesting trick. To cure her son, the later Caliph al-Amīn, of his predilection for eunuchs, she selected pretty young girls of slim stature, had their hair cut like that of boys, dressed them in jackets with tight belts, and had them appear thus before the young Amīn. These slaves were called boy-girls, and they became the fashion in the spoiled and luxury-loving society of Baghdad for at least a hundred years. Tavern girls subsequently appeared in the same fashion.

An Arab source of the eleventh century quotes a letter condemning passive pederasty, written by the Iraqi writer Abu l-'Aynā (d. 896) to a contemporary. "It is strange that you allow people to use you sexually instead of your taking your pleasure . . . Why do you pay the dowry for a bride, anyway, when you need men and have no love for women. Your women are with your neighbors and your men with your youths . . . O pity the bride whose gown is not removed . . . " [133, 161]

It is consequently not surprising that in these circumstances some women looked for alternative means of satisfaction, in lesbian relationships, for example: not difficult, of course, within the harems. Nevertheless, an Arab historian with an appreciation for the dramatic, reports that Abbāsid Caliph Mūsā al-Hādi presented his courtiers with the perfumed heads, decorated with diadems, of two beautiful young women from his harem, who had been decapitated after being caught flagrante delicto. [162, VIII, 221] Yet this says less about the high morals of the Commander of the Faithful than, in all probability, about his sense of property in regard to the ladies of his harem. Conversely, pederasty was indeed condemned by Orthodox Muslims, but it was not considered to be detrimental to honor in high society.

At a later time, there were women who deliberately became lesbians for intellectual reasons. Thus, a sexological treatise of the twelfth century by a Jewish convert to Islam reports:

"There are also women who are more intelligent than the others. They possess many of the ways of men so that they resemble them even in their movements, the manner in which they talk, and in their voice. Such women would like to be the active partner, and they would like to be superior to the man who makes this possible for them. Such a woman does not shame herself, either, if she seduces him whom she desires. If she has no inclination, he cannot force her to make love. This makes it difficult for her to submit to the wishes of men, and brings her to lesbian love. Most of the women with these characteristics are to be found among the educated and elegant women, the scribes, Koran readers, and female scholars." [66, 16]

The *adab* literature also contains chapters on jealousy between men and women; men were regarded as more jealous, since women were accustomed to sharing their husbands with co-wives and concubines. Female guile or maliciousness is a favorite subject, including tricks by which wives deceive their husbands with lovers, or try to eliminate their co-wives (an indication that women could also be jealous).

There are also discussions of whether a virgin is preferable to a deflowered woman, and whether it is better to take a young or an old wife. The first alternative is generally favored in both cases, but there is also evidence in support of the alternatives. Finally, there are quite a few chapters on female fidelity, or infidelity. In his work on fine manners, *The Book of the Embroidered Cloth* (about 900) Ibn al-Washshā of Baghdad takes the view that in general women are unfaithful, but for obviously didactic reasons, he also tells stories of faithful women. For example, the third Caliph Uthmān Ibn Affān heard from one of his companions that he had married a woman from the tribe of the Kalb and, in a letter, asked him about her genealogy and appearance. His friend told him the name of her father, a distinguished man, and wrote that she was white-skinned and tall. Uthmān then established contact with the woman's father and asked him for one of his daughters. His request was granted.

It is related in this description of the wedding night, that when the girl came to Uthmān, he was sitting on a cushion, and threw one to her so that she could sit down opposite him. He then removed his turban, and it could be seen that he was bald. He said to her: "Daughter of Farāfisa, my baldness should not alarm you, behind it is that which you like." She replied: "I am a woman for whom a distinguished man of mature age and in a ruling position is the best of husbands." He then asked her: "Will you come to me or shall I come to you?" She answered: "From the aversion of heaven, I have nothing worse to withstand than the distance which is now between you and me." She then stood up, went over to him, and sat down next to him. He gently stroked her hair and prayed for God's blessing. After this, he bade her: "Remove your veil." This she did. Then he said: "Take off your shirt." This she did, too. Next he demanded: "Undo your girdle!" but she answered: "You must do that." He then did so, and she became his dearest wife.

When at a later date Uthmān's murderers entered his room, she threw herself in front of her husband to protect him, as a result of which two of her fingers were cut off by a sword. After the death of Uthmān, which she could not prevent, Caliph Mu'āwiya sent for her to ask for her hand. At this, she extracted her front teeth so that no other man would desire her, and it was as she wished. [89, 83f.]

In Persian poetry, the words of earthly love are mostly enhanced in a mystical fashion. For Hāfiz and his predecessors, for example, earthly love is "a symbol of the all-embracing yearning for God." [25, 48] It "consequently remains something transitional; the character of unfulfilled, unfulfillable yearning is necessarily associated with it. Final fulfillment comes only with death or the complete obliteration of the self." [25, 49] But this goes beyond the scope of our subject.

While Arabic *adab* literature of the Middle Ages was noted for its anecdotes, a literary genre that has remained alien to Arabic literature achieved high standard in Persian literature: the epic. In Persian love poetry, mostly full of mystical images, it is often unclear whether the beloved who is celebrated in words of earthly love is a man or a woman, since in Persian there is no grammatical distinction for gender. However, love of women is glorified in some Persian romantic epics, and precisely these epics have supplied a great deal of inspiration for the painting of miniatures in Islamic art.

The love story of Khosrou and Shīrīn, or Ferhād and Shīrīn, was the subject of more than two dozen works of Persian literature, and even of the screenplay of a film. Numerous Turkish authors have also concerned themselves with the subject. Even at the beginning of the 1930s in Turkey, relatively large editions of the popular story of Ferhād and Shīrīn were published repeatedly, and guests in coffee houses were entertained with a magic lantern version of this romantic story. In 1942, the Azerbaijan poet Samed Burgin wrote a romantic epic entitled "Khosrou and Shīrīn," and Nazim Hikmet, the well-known Turkish writer, took up the subject in his drama "A Legend of Love" in 1948.

Traces of the Khosrou and Shīrīn story are to be found in works by early Arab historians and geographers. It must have been a folktale that survived from pre-Islamic times, and never lost its popu-

176

larity. Firdousi, author of the Persian national epic, the *Shāh-nāmeh*, "The King's Book", was the first to put it into poetic form. Its most splendid version as a romantic epic, and the model for all that followed, was the work of Nizāmī, who was born in Qum in 1141 and spent most of his life in Azerbaijan. He wrote the work in 1180 as the second of his five epics, which are known by the name of *Khamseh* (Quintette).

Nizāmī makes it quite clear that in Shīrīn—probably the most moving female figure of New Persian literature—he has immortalized his beloved wife Āfāq, who was a slave of Turkish origin presented to him by the ruler of Derbend, and who died at an early age. We can certainly agree with the Russian Iranist Bertel, who considers that all the passages of the epic, in which Shīrīn refuses to become the mistress of Khosrou, because she wants to belong to him only as his lawful wedded wife were inspired by the behavior of Āfāq.

The plot of the story is briefly as follows: The painter Shāpūr describes the Armenian (Christian) princess Shīrīn to his friend and drinking companion Khosrou Parvīz, the young, handsome, light-minded son of King Hormoz, in such glowing terms that Khosrou begins to love her, finds no peace, and cannot sleep. He begs Shāpūr to bring Shīrīn to him. The painter sets out for Armenia and, with a picture of Khosrou, succeeds in awakening love in Shīrīn as well. Urged on by Shāpūr, she rides to Khosrou's residence at Mada'in (Ctesiphon) the very next day on a fantastically swift horse belonging to her aunt, Queen Mehīn Bānū. During the journey, as she is about to bathe in a cool spring, she catches sight of Khosrou, now riding to Armenia himself. They fall in love, but without recognizing each other. They miss each other twice and meet only after Khosrou, who has in the meantime succeeded his father on the throne but been driven away by his people, seeks refuge in Armenia. But Mehīn Bānū warns Shīrīn of the tricks of men, and so she resists Khosrou's attempt to talk her into freely enjoying life. She advises him to practice self-control as the foundation of all power and to reconquer his kingdom first of all. Khosrou rides away in anger. The Emperor of Byzantium gives him his daughter Maryam as his wife and helps him reconquer his kingdom. Following the death of her aunt, Shīrīn ascends the throne of Armenia, and the country flourishes under her just rule. But when she hears of Khosrou's marriage, she fears that her confused feelings will not permit her to be a good ruler any longer. She hands over the business of government to a minister and rides to her castle in the mountains near Ctesiphon. Through Shāpūr, Khosrou begs her to come to his castle for at least one night, she angrily refuses. Also through Shāpūr, she makes the acquaintance of the architect Ferhād, who is to build a milk pipeline from the distant meadows where the cows are, through the mountains, and up to her castle. When Ferhād sees Shīrīn, he falls in love immediately. Khosrou, who wishes to get him out of the way, charges him with the apparently impossible task of driving a road through a mountain that has never been crossed before. He promises to give up Shīrīn if Ferhād succeeds in building the road. Since the architect, stimulated by the power of his love, makes good progress, Khosrou resorts to a trick; he sends news that Shīrīn is dead, and so Ferhād, desperate with grief, throws himself to his death from the rocks.

After the death of Maryam, Khosrou consoles himself with another woman, but after a short period of happiness his feelings for Shīrīn return. Since he finally realizes that he can bring her home only as his lawful wife, he has her brought to his castle as his bride, and the wedding ceremony takes place. When, even on this night, Khosrou tries drunkenly to approach her, she repulses him, and it is only the next morning that she gives herself to him. She subsequently counsels him to be just in his government.

Years later, Khosrou's son from his marriage with Maryam has him murdered as he lies asleep on his couch. The king experiences a great thirst as death comes to him. But, rather than disturb Shīrīn who has spent so many sleepless nights on his account, he dies without waking her. Shīrīn's love has thus changed the egoist. Shīrīn mourns Khosrou for a long time. She only pretends to submit to his son's wooing of her, and destroys all the things that remind her of her beloved husband. In the burial chamber where Khosrou lies on his bier, she plunges a dagger into her breast.

Another epic from the *Khamseh* of Nizāmī is "Layla and Majnūn," which was also imitated by Persian and Turkish poets. In this

178

Arab story of the unfulfilled love of the Bedouin Qays for Layla, whose hand he was refused, Qays becomes Majnūn, the "crazy one" (from love), who seeks refuge with the animals of the desert and eventually dies for love. Even in this century, the story was told by Bedouins of the Syrian desert, but various Arabic versions of it were known as early as the tenth century, and were recorded in the "Book of Songs." In the Arabic version, however, Layla is almost always a passive figure, who is loved and feels love, too, but without being allowed to express it. The following lines are attributed to her in the Arabic version:

Whatever happened to Majnūn,
I felt the same as he,
But he could express his love openly,
While I pined in silence away.
[143, 24]

Nizāmī's love for Āfāq is obviously reflected in the figure of Layla, too. Yet Majnūn is the principal figure in the tale, fated to feel love that is never to be requited. "A love which is not everlasting remains the plaything of sensual enjoyment and fades like youth." [122, 48] However, another moving factor is expressed here, the social coercion to which Layla, as a woman, is exposed. She must subordinate herself to her father's will, who marries her to a man she does not love. The only thing she can do in order to be true to Majnūn is to refuse to give herself to her husband. She says of Majnūn:

"He does not need to fear anybody, he can go where he
wishes, can shout, say and put in verse whatever he feels.
But I? I am a prisoner here. I have nobody to whom my
heart can talk, whom it can trust. Only shame would be my
fate . . . A woman may conquer a hero and enslave him so
that he lies prostrating at her feet, but she still remains a
woman and cannot act in the same way as he can . . . "
[122, 226ff.]

179

To find out how her beloved is faring in his solitude in the desert, she gives a letter to a rider to take to Qays. It is all about her love:

"I am with you with all my love and, tell me, who are you with? Like your happiness, I am separated from you, but I am your companion, even when I am far away from you . . . Do you understand me, my dear? I have given everything to share your pain with you, everything except one thing: I have not come to you in person because this one thing is not possible for me. But what does it matter? It is true that our bodies are separated, but my soul does not leave yours for one moment. I know how you are suffering and how your heart is breaking." [122, 232ff.]

She endeavors to console him about the death of his father: "Do not let your heart be so heavy, and do not think that you have nobody. Am I then nobody? Does it not help you that I am here? And belong to you—only you?" [122, 236]

Majnūn answers her and describes her as his unattainable mistress and his heavenly grove. He laments that he has lost himself on her account. Thus Layla's love seems to us much more emotional and personal than his. Layla dies; his unrequited love has already killed her husband. As she dies, she reveals her feelings for Majnūn to her mother and asks her to tell him that she loved him, and remained true to him until the last. Her mother is to dress her as a bride. Majnūn's grief for Layla is so great that he ultimately dies at her grave.

Another frequently copied epic is "Yūsuf and Zulaykha" by the Persian Jāmī (1414-1492). This is the poetic presentation of the "best of stories," as it is called in the Koran at the beginning of the 12th *Sūra*, the Joseph *Sūra*, a story known to us from the Old Testament. Muhammed adapted it from Jewish tradition. In Jāmī's version, it is the tale of the devotion of a woman, Zulaykha, to Yūsuf, of whom the poet says that "the most beautiful of the beautiful faded into nothing before him as the stars disappear in the glory of the Sun." [51, 21] Zulaykha, the daughter of a king, sees Yūsuf one night in a dream, and his beauty fills her with profound, consuming love. In further dreams, he reveals himself as a man of flesh and blood for whom she should keep her purity, and he indicates that he is the Vizier of Egypt. Her royal father, in whom she confides, asks the Grand Vizier of Egypt to take her as his wife. When she arrives in Egypt with a splendid retinue and magnificent dowry, she realizes that her future husband is not the man she saw in her dream, and is plunged from the heights of happiness into the depths of despair. Another dream advises her that she can only achieve her real goal through the Vizier; "Be quite comforted regarding his behavior, for he will leave your silver lock untouched." [51, 53]

As the wife of the Vizier of Egypt, treasures abound for her but her yearning remains unfulfilled. The poet then relates the story of Yūsuf the Canaanite, more or less as we know it, of the love of his father, of the jealousy of his brothers, who throw him in an old well from which he is eventually rescued and brought to Egypt with a caravan. He is so handsome that even the king wishes to buy him, but Zulaykha begs her husband to acquire him as a substitute for a real son, and so it happens. She clothes Yūsuf in silk and gold and tries to win his love. Her agony increases the more he rejects her, since he considers himself a true and grateful slave and the friend of the Vizier. She resorts to all kinds of tricks, as a consequence of which Yūsuf is finally cast into the dungeons. Zulaykha is tortured with remorse, since her beloved is now further away from her than before. It is only when Yūsuf is able to interpret the king's dream of the seven fat and the seven seven lean cows that he is released. The king makes him his Grand Vizier. Zulaykha's husband dies, and, pining for her lost beloved, Yūsuf, she rapidly becomes old. Impoverished and alone, she lives in a hut of reeds. Still filled with love for Yūsuf, she meets him one day on the road, but he refuses to listen to her. At this, she destroys the statue of her heathen god and embraces the religion of the true God. When she goes to Yūsuf a second time, he has her brought before him and she reveals who she is. He has to weep at the harshness of her fate, and, at her request, he prays to God to restore her youth and beauty. She then stands before him as a beautiful virgin and once more declares her love for him. The angel Gabriel commands him to marry her. Their love is fulfilled in passionate embrace on their wedding night:

> *Tenderly inclining to her, his kiss met hers,*
> *Enchanted, intoxicated with the fire of love.*
> *That lasted long, as if the world were forgotten . . .*
> *But the kiss was only the foretaste of love,*
> *Like salt, tantalizing the tongue before the meal,*
> *That the desire to feast more quickly comes.*
> *Thus the kisses aroused Yūsuf's passion, too,*
> *Until he clasped the body of the beloved in his arms*
> *And below the navel found the virgin's jewel,*
> *Untouched as when she left her mother's womb,*
> *He thereupon hastily freed the arrow of love,*
> *Wanting the pearly treasure in the hidden shrine.*
> [160, 206f.]

Years of happiness now follow in which children and grandchildren are born to them, until Yūsuf, weary of this world, begs God to take him. His prayer is heard. Zulaykha is afflicted by bitter grief, until death comes to her at his grave. She is laid to rest at Yūsuf's side.

In Islamic mysticism, Layla and Majnūn symbolize the love of man for God which cannot be fulfilled on earth. Zulaykha, the woman who loses herself in her complete dedication to love, just as Majnūn "abandons" his personality for love, becomes the image of the soul searching unceasingly for God. In his introductory chapter, the poet Jāmī, a member of the Naqshbendī order, considers sensual love as only a step on the way to true love:

> *If you have proved yourself in hundreds of kisses—*
> *Love alone can free you from yourself.*
> *So feel love, even sensually,*
> *It paves the way to real love.*
> [51, 18]

"My eyes shall gaze for ever only at your beauty"
[164, I, 179]

The cypress in the grove is not as tall as you.
The Pleiades cannot match the brightness of your face.
[43, 159]

These lines describe Rūdābeh in the *Shāhnāmeh,* the Persian national epic of Firdousi. In celebrating beautiful people, medieval Arabic, Persian, and Turkish poetry delights in elaborate and high-flown comparisons. The Syrian poet al-Mutanabbi (915-965) calls the faces of beautiful women "full moons that rose in veils and necklaces." [13, 18] To appreciate this, one must know how pleasantly cool moonlit nights are in the Orient, after the hot sun of the day. The sun is also used, although more rarely, as a comparison to a beautiful human countenance. But it is not simply a question of comparisons; terms from nature, such as flowers, trees, precious stones, scents, or celestial bodies, also serve as metaphors. A beautiful woman not only resembles the cypress, she is also "a swaying cypress," her lips are like coral or rubies, her eyes narcissi, her hair amber or musk, her face, framed by dark hair, is the moon or the sun between dark clouds, and her words are liquid honey. The same colorful metaphors are used to describe a handsome man. Images and metaphors are also supplied by the speech of combat: moonlike faces "shooting arrows whose feathers" are "eyelashes, piercing hearts before the flesh." [13, 18] It may sometimes be difficult for us, with our more prosaic standards, to follow the elaborate speech of this poetry, or to appreciate it, especially in translation. However, even in

Arabic, Persian, and Turkish, these images became rigid and were no more than clichés. Their full effect, especially in Persian poetry like that of Nizāmī, was achieved only by subtle association with other metaphors, elaborate plays on words, and comparisons.

The virgins who, according to the Koran, make the sojourn in Paradise pleasant, are dark-eyed. Their name, *hūrīs*, is derived from an Arabic word that describes eyes with a particularly marked contrast between black and white. In Islamic countries, blue eyes were regarded for centuries as a bad omen, presumably because enemies from the North—the Crusaders, for example—were frequently blue-eyed. "Blue-eyed devil" was a word of abuse in Iran, even at the beginning of this century. Blonde slaves had their hair, eyebrows, and eyelashes dyed black to conform to the prevailing ideal of beauty.

According to this ideal, eyes had to be dark and almond-shaped, resembling the Arabic letter ṣād, under thick, arched, black eyebrows, which met above the root of the nose. It was considered particularly attractive when a birthmark embellished the cheek of a young girl or boy. Pearly white teeth, a small mouth, and a straight nose were regarded just as charming, as was the contrast between small breasts, slim waist, and heavy hips crowning ample thighs. An Arab text of the fourteenth century describes the beautiful body of a singing girl in the following words:

"Then she raised her garments to her neck and she looked like a silver reed, illuminated with golden water that shimmered over something like a sandhill she had breasts like roses on which two pomegranates or two small ivory cups swell up, filling the hand that touches them, and a slim waist, below which a swaying posterior quivered . . . a round navel, so beautiful that my fantasy cannot describe it, below it a crouching hare or the brow of a treacherous lion, generous thighs and full calves, guarded by the ankle-rings, and narrow feet." [5, 134]

It has been noted several times that men not only appreciated the physical beauty of a woman, but also liked her to speak well. "When she speaks, it is as pleasant as when a shepherd hears a raindrop fall after long years of drought," such is the description of a singing girl from Baghdad in the eleventh century: "She decorates herself with words, as pleasant as an ecstasy or flowers from the gardens of Paradise, sweeter than cool water," is another one. [18, 54f.]

While poets celebrated human beauty in colorful words, others did not hesitate to define the ideal of female beauty in a so-called scientific manner:

The experts agree that the following should be lauded with regard to the face and body of a woman . . . Four black things: the hair of the head, eyelashes, eyebrows, and the black in the eyes. Four white things: the skin, the whites of the eyes, the teeth, and the eyeballs. Four red things: the tongue, the lips, the cheeks, and the buttocks. Four round things: the face, the head, the ankles, which should not protrude, and the bottom. Four long things: the neck, the figure, the eyebrows, and the hair. Four fragrant places: the nose, the mouth, the armpits, and the vulva. Four broad places: a high forehead, large eyes, a full upper part of the body, a smooth face. A single narrow place: the vulva. Four little places: the mouth, the hands, the feet, and the breasts." [8, 4ff.]

But even an Arab text, the *Book of Marriage* by a Syrian physician of Aleppo from the eleventh century, in which the woman is regarded primarily as a sexual object for the man, does not describe only the physical features appreciated in a woman. She also has to be "kind" and have "a pleasant laugh, since that is the first thing with which a wife wins the love of her husband. . . . She should speak softly and her voice should be melodious." [8, 6ff.] It may perhaps be concluded that this describes what would now be called "charm."

It might be asked whether women in Islamic countries during the Middle Ages, most of whom went out only when veiled, were at all familiar with the exciting world of fashion. There is considerable evidence, besides that of the miniature paintings, that they did indeed know about fashion and, if they had the necessary financial resources, liked to follow stylish trends. In the early period of Islam, simplicity was still the general rule in material life in the Arabian Peninsula. Particularly as a result of Persian influence, however, the upper classes soon acquired a marked predilection for splendor and luxury. The conquest of foreign countries with their riches provided the material requirements for this.

The Hadīth-literature of the eighth century reflects the confrontations that must have taken place between the devout, who advocated a simpler way of life, and those who sought luxury. There are traditions that say that Muhammed forbade men to wear garments of silk or brocade, or conspicuous colors such as yellow and red; that men and women were not permitted to wear trains of excessive length or with wide sleeves; and that a certain headgear obviously of an exceptionally extravagant kind was banned for women.

However, such rules could not prevail over the long run. Arab and Persian historians and geographers of the time, like European travelers of a later date, often tell of a level of material magnificence of the upper classes of Islam that seems almost like a fairy tale to us. Clothing played a principal role. Men in positions of leadership, as well as women, attached importance to luxurious garments, usually in glorious colors.

An Arab historian says of the Abbāsid Caliph al-Mutawakkil of Baghdad (ruled 847-861) that he preferred clothes of a silky fabric which was subsequently named after him: *mutawakkilī*. It is reported that all the members of his household imitated this fashion, which then spread to the rest of the population. This fashionable cloth soon became expensive, and the workshops which produced it expanded, to satisfy the demand. [152, 75]

The Mughal Emperor Akbar not only took a special interest in the development of the textile industry in his country, but also changed the names for certain garments, and thus created "new and pleasing terms" for them. As his friend and minister Abu l-Fazl writes in his report on the Imperial Household, Akbar also had a special system for listing his personal wardrobe, from which it can be guessed how large it must have been. His clothes were classified according to the day, month, and year of acquisition, and also according to price, weight, and color. The hues that are mentioned are not simply red, blue, green, or yellow; they are described in terms such as ruby-red, gold, orange, brass, cotton-blossom, sandalwood, honey, almond, lilac-brown, and so on. [6, 91 ff.]

The custom of bestowing garments of honor is also a clear indication of the value attached to exquisite articles of clothing. Already widespread in the Ancient Orient, it was also practiced under the Umayyads. As with the conferring of orders during the Middle Ages in Europe, here, too, could be found distinctions of rank and reputation, as well as special ceremonies. If one of the high dignitaries or officials had not yet been awarded this distinction, he endeavored to acquire it (by more or less acceptable means), since he wanted to demonstrate to his subordinates the esteem in which he was held by his exalted superiors.

Differences in clothing for certain professional groups, such as scholars or legal experts, appeared during the early Abbāsid period. Certain colors became associated with certain families; for example, in the second half of the fourteenth century, black was the color of the Abbāsids and green the color of the Alīds. Jews and Christians were usually required to wear clothing different from that of the Muslims. An edict of the Caliph of 849 prescribed that members of other faiths should wear honey-colored headgear and belts; but those affected often preferred to ignore such regulations. As early as the beginning of the second half of the eighth century, a Council of Sages decreed that Christian women had to wear blue coats, Jewish women yellow ones, and Samaritan women red ones.

It would be a mistake to think that this was a forerunner of the Jewish star used in Nazi Germany. The intention was, clearly, that people of other faiths should be distinguished from Muslims, but, in view of the tolerance displayed by Muslims toward Jews and Christians for the whole of the Middle Ages, this is rather to be seen in the same light as the distinctive clothing for the various professions.

Trousers, a garment exclusively for men for centuries in Europe (where the expression "to wear the trousers" is synonymous with being in charge), were for a long time part of a woman's basic wardrobe in Islamic countries. The Arabs probably adopted them from the Persians, and it may be assumed that they were worn by women earlier than by men. At any rate, in the hadith-literature, it is expressly recommended that women should wear this garment, the justification being that trousers were the best covering. However, women's trousers in the Islamic countries during the Middle Ages were never tight and figure-hugging (other clothes were worn over them, as well) as has long been the international fashion of our time. A *hadīth* states that "Allah bestoweth mercy on women who wear trousers." The traditions mostly define a seemly length as down to the ankles. Over the course of centuries, the material, width, and color were determined by fashion, and sometimes by social and local factors as well. For example, silk trousers were a Persian specialty, whereas white linen was preferred for quite a long time in Egypt. It is said that at times red leather trousers were worn by the prostitutes of Cairo.

Trousers were gathered at the waist by a special belt, the *tikka,* which was very elaborate, although generally hidden by the other clothes. Inscriptions, usually erotic poetry, were a favorite motif for decoration of these belts which, like women's garters in Europe, also served as signs of love. On the occasion of her wedding, the daughter of the ninth-century Tūlūnid ruler Khumārawayh Ibn Ahmad Ibn Tūlūn of Egypt, is said to have received a thousand *tikkas* ornamented with precious stones—but certainly not for these purposes.

A shirt was worn over the trousers. This was probably introduced by the Romans, who had seen it in Germania and Gaul, in pre-Islamic times. To begin with, cotton was probably worn, but later more transparent materials were preferred. Thus it is reported of the beautiful slave of an Umayyad: "She wore a shirt of material as delicate as dust, under which the white of her body, the roundness of her navel, and the design of her sash was to be seen." [77, 69] It was only after the decline of the textile industry that the material for such shirts was imported from Europe. Thus, at night, a king's daughter in a late tale of *Arabian Nights* wears "a fine Venetian shirt with two golden hems, decorated with the finest embroideries." [164, II, 373] Generally,

over the centuries, women's clothing in the countries of Islam differed less from men's clothing than it did in Europe during the
Middle Ages.

This is what European travelers such as Chardin, Olearius, and
Tavernier report, and Islamic miniature painting indicates that it was
already so at an earlier date. In one of the first Arab sources containing information on clothing, the *Book of the Embroidered Cloth* by
Ibn al-Washshā to which reference has already been made, the chapter on the clothes of the elegant lady lists only what distinguishes her
from a fashionable man. He mentions smoke-colored wraps and various kinds of coats, mostly designated by their origin or their material
also wide sleeves, white trousers with a train, veils from Nishapur,
black head scarves dyed with spikenard, and collars with clove
chains. Since Ibn al-Washshā assumes that these garments are
known to his readers, he does not describe them. He only sets out to
give guidelines on what was seemly, in his time, for a woman or man
who wished to appear respectable.

The color of clothing in Ibn al-Washshā's time gave an indication
of moral standards; it might also be a pointer to marital status or certain social features. Thus the lady of the world during this period did
not wear dyed cloth, but only materials in their natural colors. Men
wore white, which was recommended by the traditions, but white
(with the exception of trousers) was worn only by divorced women,
blue and black only by widows and professional mourners. As
regards the *tikkas*, the belts or sashes for the trousers, both men and
women could wear half silk, but brocade and braided silk tassels were
reserved for men.

Wide shirt sleeves were also in fashion during the Mamlūk
period in Egypt, but they often met with the disapproval of the rulers.
Thus Emir Kumushboghā, viceroy of the country during the absence
of the Sultan, in 1390 prohibited shirt sleeves which were wider than
twelve ells, still a very considerable size. Since some women were
not willing to observe this edict, he sent his slaves through the markets and streets with instructions to shorten excessively wide and
long sleeves with their knives. When the Sultan returned, the ladies
followed their favorite fashion again. The shirts, which had to be

long according to religious law, were often only of knee length, at least in the fourteenth century. A wrap, the *mi'zār*, was worn over the shirt. Egyptian women of this time also wore trousers: the slave-sultana Shajarat ad-Durr, who was murdered and thrown in a trench by the girls of her harem, was found dressed only in shirt and trousers. Over their shirt and trousers, they wore a dress-like gown with short, wide sleeves, plus a wide white coat held together by a belt. Part of the coat covered the hair, and a cloth wound into a turban, often richly embroidered and ornamented with precious stones was worn on the head.

The wearing of turbans by women frequently met with the disapproval of religious scholars, but repeated utterances on this subject show that this fashion was followed regularly by women. Indeed, judging by the miniatures, it seems that female headgear was more influenced by fashion than were other garments. It was often an indication of social status. Ulayya, the beautiful half-sister of the Abbāsid Caliph Hārūn ar-Rashīd, is said to have created the fashion of wearing headbands, the aim being to conceal a birthmark she had. These headbands were often ornamented with jewels, and also with verses or quotations from the Koran embroidered in silver or gold thread. The following lines are said to have been embroidered on the headband of one of Hārūn ar-Rashīd's female slaves:

Tyrant, you were cruel to me in love,
May God judge what happened between us!
[68, 22f.]

For centuries, belts and shirts were also decorated with such sayings. Outer garments worn by the upper classes were ornamented in like manner at the neck and on the sleeves, both above the elbow and at the wrist. When worn by rulers, this strip of lettering, known as *tirāz,* was not, of course, an erotic verse as above, but usually proclaimed his name, titles, and often felicitations or blessings.

On account of their occasional extravagance, female head coverings in Islamic countries seem to have attracted official criticism more often than any other article of clothing. It is reported that in 1471, the

Mamlūk Sultān Qayitbey forbade the women of Cairo to wear certain kinds of silken headgear or caps decorated with a kind of coxcomb. He decreed that the paper foundations for these caps must be one-third of an ell long, and must carry the seal of the Sultan on both sides. His chief of police was instructed to patrol the markets and to beat and pillory all women found wearing the kind of headgear he had banned. Understandably, this made women apprehensive, and they preferred to go out bareheaded.

The women did not leave the house without their veils, however, of which there were various types: a black one of a kind of netting, which either covered the entire face or had holes for the eyes, and the *burqu'*, a white or black veil which covered the face up to the eyes.

The Egyptian historian al-Maqrīzī (d. 1442), who as a police official must have known what he was talking about, reports that the wealthy women of his time were wildly extravagant regarding clothes. According to him, the wife of an Emir spent ten thousand gold dinar on an elegant pair of trousers, and a wife of the Sultan Baybars paid thirty thousand dinar for a dress she had made for the occasion of her son's circumcision. To convey an idea of the crass social contradictions that prevailed in Egypt at that time (and that continued for the whole of the Middle Ages in Islamic countries), one must realize that a water carrier in the early Mamlūk period earned I to 1.5 dinar per month, a minor official 2 to 3 dinar, and a royal Mamlūk, who held a fief, between 83 and 125 dinar. [15, 297, 284] In the first half of the fourteenth century, one *ratl* (449. 28g) of mutton cost 0.03 dinar. [15, 295]

Trousers, a long shirt, a dress-like topcoat, and, outside the house, a veil for the face were the basic items of a woman's wardrobe also in the East of the Islamic realm, which, from 1258 on, was under Mongol and then Persian rule. In the Mongol period, princesses and ladies of the Court indulged in an exceptionally extravagant piece of headgear, the *bōqtāq*. It may be assumed that ladies with this bush of feathers on their heads could walk only in a stilted fashion.

In the first half of the fifteenth century, the ladies of Tabriz and Herat wore a kind of topcoat, which reached down to the ground, was often left open at the front, and had narrow sleeves extending over the hands. The belt had already been adopted from male fashion, and was worn loosely over the hips. Now preferred as covering for the head were softly hanging cloths, which exposed the front of the head and hung down over the shoulders and back. In general, fashion in the fifteenth century made women look more graceful. As the century wore on, clothes became increasingly varied and luxurious.

Once the Safavids became established in Persia and brought a united Persian Empire under their central control, the country experienced an economic and cultural upswing. A rich material civilization emerged, in which high fashion of exceptional magnificence was the hallmark of the upper classes. Qazvin, and later Isfahan, the residence cities of the rulers, were fashion leaders for the whole of the East of Islam.

Fashions in female headgear changed so rapidly that it is difficult to list them in detail. In about 1530, there were brightly patterned cloths with a bush of feathers over the forehead. Very splendid indeed was the *tāj-kulāh*—literally the "crown hat"—worn by Persian princesses in about 1550. In the beginning, it consisted of a narrow crown worn over a flat cap. Fig. 31 shows what it looked like in the middle of the sixteenth century. An attractive fur-trimmed cap is to be seen in Fig. 32, a miniature from the mid-seventeenth century. Other miniatures show cloth head coverings attached to a triangular headband.

In comparison to the rapid change in fashion in headgear, hair styles do not seem to have changed very much at all. Braids are to be seen in illustrations from the thirteenth century, worn by men as well as women. The French jeweler Chardin, who was in Persia on several occasions in the 1660's and 1670's and whose record of his travels is one of the most comprehensive and detailed that we possess, says that the hair styles of the women at that time were not elaborate. The hair was combed back and plaited in several strands.

The beauty of the hair style is that the plaits are thick and reach to the ground. Silken plaits are also attached to them to make them longer. The ends of the plaits are decorated with pearls and a bouquet of precious stones, or with gold and silver jewelry. Under the veil, the head is covered only by the tip of a delicate, triangularly cut headband of different colors, which is held over the forehead by a ribbon about one inch wide. The ribbon is embroidered or ornamented with precious stones, depending on the rank of the wearer. Only married women wear it. Girls wear small caps instead of the headcloth or the tiara. [30, IV, 12]

E.W. Lane reports that in Egypt in about 1830, the hair styles of the women consisted of 11 to 25 plaits, which hung down over the back; they were made longer by braiding in black silk ribbons, and were ornamented with gold jewelry. [99, III, 211f.]

The head coverings of the women differed not only according to

Young woman making her toilet.

their marital status but also according to the professional status of their husbands. This information comes from the Dutchman Cornelius Le Brun, who was in Persia from 1702 to 1704. He says that military men, for instance, dressed quite differently from lawyers, and this also applied to their wives. In addition, there was not only a great difference between the clothing of married women and young girls, but also between old and young women. Le Brun considered the clothes of the Persian ladies of this time to be very attractive, and his remarks are worth hearing:

> *They also have a while, gold-embroidered veil hanging down over their shoulders, necklaces of precious stones and pearls, and golden chains which hang down to the bell and carry a little jar of perfume. Their outer garment is of brocade with flowers of gold or silver. But sometimes they wear one which is just of one color. Beneath this stola, they wear a jacket extending below the waist. Their shirts are of taffeta or of fine silk, embroidered with gold. They also wear trousers and skirts, fabricated by craftsmen, and boots, which rise four fingers above the ankle and are made front embroidered materials, velvet, or very richly decorated cloth. Their slippers are of green or red leather and have high heels in the same color. They are doubled and decorated with little flowers. Their belt, two or three inches wide, is ornamented with precious stones and pearls. At stomach level, they wear sashes which extend above the belt. In winter, they put on over this clothing a padded jacket of cotton cloth which reaches the width of a foot below the belt and, when it is very cold, a robe of gold or silver brocade, lined with sable or other furs. When they leave the house, they are wrapped from head loot in a large white veil, covering everything except their eyes. This veil is usually made from a single piece of cloth. They also wear bracelets of precious stones, and their fingers are ornamented with rings. The women of lower status clothe themselves as well as they can. The wives of the nobiliy or of military commanders wear netting of silk or something similar over their*

194

clothing, and this has a very pretty effect. [100, 217]

Scarcely any of the other travel accounts makes mention of these differences in clothing which resulted from social position.

The Englishman James Morier, who visited Persia between 1810 and 1816, reported of the Shah's First Lady that her clothing was embroidered with such a profusion of jewels that she could hardly move under the weight. Her trousers in particular carried so many pearls that they looked like a mosaic, while the legs of the exalted lady seemed like pillars. The English ambassador's wife, who told him this, was sent clothes as a gift from the Court on the day following her visit. Of these, the most remarkable were brocade trousers which were so stiff that they could stand by themselves. [118, 61f.]

From about the middle of the nineteenth century, the European influence on policy and economics, which had really been felt since the beginning of Qājār rule in Persia, also affected fashion. The ladies wore crinoline-like skirts with hip-length jackets, but when they left the house they preferred to wear trousers. A dark cloak enclosed them down to the knees, and a white veil covered their faces.

A very impressive image of the clothing of a Turkish lady of 1717 is conveyed by Lady Wortley Montague. This very emancipated member of the English aristocracy was probably the first European woman to dare to travel around Turkey. In contrast to male travelers (other than physicians), she had the advantage of being able to enter the harems. With feminine awareness and much sympathy, she sensed the atmosphere of the women's world of the Turkish upper classes of that time, and in her letters she describes it with great enthusiasm and with the desire to awaken the understanding of the reader. She sketches herself in Turkish clothing to her English correspondent:

> *The first peice of my dresse is a pair of drawers, very full, that reach to my shoes and conceal the legs more modestly than your Petticoats. They are of a thin rose colour damask brocaded with silver flowers, my shoes of white kid Leather embrodier'd with Gold. Over this hangs my Smock of a fine*

Turkish lady with maidservant on the way to bathe.

white silk Gause edg'd with Embrodiery. This smock has wide sleeves hanging halfe way down the Arm and is clos'd at the Neck with a diamond button, but the shape and colour of the bosom very well to be distinguish'd through it. The Antery is a wastcoat made close to the shape, of white and Gold Damask, with very long sleeves falling back and fring'd with deep Gold fringe, and should have Diamond or pearl Buttons. My Caftan of he same stuff with my Drawers is a robe exactly fited to my shape and reaching to my feet, with very long strait falling sleeves. Over this is the Girdle of about 4 fingers broad, which all that can afford have entirely of Diamonds or other precious stones. Those that will not be at that expence have it of exquisite Embrodiery on Satin, but it must be fasten'd before with a clasp of Di'monds. The Curdée is a loose Robe they throw off or put on according to the Weather, being of a rich Brocade (mine is green and Gold) either lin'd with Ermine or Sables; the sleeves reach very little below the Shoulders. The Headress is compos'd of a Cap call'd Talpock, which is in winter of fine velvet embrodier'd with pearls or Di'monds and in summer of a light shineing silver stuff. This is fix'd on one side of the Head, hanging a little way down with a Gold Tassel and bound on either with a circle of Di'monds (as I have seen several) or a rich embrodier'd Handkercheif. On the other side of the Head the Hair is laid flat, and here the Ladys are at Liberty to shew their fancys, some putting Flowers, others a plume of Heron's feathers, and, in short, what they please, but the most general fashion is a large Bouquet of Jewels made like natural flowers, that is, the buds of Pearl, the roses of different colour'd Rubys, the Jess'mines of Di'monds, Jonquils of Topazes, etc., so well set and enammell'd tis hard to imagine any thing of that kind so beautifull. The Hair hangs at its full length behind, divided into tresses braided with pearl or riband, which is allways in great Quantity. [117, 326 ff.]

The countries of the Arabian Peninsula, at that time provinces of the Ottoman Empire, which had long been experiencing a decline in its power, presumably followed the lead of the capital in matters of fashion. However, even the Italian nobleman Pietro della Valle, who traveled the Near East a century before Lady Montague, reports that the women of Baghdad—once the splendid metropolis of the Caliphat—clothe themselves like the Turks but "still in the old manner . . . since the new fashions, such as those that appear at the Turkish Court, reach them so late." [173, I, 210a/b] This is not surprising, considering the channels of information and communication of the time.

Everything that has been said here about clothing and fashion in the Islamic countries applies to the ruling classes, who considered it their privilege to live in luxury. The great mass of the people never possessed the necessary financial resources. In the *Arabian Nights*, there is a description of how a woman disguises herself as an itinerant vendor; she puts on a patched robe, wraps a honey-colored veil around her head, an indication for being a Christian or a Jew, takes a stick in her hand, and picks up a basket containing the merchandise. [164, III, 226]

Pietro della Valle describes the clothing of Bedouin women, for which the term "fashion," even now, is inappropriate, although the more prosperous ones had a kind of "Sunday-best" wardrobe, consisting of a "violet-brown or Turkish-blue shirt reaching down to the feet." It had such wide sleeves that babies who had to be suckled could be put to the breast through the sleeve. When it was cold, he reports, Bedouin women pulled over the shirt "a coarse sleeveless upper garment, known as an *aba,* which is not so fine nor so wide as when they want to show themselves but narrow, such as all the women wear." They wrapped their heads in black linen and concealed their faces with a black or blue veil. [173, I, 207a] Della Valle observes that the fellah women did not wear veils.

We have yet to take a brief look at fashion in India of the Mughal period. The first Mughal rulers of the sixteenth century came to the country as alien conquerors, and had scarcely anything in common with the subjugated Hindus. Under their regime, clothing—like the entire culture and civilization of these rulers—was marked by features predominant at the time in Persia and Turkestan. This is evident from the miniature in Fig. 36.

From the end of the sixteenth and the beginning of the seventeenth century, the constantly growing influence of the Indian environment on Mogul culture became increasingly apparent in fashion as well. The lady in the miniature in Fig. 34 demonstrates this. Emperor Aurangzēb (1659-1707) was offended by the erotic and transparent garments that were worn. Thus it was that a long jacket of gold brocade with flower embroidery came into fashion, at least for the winter months; it was worn on top of the other clothing. The Venetian Niccolao Manucci, who spent several years at the Mughal Court as physician-in-chief to Shah Ālam, the eldest son of Aurangzēb, reports that ladies' dresses did not usually weigh more than one ounce, that they slept in them, and that they wore them only once before giving them to their maidservants. "During the cold weather . . . , they wear the same clothes, covering themselves on the top of the other things, however, with a woollen *cabaye* (*qabā*, a long open gown), of fine Kashmīr make. Above their other clothes they put on fine shawls, so thin that they can be passed through a small finger-ring." [108, II, 341]

Here, too, at this time, the head coverings of the ladies were symbols of rank. "Some of these princesses wear turbans by the king's permission. On the turban is a valuable aigrette, surrounded by pearls and precious stones. This is extremely becoming, and makes them look very graceful. . . . During festivities, such as balls and the like, there are dancing-women who have the same privilege." [*Ibid.*] This shows the regard in which dancers were held at Court.

The love of jewelry was closely associated with the love of luxurious clothes. Both men and women in the Islamic countries paid a great deal of attention to complementing the splendor of their clothes with the right jewelry. Sometimes they indulged this inclination to excess. In the *Arabian Nights* it is said of Zubayda, wife of Hārūn ar-Rashīd, that she "could scarcely walk under the weight of her jewelry and dresses." [164, I, 325]

In the "Book of the Embroidered Cloth" by Ibn al-Washshā, it is written that fashionable ladies liked to wear close-fitting necklaces of fermented cloves, or long cords of costly camphor or ambergris pearls over their collars. (This predilection for perfumes will be examined later on.) Long chains of sweet-smelling cloves are still sold in the *sūq* of the Kurd town of Sulaymaniyya in Northern Iraq, and short necklaces of the small whiteful blossoms, probably a species of narcissus, may be bought in Cairo. They have an excitingly sweet scent, which clings for a long time to the skin and cloth.

Ibn al-Washshā lists other jewelry favored by the ladies of Baghdad of his time. They include link chains and pierced amulets to which tassels of braided gold or silken thread were attached. Among the precious or semiprecious stones were black obsidian, pure rock crystal, genuine pearls, corals, amber, and all kinds of corundum.

The women decorated their head coverings, of whose shape nothing is now known, with pearls and jewels, and they embroidered their headbands with silk and gold. They wore signet rings in which brilliantly colored precious stones such as rubies, emeralds, and sapphires were embedded. The etiquette of the time, however, prevented a lady from wearing rings of silver, enamel, or iron, with carnelian, turquoises or garnet stones. Only men and female slaves could wear such rings.

In a text of the eleventh century, a desirable and prosperous singing girl of Baghdad is reported to have worn a rosary of a special kind of dark ambergris and sandalwood taken from a carved wooden lattice in the Caliph's compartment of the mosque, that indicates religious and worldy power and is at the same time, evidence, even if fictitious, for the obvious interlacing of courtly pleasures in both. Both ambergris and sandlewood were carved in the shape of large pearls, and worth a thousand dinar. Her jewelry is admired in rhymed prose: "The jewel on her breast flashes like lightning in clouds dark, like in the night the lamp's spark, like flowers in full bloom in the meadow of spring or in the June sky's nightly blue the Pleiades' ring. Her bangles shine like the half-moon the same, her anklets like rings of flame." [18, 53]

Trade in jewelry was of considerable importance in the Middle East of the Middle Ages. Rubies came from India and the Yemen, pearls from Southern Iran and the coast of Oman, corals from the coasts of the Red Sea, sapphires from Ceylon, emeralds from Egypt, and ivory and gold dust from Abyssinia and East Africa. Precious stones, as is apparent from the *Book of the Embroidered Cloth*, were also subject to the whims of fashion. Diamonds, now regarded as the most precious of precious stones, were used only for drilling and as poison in Khorasan and Mesopotamia around 1000 A.D. Wealthy people used them to commit suicide. The most valued stones of this time were sapphires, emeralds, and rubies; pearls were also highly valued. By the twelfth century, however, rubies were so common, even among the lower strata of the population, that more prosperous citizens used only the large specimens, making them into salve boxes, beakers, and the like. Chardin relates that a Persian lady of the middle of the seventeenth century might pin aigrets of precious stones on her head or to her headband, that she might wear a collar of pearls extending from underneath the chin to the ears, and that she often wore, on the left nostril, a ring that hung down like an earring and had two pearls and a ruby on the lower edge. It was especially the slaves and children of the wealthy who wore these rings. The Persian ladies of Isfahan, however, did not pierce the nose. The ladies also ornamented themselves with loose bangles of precious stones. Gold or pearl necklaces hung down on the breast, and were held there by golden perfume boxes, studded with jewels. Young girls mostly wore only narrow golden bracelets fastened with a precious stone. [30, IV, 44ff.]

When the Mughal Empire was at the peak of its power and outward glory, the ladies also wore an exceptional amount of jewelry. In the past, two pearls and a pendant in the ear had sufficed, but now the ears were ornamented with more pearls and several small rings at the edge. In addition to bangles on the upper arm, wide golden bracelets bordered with pearls were worn at the wrists and circlets at the ankles.

Manucci says that the jewelers were kept very busy at the Mughal Court of 1700. "The best and the most costly of their productions are for the king's person, the queens, and the princesses. The latter pass the time in examining their jewels and showing them to others." As a physician, he had access to the imperial harem, where he observed that the ladies, when they sent for him, had their ornaments and jewels fetched "solely as an opening for a conversation." He reports that the princesses not only had strings of pearls around the neck and over the bosom, but also wore bunches of pearls decorated with jewels over their forehead, diadems as ear-pendants, armlets and bracelets, rings on their fingers, belts of gold studded with precious stones, trouser strings with bunches of pearls at the ends, rings and strings of pearls at their ankles. "All these princesses own six to eight sets of jewels, in addition to some other sets of which I do not speak, worn according to their own fancy." [108, II, 339ff.]

From about 1750, the Mughal ladies began to wear nose rings. They later adopted the pearl necklaces crossed over the breast worn by Rajput women.

Ibn al-Washshā describes rings worn by the men of Baghdad around 900. Gold was not favored, since according to Islamic traditions, Muhammed had forbidden the wearing of gold rings by men.

Of course, only the really wealthy could afford such expenditures. As early as the tenth century, there are reports that less prosperous women borrowed jewels and ornaments from the jewelers, so as not to be outdone by their more prosperous sisters.

At various times, rulers attempted to impose a kind of social discipline on their subjects. Tavernier, a French goldsmith and jeweler, who was in Persia on several occasions between 1631 and 1665 at the time of Shah Abbās II, relates that often a courtier who had an income of seven to eight *tomān* per year would spend four to five *tomān* on clothes. Abbās II did nothing about this, unlike his forefather, Shah Abbās I (1587-1629), who once ordered a courtier "to be given so many strokes on the soles of his feet that he gave up the ghost a few days later"; the courtier had worn golden stockings which he could not afford on his pay. [165, I, 275]

Unfortunately, relatively little of this profusion of jewelry has survived. On that which still exists, certain motifs, such as birds, trees of life, and the shape of the half-moon or crescent, are found time and again. The bird motif is found even in the pre-Islamic Persian jewelry of the Sassanid period. People also liked to inscribe benedictions for the wearer; these could be either displayed prominently, or carefully concealed. It may be supposed that women (and not necessarily only women) have always and everywhere attempted to give their natural beauty added attractiveness in accordance with the ideal of beauty at the time.

The basic condition for this in the Islamic countries was the thorough cleansing of the body after every form of bodily contamination specified in Islamic law. The public baths were also visited after journeys, after long illnesses, and, quite simply, for the pleasure of a sociable activity. Only the extremely wealthy could afford to install baths in their own houses. A seventeenth-century European view of this frequent bathing is conveyed by the French jeweler Tavernier: "They have a different idea of washing, which is prescribed by law, namely, to take a bath after they have approached their women, and some of them are so superstitious that they go to the baths almost every day." [165, I, 273b] What he refers to are the Islamic prescriptions of bodily purification after intercourse.

The cosmetic procedures carried out in the bath included thorough rinsing with cold water, perspiring in a room filled with hot steam, soaping, and rubbing down or a massage. The hair was undone, washed, rubbed with rose or orange blossom water, and braided again in plaits. Men and women had their body and pubic hair removed in the baths. For this, the skin was rubbed with *nūra,* a kind of cream or salve of quicklime and arsenic trisulphate. After being allowed to take effect for a short time, it had to be washed off rapidly, together with the hairs, since frequent use roughened the skin. For the skin care that followed, use was made of an ointment of rice, barley, broad-bean or chickpea flour, which had been blended with rose or myrtle water. The women also underwent quite a painful treatment for the removal of facial and leg hair; a mixture of thick syrup and turpentine was applied to the skin, allowed to dry, and then peeled off with the hairs.

A woman was considered untidy if body hair was not removed. An Arab author slanders a singing girl with verses that begin: "She has a pudenda which is as prickly as the face of Khazar lout." [62, 77] Lesbians in Baghdad of the eighth century did not shave the pudenda.

Since expressive dark eyes basically define the ideal of beauty in Islamic countries even up to the present century, and as the eyes were the only part of a veiled woman's face that could be seen, eye makeup was of considerable importance. Blackening the edges of the eyes was the custom even in the Egypt of the Pharaohs. Here, as later in the Islamic countries, antimonite (antimony sulfide) or galena was used for this purpose. The Arab designation for this is *al-kuhl* (a word which the sixteenth-century physician Paracelsus arbitrarily applied to the spirits of wine, known to us today as alcohol). In Persia, the blackening agent was called *Isfahānī* or *Surma* after the place where it was found.

The physician Russell was obviously allowed to see something of the makeup secrets of the Syrian women of his time, since he describes how it was applied: The powdered *kuhl* was placed on a short, smooth probe of ivory, wood, or silver. "The probe being first dipt in water, a little of the powder is sprinkled on it the middle part is then applied horizontally to the eye, and the eyelids being shut upon it, the probe is drawn through between them, leaving the inside tinged, and a black rim all around the edge." [142, I, 111] Iraqi women of the present day still make up their eyes in this manner. Russell also reports that the women used to dye their eyebrows black with *khatat,* a concoction of equal parts of oil and bruised oak-apples, to which sal ammoniac, burnt copper, and henna leaves were subsequently added, but that this was no longer in fashion. *Kuhl* was also used by men, and the eyes of newborn babies were treated with it, since it was thought to have medical properties.

Many sources state that men dyed their hair and their beards, since they did not like white hair. Even the first Caliph Abu Bakr is said to have dyed his hair red with henna. Black hair was generally regarded as most desirable, and black dye, made from woad leaves or pomegranate peel, for instance, was used for this purpose.

Henna was used for centuries by men and women in the Arab countries, Persia, Turkey, and Mughal India, to lend a reddish color to the palms of the hands or just the finger tips, fingernails, and toenails. For this, henna was dried, pulverized, and mixed with pomegranate or lemon juice, or sometimes just with water to obtain a paste. The parts to be dyed were then rubbed with the paste in the evening and a cloth bound over them. In the morning, the cloth was removed, and the henna fell away as dust. [173, II, 89ff.] In some regions, flower patterns were drawn with henna on the hands and feet. However, in the nineteenth century it was only among the lower strata of the population that henna was still in use in Turkey as a dye for the hands and feet.

The author of the Arab *Book of Marriage* of the eleventh century, from which passages have already been quoted, records a whole series of formulas for cosmetics, with the assertion that the use of these preparations could enhance the sexual attractiveness of women. In a society in which polygynous marriages were possible, a relatively large number of women in the harems of the wealthy often lived in a state of isolation, which made them dependent on one another. But it also led to a very strong sense of competition. In his *Book of Marriage*, this Syrian physician provides formulas for making straight hair curly and curly hair straight, as well as for dyeing the hair black or red. He also mentions cleansing agents, at least some of which are probably still being used by modern cosmetics industry, such as rice, barley, and almond flours, borax, and fish oil. However, in a certain similarity to the European primitive pharmacy of the Middle Ages, but with much more refinement and cultivation he also knows of mixtures in which natural substances and others are blended to produce astonishing effects. Thus he mentions a cosmetic that "gives the face a bright and radiant rosy hue and causes freckles to disappear, eliminates traces of leprosy, smallpox, scars, and all black spots, so that one brother would no longer recognize the other when he has used it for seven days." He then lists a complicated mixture of peeled cherries, grapevine roots, saffron, candy, gum arabic, bat's urine, boiled bran water, human milk, egg white, almond oil, fig juice, dried and powdered sea onion, celandine, peppermint, chickpea flour, milk vetch, rice flour, pistachios, Roman mustard, Armenian borax, and, for binding, water, oil, and egg white. [8, 27ff.] He also quotes formulas for teeth-cleaning agents and for mouth-odor pastilles.

Whereas most of us today try to achieve the ideal of a slim figure, and more or less silently regret giving up many a favorite dish, this text has the following to say: "Since a man likes a woman to be fat and plump, for he then experiences, when he sleeps with her, a pleasure which he does not have with a thin woman, I mean, a slight woman, we list here foods which make a delicate woman fat, make her flesh firm, give her skin a clear color and enable her to win the favor of her husband when she always eats them." [8, 60ff.] Among the fattening substances named by the author are mixtures of various kinds of nuts with honey. Foods rich in calories were also taken by women when they went to a public bath.

Finally, there are formulas for deodorants and scents, with the reasoning: "The cosmetics which we have named so far are of no use if pleasant scents are lacking." [8, 76] The liking for pleasant odors, which the people of the Middle East have always had, is legendary.

It would seem to be based on a highly developed sensuality, and reflects a high degree of civilization. The Islamic traditions record that Muhammed had Ā'isha rub his beard with sweet-smelling *ghāliya* salve. Even Herodotus calls Arabia the land most blessed with pleasant scents. The Koran, *Sūra* 56: 89 (88), speaks of Paradise not only as the "Garden of Delight" but also of "an evening breeze and fragrance." Islamic religious law exhorts the faithful to perfume themselves on Friday, the sabbath of the Muslims, but a woman should not do so when she goes to the mosque. The same applies to the period of mourning prescribed by law after the death of her husband. Frankincense was burned in the mosques on days of prayer, but the mosques were perfumed as well. It is thus related that the mother of the Abbāsid Caliph al-Muqtadir (908-932) had the Ka'ba in Mecca and the Holy Rock in the Dome of the Rock (Mosque of Umar) in Jerusalem perfumed every Friday with *nadd,* a mixture of musk and ambergris. [183, 424]

At receptions given by the Caliphs and the great men of the Empire, the rooms were scented with aloe, camphor, saffron, and rose water. Frankincense was also burned. Of the Mughal Emperor Akbar, it is reported by his friend and minister, Abu l-Fazl: "His Majesty is very fond of perfumes, and promotes them out of religious motives." [6, 73] Tavernier relates that in seventeenth-century Persia, visitors were offered pipes with aloe wood. Prior to this, however, they were offered rose water in vessels of gold or silver, depending on the rank of the guests, with which to wash their face and hands. They then dried off the water by bending over aloe smoke, whose scent clung to the hair and the beard. The principal constituents of perfumes were musk—Muhammed is said to have termed it the best of all essences—camphor, aloe, ambergris, and saffron. Other aromatic substances included spikenard, cloves, sandalwood, nutmeg, roses, cinnamon, cardamom, a series of other vegetable substances, and the secretion of the civet cat.

Even at a relatively early date, however, perfumes were synthesized. A treatise on perfumes by a famous Arab scientist of the ninth century contains formulas for imitating these precious essences, which can be sold "for good money without anyone noticing the deception." [186, 2 ff.]

The perfumed ointments *nadd* and *ghāliya,* mixtures of musk and ambergris, or ambergris, musk, and aloe, were held in particularly high esteem. The books of formulas state that special variations were produced for illustrious historical personalities, and that the formulas became increasingly more sophisticated in the course of history.

Like necklaces of camphor and cloves, and shirts perfumed with ambergris, *ghāliya* salve was a popular gift for the singing girls of Baghdad from their admirers around the year 900. The paste was dark in color, and, like musk and ambergris, was customarily used in an amorous pastime, namely, the writing of verses on the forehead or cheeks of singing girls and slaves. The singing girls also used it for sealing their love letters, while the boy-girls already referred to employed *ghāliya* for painting mustaches on their faces. However, by then, in contrast to earlier periods, it was regarded as a characteristic of the demimonde, since Ibn al-Washshā calls it the perfume of the singing girls and the homosexual pleasure-boys.

Some perfumes are reported to have been invented by women, who either created them for their own use or were commissioned by others. Nūr Jahān, the clever and attractive wife of the Mughal Emperor Jahāngīr, is said to have developed a kind of rose essence with which she won the admiration of her Imperial husband. [108, I, 163 f.]

French and English perfumes are now sold in the Islamic countries to those who can afford them. There are, of course, still shops where the classic perfumes of the Middle East are sold, but these are generally in parts of the city frequented by tourists. They are designed to cater to those who wish to take home with them something of the atmosphere of the Orient in the shape of a dearly bought phial of lotus, sandalwood, or aloe perfume.

Development in the Muslim world bas been marked for about the last 150 years by a process which has not run its course without contradictions; the process of displacing old traditions by innovations from outside. For roughly two generations this has also made itself felt, in various degrees in the individual countries, in women's fashion, as it did earlier in men's. Yet, once again, dress only emphasizes social differences. Only the upper classes in most Islamic countries have followed international fashion trends. In Iraq there was an attempt to create an haute couture which has been based on pre-Islamic dress of Mesopotamia. Women from the petite bourgeoisie and the urban proletariat, as well as women from the country, still wrap themselves in black cloaks which are called *milāya* in Egypt, *abāya* in Iraq, *chādor* in Iran, and *charshaf* in Turkey. White cloaks are widespread in North Africa. It is not unusual, however, to meet young girls, for example in Baghdad, who wear denim skirts under their *abāya*. In Orthodox Islamic Libya, even the female television announcers appear in *milāyas;* however, there is no obligation to wear a veil. Supposedly, young Saudi Arabian women, who have to wrap themselves up when in their strongly Orthodox homeland, change their traditional clothing for skintight jeans and tight pullovers in the airplane when travelling abroad.

Yet these are only external manifestations of a process which we will go into further later on. In this book, it will be possible only to provide an insight into the development and problems of women's liberation which have arisen against the respective historical backgrounds, and which have not been satisfactorily resolved to this day. A claim to completeness cannot be made.

35

There were women who were famous for their calligraphic expertise. This elegant Persian, in the process of writing a letter, is wearing strings of pearls around her face and neck, and has dashingly wrapped over her head a brightly colored cloth topped with a peacock feather. She has thrown her veil of delicate white material over her shoulder, and her corkscrew locks hang down over both ears.

36

This Mughal lady has made herself comfortable in an easy chair. She wears the Mughal fashion of the sixteenth-century, before Indian influence became apparent: a long, shirt-like gown reaching down to her feet and gathered in at the waist and between the breasts, a high cap, not unlike a hennin, decorated with a plume of feathers and pearls, a patterned scarf around her shoulders, and a ring on her thumb of her right hand. Instead of a stone, it is set with a little mirror which was preferred by the ladies of the time. She has discarded her red slippers.

37

With his arm around his beloved, the young man passes her a cup of wine with one hand and some fruit with the other.

38

A love scene from the Shāhanāmeh. *Zāl has fallen in love with the beautiful Rūdābeh from hearsay and she with him. At night, when the harem guards are asleep, he climbs up a rope ladder into the palace where she and a maidservant are awaiting him on the roof terrace. In this night, they swear everlasting love.*

39

From a Persian epic. The princess kneeling before the ruler tenderly embraces his thigh while he tickles her chin. Three maidservants are waiting at the door with refreshments.

40

*From her litter on a camel, a beautiful lady has watched two admirers
fighting for her hand. The duel has ended disastrously for one of them.*

41

Despite the passionate embrace, the countenance of this pair is radiant with peace and beauty.

42

*Intimacy for two alone was certainly not always the rule in the
harems of great personages.*

43

Layla is dead. Overcome by grief, Majnūn dies at her grave. The beasts of the desert which had once consoled him in his solitude, gather around him. In the background is again a Bedouin camp with herdsmen and their animals, a woman milking, and another at the spinning-wheel.

44

Also in his epic Haft Peykar (Seven Pictures), *the Persian poet Nizāmi celebrates a woman's wisdom founded on love. He gave a new accent to the old saga of Bahrām Gūr and his favorite slave Āzādeh who has already appeared in the* Shāhunāmeh. *In Firdousī's version, Bahrām Gūr has Āzādeh killed because she only remarks smilingly, "Practice makes perfect," instead of expressing due admiration for the fine shot he has made. In Nizāmi's epic, she takes refuge from the angry ruler. Much later, to his surprise, he sees a woman carrying a full-grown cow up sixty steps. She calmly explains that "practice makes perfect," since she has carried it thus from the time it was a calf. He then recognizes her, regrets his earlier anger, and is reconciled with her.*

45

The fairy tale of Tobias, originating from the philosophical and didactic literature of the Near East, was given a literary presentation in the Biblical Apocrypha and was very popular throughout the Near and Middle East. In this Indian miniature, where Persian influence is still apparent, Tobias has become an angel to whom the painter has given the appearance of a beautiful young woman. She is wearing a trouser-dress of a magnificent pattern and with wide legs, pearl pendants in her ears, close-fitting necklaces, and strings of pearls around her feet. Her imaginary headdress is probably what the artist considered appropriate for an angel.

46

A wall tile conveys an impression of the ideal beauty of seventeenth-century Iran. Eyebrows joined above the nose curve high above black almond-shaped eyes. She has corkscrew curls on either side of her face.

On the Search for Identity

Tear away the veil, woman of Iraq,
Unveil yourself for life needs transformation.
Tear it away, burn it, do not hesitate,
It has only given you false protection!
[188, 335]

This was the appeal of the Iraqi poet Jamīl Sidqī az-Zahāwī to his countrywomen in the first quarter of the twentieth century. As early as the second half of the nineteenth century, the veil, for enlightened intellectuals in some countries of Islam, became the symbol of the exclusion of women from public life and from practically all forms of education, trends that had increased markedly in the period of the decline of the Islamic world.

Toward the end of the eighteenth century, the countries of the Middle East were politically, economically, and culturally at low ebb. In this state, they presented an attractive prize for the colonial powers, England, France and, to some extent, Tsarist Russia (with regard to Iran and Turkey), who were seeking to expand their spheres of economic and political influence. The first contacts with Western Europe, such as the journey by a small group of Turkish politicians to France in 1720, the later activities of European specialists in some Oriental countries, and, above all, Napoleon's expedition to Egypt in 1798-1801, made it terrifyingly clear to enlightened politicians and a small intellectual elite just how backward their countries were in comparison with the highly developed civilization and technology of Western Europe. They realized that the only way to resist the expansionist aims of the powers of Western Europe was to adopt the foundations of Western civilization and use them to their own advantage. This was considered to be quite compatible with the principles of Islam, whose open-mindedness in the first Islamic centuries was recalled.

A start was made with military and administrative reforms, since the politicians were primarily concerned with preserving and expanding their power. Study groups from Turkey and Egypt, established contact with new educational principles and other aspects of European society. The ideas of the French Enlightenment and the French Revolution and such concepts as nationalism, constitutionalism, and democracy penetrated the Middle East. Schools and the first universities were founded on European models, and European teachers were recruited. The report on his sojourn in France written by the Egyptian Rifā'a af-Tahtāwī shows the great impact the social and intellectual position of French women made on Muslim intellectuals, although, of course, he describes only the middle class, with whom he had the most contact. He had accompanied the first Egyptian study group to Paris, where they stayed from 1826 to 1831, and his report reveals the differences between the two worlds, particularly the virtual ignorance of the one, the Orient, about the other, Europe. Rifā'a af-Tahtāwī tells his countrymen that Frenchwomen not only travel unaccompanied but also pursue scientific interests. In France, he comments, the saying that man's beauty lies in his understanding while woman's lies in her speech did not apply, since understanding, talent, perception, and knowledge were also expected of women. He finds that French women "are equal to men in all things." [135, 89] To an Oriental accustomed to an extremely patriarchal family structure, Western forms of politeness appear highly suspicious: "In many things the men are the slaves of the women." [135, 59] Although this pious Muslim finds it necessary to criticize the morals of some Frenchwomen, he has the ability to differentiate, and says that a woman's virtue does not depend on whether or not she is veiled, but on her education and other such factors, mostly of a mental nature. Rifā'a at-Tahtāwī was subsequently to become one of the first Egyptians to advocate that girls should be given an appropriate school education.

222

For centuries, people of Islamic countries had believed that they were superior to all other lands, and in the Golden Age of the Califate this had not been very far from the truth. The religion of Islam was considered to be the reason for this superiority. Now they had to acknowledge that the civilization and technology of Western Europe had reached a far higher level of development, although they did not deny the fact that rethinking was needed and many things had to be seen from a different angle, people were nevertheless still convinced that Islam was the best of all religions. Like the nationalist tendencies in the countries of the Muslim Near East, the movement for "Women's Lib" or any of the efforts to better women's life conditions in these countries, should not be seen isolated from similar developments in Western Europe. Male and female members of the religious and intellectual upper classes initiated emancipatory nationalist and social developments in permanent confrontation with sometimes overpowering outside influences, while looking for and thinking over genuine historic traditions and social and religious values, which might support these influences, and help to adapt them as principally rooted in Islam.

The Egyptian modernist Muhammad Abduh was the Grand Mufti of Egypt from 1899 until his death in 1905. He emphasized time and again that Islam was the most rational of world religions; yet in the last decades of the nineteenth century he also undertook a reinterpretation of the Koran in which, for instance, he wished polygyny to be considered as a historical and social issue, and noted that Islam did not recommend it as an absolute, but only under certain historical and social conditions.

The publicist Qāsim Amīn (1865-1908), who had been one of Abduh's pupils at the Islamic al-Azhar University, published a book in 1899 entitled *The Liberation of Woman.* The author stresses that the degradation of women in Islamic countries, which had increased in the course of the centuries, did not have its origin in Islam but had been absorbed from the views and customs of peoples who had subsequently become Muslims. This opinion throws light on the emergence of Arab self-consciousness and nationalism. According to Qāsim Amīn, respect for women and equality of the sexes are basic principles of Islam. He refers to the early days of Islam when one of Muhammad's wives, Umm Salama, accompanied him on various expeditions and tended the sick and the wounded, whereas in contemporary Islam, women were not permitted to perform such humanitarian services. Amīn sees the real reason for the low social status of women to be the political absolutism that prevailed for centuries in the Orient, leading to the abuse of power and to corruption of the individual. Since everyone corrupted in this way endeavored to tyrannize those in close contact with and dependent on him, women, as the weaker sex, had been victimized. He argues that a free society can be established only when all its members are free. The lower social position of women, as well as patriarchal tyranny affirmed by convention, did not justify its continuance. Women had a right to education, a share in social life and the practice of a profession, since they were no less human beings than men. The verses in the Koran that had subsequently been quoted to justify the obligation to wear a veil, as well as those referring to polygyny and *talāq*, needed to be interpreted differently and had to be understood in the context of the age in which they had first appeared. Qāsim Amīn's book was violently attacked. Two years later, he published a slightly revised version entitled *The New Woman*, which once again outlined his views.

A few decades earlier, a start had been made to give women a chance to obtain an education. In 1873, the Egyptian Khedive Ismā'īl opened the first school for girls in Cairo. He also issued instructions that the pupils were not to wear their veils when leaving the house. But this effort was apparently premature, since young Egyptian girls and women were not adequately prepared for such a measure.

The first college for the training of women teachers was opened in Turkey in 1863, the idea being to prevent upper-class families from bringing foreign women into the country for the education of their daughters. As early as 1893—a time of harsh political tyranny under Sultan Abdulhamīd—women were permitted to attend lectures at the Medical Faculty of Istanbul University; from 1899 on they were allowed to pursue a regular course of medical studies. It was an urgent necessity in Turkey, because only a few women in the Muslim countries of that time would allow themselves to be treated by a male physician.

A decree on general compulsory education was enacted in October 1913, which, although it could not be implemented everywhere, did provide for the coeducation of boys and girls up to the age of twelve. Even today, this is still not customary in every Islamic country. In October 1913 a women's university was founded in Istanbul, but its curriculum was close to that of a secondary school. Regular courses for women at Istanbul University began in 1914.

In Iraq, the first government girls' school was opened in 1909; in Iran, there was none until 1917, and in Saudi Arabia (where the first boys' school was opened in 1942), in 1956. According to the UNESCO statistical yearbook of 1991, girls' enrollment in schools in Arab countries increased from 27% to 42% between 1975 and 1988. In other developing countries, enrollment has remained frozen between 42 and 44%. The difference in the speed with which such innovations were introduced in the various Islamic countries depended greatly upon their political situation. Iraq, for instance, like Syria and Lebanon, was a Turkish province until the end of the First World War, whereas Egypt under the Khedives enjoyed relative independence until it was occupied by Great Britain in 1882.

On March 19, 1919, the Turkish Minister of Education opened the first lectures for women at the Philosophical Faculty of the University of Istanbul. The first lecture halls for joint use by men and women students were opened in 1921, but the young girls were still separated from their male classmates and were permitted to lift their veils only while attending lectures. In Egypt, the first women began university studies in 1928.

In his book, *Mirrors,* the Egyptian novelist Naguib Mahfouz gives us an impression of the relationship between men and women students in Egypt a few years later:

The women students of 1930 were few in number, not more than ten. Most of them were characterized by the harem. They dressed discreetly, wore no jewelry or make-xup, and sat by themselves in the first row of the lecture room as if they were in the women's compartment of the tram. We did

not greet each other, nor did we talk together. When a ques-
tion had to be asked or a book borrowed, this was done cau-
tiously and shyly, and it did not happen secretly either, but
attracted attention and led to gossip and aggressive comments.
[107, 160]

The University of Teheran was founded in 1935. In 1938, by decree of the Shah, women were allowed to study and were given access to professions and even posts in the government that had previously been barred to them. In 1928, financial assistance had been made available for some upper-class women for studies abroad.

In 1922, the first Turkish woman physician opened her practice in Istanbul, the first Turkish woman lawyer appeared on the scene in 1927; the first woman judge in 1930, and the first woman prosecutor in 1932. In the middle of the 1980s, every fifth practising lawyer and every fifth physian in Turkeyt was a woman. But in Egypt, for example, it is still not permitted for women to be either a judge or a public prosecutor. In 1937, the first Iraqi woman received the degree of Doctor of Medicine at the University of Beirut, but it was only in 1960 that an Iraqi woman won a doctorate in chemistry—and this was at a foreign university. In 1979, the first three Iraqi women lawyers were appointed judges.

Let us return once more to the subject of veil and seclusion. In 1910, a young Turkish woman attracted attention by daring to have herself photographed. For women who were not allowed to show themselves in public without a veil, this was certainly not an everyday event. At about the same time, young educated women in Turkey began to leave the house unveiled. In Egypt, on the other hand, young girls did not put aside the veil until the mid-1920s. In Iran, it was a sensation even in the late summer of 1928 when the police chief of Teheran visited a café in a summer resort in the company of his veiled wife: even today, the traditional Arab coffeehouses are reserved exclusively for men. A few weeks after the daring appearance of Teheran's police chief, men were seen walking side by side with their veiled wives in the street or riding in an open carriage to the cinema, although men and women continued to sit there in separate sections. A European observer reports that at this time in Teheran two or three women and half a dozen schoolgirls went unveiled in the streets. It was also then that the women's compartments disappeared from the public traffic, something that had been done in Turkey a few years earlier but which is debated again today in countries with overcrowded big cities. In 1936 the Shah of Iran introduced a law forbidding the wearing of veils, but many women were still so bound by tradition that the law had to be revoked in 1941. Customs practiced for centuries cannot be changed overnight at the stroke of a pen. A fairly long process of education is needed, not only for the women but also for the men. The legal position of women was not in any way changed by this law. After 1941 most women from the lower urban population classes put the *chador* on again. Clothes from the West were characteristic of the upper class.

As late as 1943, Sultan Muhammed V. of Morocco astonished his entire people when he presented his daughter Ā'isha to the nation without a veil. At a session of the All-India Women's Conference at Lahore in January 1931, in which women of all creeds took part, the chairwoman of the Reception Committee welcomed the guests. Her words were broadcast over loudspeakers, but she herself sat behind a screen, concealed from view, in the same way as the noble ladies in Medieval Islamic Society had sometimes taken part in negotiations from behind a curtain.

The *milāya, abāya, chādor, charshaf,* or veil also offered women protection. When progressive Egyptian women took part in the uprising of 1919, the *milāya* enabled them to hide weapons. This was, incidentally, the first great opportunity for Egyptian women to demonstrate that they wanted to participate in the political struggle of the country. Iranian women also carried weapons under their *chādor* in the riots that occurred at the end of 1978.

Nowadays, women of social strata who in bygone centuries did not wear the veil, are veiled. Because the veil would have been a hindrance when working, peasant women in former times did not wear veils as they do now. Clearly this is a reaction against the upper classes with their westernized way of life. While at the beginning of the emancipation development the struggle against the veil was a main point, for the past twenty years restoring trends are increasing.

Women's organizations play an important role in the struggle for women's political rights and for legal reforms in the Islamic countries. In Turkey, the first women's clubs and societies were formed before the First World War. In Iraq, the first women's organization was founded in 1924 and was led by the sister of the poet az-Zahāwī, quoted at the beginning of this chapter. This was only a year after the first women's political organization came into existence in Egypt.

To begin with, the principal aim of the Egyptian organization was to win the right to vote as the most important basic political right of women. In fact, this aim was not achieved until some years after the Egyptian Revolution of 1952, namely in 1956. In the first Egyptian constitution following complete political independence that year, it was declared that all citizens, men and women, had the same rights. In 1957, the first two women entered the Egyptian Parliament as elected representatives; in the parliamentary period of 1964-1968, there were eight women members. In 1969, however, there were only two. In the second free election to the People's Assembly, thirty seats were specifically reserved for women, as additions to the total number of seats. The new People's Assembly had a total of 390 members, of which almost nine percent were women. In 1982-1983, thirty-five women were members of Egypt's People's Assembly.

In Turkey, where the sentence "The official religion of the State is Islam" had been dropped by constitutional amendment on April 8, 1928, women were given the franchise in three stages: in 1930 for the town councils, in 1933 for the Councils of Elders, and in 1934 for the National Assembly. Eighteen women deputies, including fourteen teachers, were elected for the first time in Turkey in February 1935. But there were only three female deputies in the Turkish National Assembly in 1950; between 1954 and 1983 the number ranged from four to twelve of a total of 535 respectively 400 deputies..

In Pakistan and Syria, women have had the right to vote since 1954, in Iran since 1963; since the mid-sixties, they have also taken part in elections in Algeria, Tunisia, Morocco, Iraq, and Lebanon. Critical investigations by women sociologists and politologists from Turkey and some Arab countries state what can be observed in

European countries, too: seats reserved for women in parliament—like functions in political parties—have been seen for a long time as indicating social and political progress and were nothing more than an alibi. The reason is that men, who are still the leaders in politics, economics, and society, do not concede to women real competence and power of decision. Sex segregation has prevailed during the elections over the centuries and still does today: men and women vote separately. In Algeria, men are allowed to vote for their wives. This has been explained by women's domination over their husbands and in their households, and the men's wish to save their wives the troublesome trip to the election office.

In this same period, women have been made ministers in some Islamic countries. The first female minister was an Iraqi as Minister of Agriculture in 1959. Women have headed the Ministry of Social Affairs (in Egypt, since the mid-seventies), the Ministries of Education and Higher Education (in Iran before 1978, in Iraq since the seventies, and in Afghanistan since the revolution), and the Ministry of Culture (in Syria, since 1980), ministries. which seemed controversial to women's role in society.

The women's organizations furthered education for women, especially for village inhabitants and the lower strata in the cities. However, it is precisely among the rural population that literacy is progressing at a slow rate, in Iran, for instance, from 1 percent in 1956 to 3.6 percent in 1966. Between 1960 and 1970 the percentage of female illiterates in the Arab countries decreased by 5% (to 85%), that of male illiterates, however, by 10% (to 60%). [144a, 52] Illiteracy rates in general are decreasing in Islamic countries. Although statistics in developing countries have to be read with a skeptical eye, they mark a general tendency of increasing literacy. UNESCO statistics for 1991 show an estimated rate of illiteracy for 1990 in Iran: among males, 35.5%, among females, 56.7% In Turkey, where illiteracy rates have for decades been lower than in Iran or the Arab world, among males, 10.3%, and among females, 28.9%. In Arab countries there are great differences for example between Lebanon (males 12.2%, females 26.9%) and Sudan (males 57.3%, females 88.3%). This last is an increase from 1973, when the male rate was 55.2% and the female rate 82.1%. Sudan and Iraq are the only countries for whom statistics show an increase in illiteracy. The causes for the declines are, in Iraq, the two wars in the Gulf, and in Sudan, the worsening social, economic and political condition.

The women's organizations also provide information on hygiene, and endeavor—often in the face of great resistance from the women concerned—to encourage family planning. In addition, they hold courses, for example, in needlework and typewriting.

By reason of the taboos that still prevail concerning the mixing of the sexes, women still prefer certain professions. Graduates are mainly employed as teachers in girls' schools, as professors in women's faculties (which are still to be found in universities of Islamic countries), and as doctors, for the most part as gynecologists and pediatricians. Women with a medium level of education work, for example, as nurses in women's and children's wards, and only fairly recently with male colleagues as administrators or laboratory technicians as well. In factories in Egypt, Syria, and Iraq, the author often saw departments exclusively reserved either for men or women workers. The reason given for this was the mostly conservative attitudes of the lower strata of the population. Fathers, it was said, would refuse to send their daughters to work in a factory where they would mingle freely with male co-workers. It was also suggested that separation of the sexes was a first step in persuading women of this class to work outside the house at all.

The well-known Moroccan feminist, Fatima Mernissi, who took her doctor's degree in sociology at an American university in 1974, wrote in her thesis that in Morocco a girl who had to go out to work was regarded as being on the lowest step of the social ladder. To refrain from public activities and from any kind of work outside their home was still the privilege of the wives of wealthy men. She wrote, that many men, who were unable to feed their families adequately because of unemployment, allow a woman to work outside her own house and, especially, under the supervision of men because it would give them, the feeling of being a pimp. [114, 185]

Only for the few women in professions with a high social prestige, such as physicians, lawyers, and teachers, does a professional activity mean true emancipation. The opportunity for a womens' labor force in general is dependent on the economic and demographic situation of a country, as well as on the ability of women to work and the need of the family for a second income. Economic underdevelopment and surplus labor force in many countries such as Morocco, Tunis, Egypt, and Turkey, cut down the possibilities for women to work outside the house. In general, a social value system according to which the honor of a family depends on the virtue of its female members does not favor women working. Such a system results in sexual segregation, a strong gender specific socialization, early marriages for girls, and protection of girls and women, which leads to supervision first by the father and then by the husband (especially in the middle and lower strata of the society). Countries which claim to be progressive, try to integrate women into professions unusual for them according to conceptions of sexual segregation, such as traffic policeman, worker in a gas station, and even judge and diplomat. Nevertheless the female working rate is much lower than in other developing countries. Working in agriculture, which is the rule for women in underdeveloped countries such as Yemen, is not included in statistical surveys.

Some fields of activity, such as domestic service and retail trade, which are now in the Western world largely reserved for women are still the domain of men in Islamic countries or, at most, of foreign women. It probably seems strange to Westerners when in Baghdad, for instance, in one of the little shops of the *sūq,* we see a young woman, wrapped in an *abāya,* buying the sheerest of underclothes from a male clerk.

The women's organizations have also called for reforms in family law in the Islamic countries, a demand that is still current. In fundamentalist Saudi Arabia, since its foundation in 1927, the *sharī'a* is legally binding. Libya reestablished the *sharī'a* in 1971, with some alterations such as the fixing of a minimum marriage age and greater rights for women to demand a divorce. In 1979 the Iranian government annulled the legal reforms introduced by the last Shah.

Most countries adhere to the *sharī'a* in a form that includes new elements. In this way, an effort is being made to obtain legislation

231

that is in harmony both with Islam and with the needs of modern life. To begin with, the approach was to adopt from each school of law those principles that seemed most suitable for the present time.

Turkey adopted Swiss civil law, practically word-for-word, on October 4, 1926. It was the only Islamic country to make a clean break with the *sharī'a*. However, introduction of the obligatory civil marriage has shown that a body of law cannot simply be transplanted to a country where it is not part of tradition. To the present day, the Turkish rural population has clung to the form of marriage performed by the *imām*, the prayer leader, although the law does not permit this ceremony even to be performed if not preceded by a civil ceremony. The marriage ceremony performed by the *imām* still permits polygyny and *talāq* (the repudiation of the wife). One result of the conflict between the old and the new was that between 1933 and the present time, the Turkish government was obliged to pass at least eight "amnesty laws," recognizing, in particular, the legitimacy of the children born from such unions, but recognizing these unions as legal life companionships, too.

The only Islamic country, apart from Turkey, that has officially prohibited polygyny is Tunisia. The law was passed there in 1956 but its implementation was apparently difficult, since in 1964 it was stated again that a marriage is invalid if contracted by a person already married. Anyone attempting to contract such a marriage would be punished by law.

The Turkish law of 1917, which continued to recognize polygyny (although the wife had to agree to a second marriage by her husband), was valid until the 1950s in Syria, Lebanon, Jordan, and Iraq, which had previously been ruled by Turkey, even though it was superseded in Turkey itself in 1926. In Iran, by an amendment of 1959, the husband also had to prove to court that he was financially able to support a second wife. It may be assumed that the agreement of the first wife was and is obtained without much difficulty when she is economically dependent on her husband, or in other words, when he can put pressure on her. There are, as far as the author could discover, no numerical data for men living in polygynic marriages, or more precisely, men married to two women. (Marriages to more than two wives are not taken into account, even legally.) Yet it seems that after a decrease in polygynic marriages, there has been a slight increase over recent years. Because of strengthened Islamic attitudes, a man, even one of socially high status, may take a second wife (with his first wife's consent) without social stigmatization; however, the attitudes may differ from one country to another.

Another innovation is the prescription of a minimum age for marriage, mostly eighteen years for the husband and sixteen years for the wife. In an amendment of 1959 to Tunisian family law, this was raised to twenty and seventeen years respectively, and in Iran, in the summer of 1974, to twenty and eighteen years respectively. The reason for this was clearly the desire to control the population explosion since, according to traditional Islamic views—at least in the lower strata of the population—the status of a woman still depends on the number of children, especially sons, she has borne. In Iraq, the family law supplement of February 1978, permitting the marriage of fifteen-year-olds in exceptional cases when the judge agrees, is considered to be taking account of reality.

Some legislation, in Tunisia and (socialist) South Yemen, specified that the wife, when she is able to do so, has to contribute to the upkeep of the household together with the husband. According to the *shari'a*, she is not obliged to do so. In South Yemen, after massive reforms of family law, each of the two partners must provide for the upkeep when the other is unable to do so. This implies that the wife is no longer regarded as a helpless creature in need of protection for whom the husband must take responsibility.

The right that some schools of law give the father or guardian, to force a girl who is under age into a marriage, has also been eliminated in countries with a modified *shari'a*. In the Iraqi family law supplement of February 1978, drastic punishment is prescribed for anyone attempting this, a sign that such marriages then still took place at least in rural districts.

Limits are set to the arbitrary divorcing of the wife by the husband in Algeria and South Yemen, following modifications of the family law. In countries with a modified *shari'a*, the wife has more rights than in the past to demand divorce by a court of law, when:

physical or mental illness affects the marriage, when the husband does not contribute to the upkeep of the family, when the wife is the victim of cruelty or unbearable treatment, when the husband is absent for a long time, and, in Iraq after the last supplement of 1978, when the husband is unfaithful.

Most Islamic countries, however, still make no provision for the adequate support of divorced women, but they can keep their children for a longer time than stipulated in the *shari'a*.

The return to the original Islam, as is demanded similarly by Libya and Saudi Arabia, can also be understood in various ways. This includes, in Libya, equal rights in school and professional education for girls and boys—to a certain extent also coeducation. In Saudi Arabia's universities in Riyadh (founded 1957) and in Jiddah (founded 1970), there are girls' faculties, where female students follow the lectures of their male professors by videotape, put their questions by phone, and use the university library only on those days on which it is closed to male students. Because Saudi Arabia wants to do without any imported labor force, it encourages female work. There are companies and banks with entirely female staffs and exclusively female clients.

The patriarchal family structure in Islamic countries is disintegrating gradually. Among the upper and middle classes of the cities, in particular, the nuclear family has become usual, whereas in many rural regions the extended family is still prevalent. But obviously the nuclear family in a patriarchal society is not always favorable for women, because there they are more isolated than in the extended family, and are more subject to the dominance of a tyrannical husband. It has been observed that in some areas, for example in the older parts of Cairo, women form a network of their own, supporting and encouraging each other. Possibly, this has been a tradition for centuries. It is still unusual for a young unmarried woman, even a university graduate, to live alone and not with her immediate relatives. How greater freedom will affect the crime and suicide rates among the female population of Islamic countries, which have remained till now very low, is unknown.

Even in the middle-aged generation of university graduates,

fathers still consider it self-evident that they should find the right husband for their daughters, despite the changes that are taking place as a result of the increasing amount of coeducation at the universities.

Many young men still expect their bride to be a virgin. Latīfa az-Zayyāt, then professor at the Ayn-Shams University in Cairo, referred to the sexual confusion of young Egyptian girls of the mid-1950s in her novel *The Open Door,* published in 1960:

> *Our mothers understood their situation. We, however, are lost. We do not know whether or not we still belong to the harem, whether love is forbidden or permitted. Our family says "forbidden," but the government radio broadcasts love songs day and night. Books urge a girl: "Go, you are free!" But if she believes this, she will be unhappy since her reputation is then lost and sullied by shame.* [189, 71]

This novel was a sharp protest against the patriarchal family and the custom of having parents seek husbands and wives for their children, mostly on the basis of social status, without regard to the feelings of the young people. It is made quite clear that women in particular fall apart emotionally in such marriages. As against the rigid social convention that puts a woman's life entirely under the control of her father and husband, the authoress demands a woman's right to individual liberty and self-determination in her own country.

Arab female writing in modern times began before 1900, with the Syrian Zainab Fawwāz (1860-1914), who emigrated to Egypt in search of greater intellectual freedom, as did other members of the Syro-Lebanese upper class. In 1892, she finished her novel *al-Hawwā' wa-l-wafā', Eve and Fidelity.* Judging only from the title, it is part of the tradition of a rather new genre in Arabic literature: family novels with a didactic, moralistic tendency. The authors wanted to influence the patterns of Arab family life, then changing under economic and political influences from Europe. Her biographical dictionary, with the rhymed title Ad-*Durr al-manthūr fi tabaqāt rabbāt al-khudūr, Scattered Pearls about the classes of noble ladies,* published in Cairo in 1896, contains biographies of women famous in the

cultural, literary, and political history of Arab and European countries. The number of Arab women exceeds that of European. The
Arab maxim *al-Fadl lil-mutaqaddim,* "Priority belongs to the one who
comes first," applies perfectly: the fame of the Arab women portrayed
in the book dates back to a much earlier time than that of the
European. From a sociolinguistic point of view, it is interesting to
know that *al-mutaqaddim,* "the one who comes first or has come
first," literally means "the one who is at the head, the leading one." It
is a maxim of a patriarchal society that is proud of its traditions. The
dictionary has prefaces not only by Zainab Fawwāz, but by Arab
Jewish, and Christian authoresses of the time. It is symptomatic of the
time that educated Muslim, Christian, and Jewish ladies worked
together to prove that Arab women of former times were at least as
creative and dynamic as European women centuries later. We see
here the concerted efforts of Arab nationalism and Arab feminism, in
a time when support of Arab self-consciousness was necessary, pitted
against nearly overwhelming European influences. Today, we find
tendencies of feminism versus nationalism, because Arab (as well as
Turkish and Persian) nationalism nowadays is much more bound tra-
ditionally Islamic than was the case about 1900.

Today there is a rather large number of female poets and prose
writers. We should mention, for instance, the Iraqi poetess Nāzik al-
Malā'ika (b. 1922). Her book, *Qadāyā ash-shi'r al-mu'āsir, The
Problems of Modern Poetry* (1947) was regarded as the theoretical
foundation of a modern, nearly revolutionary poetic development in
Arabic literature, in which poetry has had strong formal traditions for
more than one millennium. There are feminists, like the above-men-
tioned Moroccan sociologist Fatima Mernissi (b. 1940) who wants to
support Arab female self-consciousness by going back to early Arab
historical sources. She writes about womens' roles in early Islam,
about women rulers in Islamic countries, about male-female relations
in Arabic-Islamic societies, and about Islam and sexuality.

The Egyptian physician Nawāl as-Saadāwī (b. 1931) wrote books
on female and male sexuality, which were published at the beginning
of the seventies and which cost her her position as the director of a
clinic. Her books depended greatly on American and European

medical and psychological research, such as the Kinsey report and Freudian and neopsychoanalytical theories which she compares to her own experiences as an Egyptian female physician. She informed about the biological and psychic fears of women and wrote about women's roles in family and society, particularly in Egypt, in a strong criticism. The heroines of her short stories and novels sometimes seem to be very European or American in their behavior and emotion.

The Egyptian Alīfa Rifaat (b. 1930) reveals in her sensitive stories innermost female emotions during and after the circumcision and a sexually unfulfilled marriage, written in a very tender, sometimes metaphoric way. In nearly every Arab country today we find female authors who, in their novels and short stories, deal with girls' and womens' social, psychological and emotional problems in the Arab male-dominated society, and with their search for social, emotional, and sexual freedom. The list of authors include the Syrian Ghāda as-Sammān, the Lebanese Hanān ash-Shaykh, the Kuwaiti Laila al-Uthmān, and the Iraqi Buthayna an-Nāsiri.

One of the subjects of modern Arabic, Persian, and Turkish fiction, even by male authors (some of whom discuss the ambivalent emotions of men in this situation), is the already mentioned *ghusl al-'ār,* shedding the blood of a girl to cleanse the family of presumed "dishonor." This is still a social reality. When an unmarried Muslim girl has a baby, both she and the child are stigmatized, the girl even when it is only guessed that she has lost her virginity without being married. Not only is she rejected by her family and by society, in some rural areas a close male relative is obliged to kill the girl for having brought shame on the honor of the family, the most precious thing that it has.

In 1973, in her book published in Beirut under the title *The Arab Woman and the Backward Conventional Society,* an Egyptian woman wrote that many women hesitate between a traditional life, restricted to home and children, and the kind of life they came to know during their studies. She told how they feel torn between the world of emancipation and meeting their responsibilities personally, and the world of the harem with their reliance on others. Incidentally, this writer attacks Islam, since it supplies arguments for the opponents of women's emancipation. [69, 9]

Nevertheless, when visiting Arab countries such as Iraq, Syria, or Egypt, one often has the impression, at least in well-educated circles, that the woman of the family is sometimes the "power behind the scenes," exercising a strong influence on the opinions and decisions of her husband. The fact that in the lower strata of the population, especially in rural districts, there still exists a very conventional attitude to the role of women in family and society, is demonstrated by a Master's thesis submitted to the University of Baghdad in 1970. The author had organized a poll in the district of Diyala, northeast of Baghdad, in which, for instance, only 30% of the lower strata (68% of the upper strata) answered "no" to the question of whether a girl's education should focus exclusively on preparation for marriage. Only 15% of the lower strata (80% of the upper strata) favored votes for women. Only 10% of the lower strata (78% of the upper strata) considered that a woman could successfully act as ambassador to a foreign country. [7]

It can be inferred from realistic works of modern Egyptian writers like Abderrahmān ash-Sharqāwī or Naguib Mahfouz, for example, that among the younger peasant women some are shaking off the fetters of the past, a past in which the female fellah was valued only as cheap labor. For an Egyptian landowner of the first half of the twentieth century, a woman laborer's wage for a twelve-hour day was less than the amount of money required for keeping a donkey for one day, half the amount required for a mule, and only a quarter of that needed for a cow. Nevertheless, one sometimes has the impression in modern Arab, Persian, and Turkish fiction, that the authors mean the young peasant women to be representations of an ideal.

It is of interest that in countries as profoundly marked by a strong ideology as are the countries belonging to the Islamic world, traditionalists and advocates of progress alike use the ideology itself as the basis of their arguments for and against change. For example, a few weeks before the Egyptian Revolution, on June 11, 1952, a commission of scholars of the Islamic al-Azhar University at Cairo issued a *fetwā*, a formal legal opinion, in which it rejected the right of women to vote and be elected, arguing that the *sharīʿa* gave only men the right to exercise public functions, and that at the election of the first Khalif Abu Bakr the electoral body had consisted exclusively of men. Ra'ūf Shalabi, Director of the Department for Islamic Propaganda and Culture at the Faculty for Religious Fundamentals of the same university, in 1975 published a book entitled *Treat the Women Well!* In it he inveighed against the Arab women's movement, which imitates European women and demands prohibition of polygyny, thus attacking the word of Allah and the revealed religion. With reference to the "emotional nature" of women and their weakness, he justifies *talāq*, polygyny, and separation of the sexes. [145]

Fundamentalist scriptures like these have increased in number in nearly every Arab country, in Iran, and even in more secularized Turkey. The Egyptian female author Zainab al-Ghazālī (b. 1917) supports the Islamic fundamentalists' policy on women in a rather skillful way. It should not be astonishing that Islamic fundamentalism, in particular on womens' questions, has its severest adherents among Muslims in the diaspora, especially Arabs and Turks; and even in the second generation, among Muslims from Islamic countries where fundamentalism is not supported by the government. This seems to be an expression of their search for their own roots, for individuation when living in a foreign society.

Most Islamic countries are therefore in a state of upheaval, which greatly affects the situation of women in family and society. Of course the development differs in each individual country and does not always run a true course. As a result of a superficial westernization, felt by many to be disappointing, a trend is to be observed, even among members of the upper classes, toward a conscious return to old Islamic traditions. In Iran since 1980, but also in other Islamic countries (though less obviously in Tunisia [20, 141ff.], has been in Algeria [20, 159ff.]), the emancipation of women based on the western model was seen to be closely connected with the failures of western colonial and imperial policy and therefore rejected by many. In Turkey, the striving for secularization that Ataturk wanted to achieve in the twenties and thirties of this century could not be fulfilled to the extent planned. In emphasizing what one considers to be the original principles of Islam, there is in many Muslim countries today a search for the power to overcome the complicated developments of the present time. But we have seen, especially from women's perspective, those varied and partially contradictory aspects that Islam has embraced in the course of its development.

Women as we have already learned, had rights in the early period of Islam that were later taken from them. At present, in the more advanced Islamic countries, there are many women who have assumed positions they deserve, not only in the family but also in scientific, political, and especially cultural affairs. Women artists and authors are no longer a rarity, and among women professors in universities—especially those of the older generation—there are some who are more impressive than their male colleagues probably because they had to overcome obstacles that the men did not. It remains to be seen what the future will bring.

Selected Bibliography

TO THE GERMAN EDITION, BY WIEBKE WALTHER

In the text, the numbers in square brackets [ ] designate sources. The first figure is the number in the Bibliography; the second indicates the page. Roman numerals refer to the volume.

Abbreviations

HO   Handbuch der Orientalistik
MW   Muslim World
N. S. Neue Serie (New Series)
WI   Die Welt des Islams

1. Abbott, N., *Aishah the Beloved of Mohammed.* Chicago, 1942.

2. —. *Two queens of Baghdad.* Chicago, 1946.

3. —. "Women and the state in early Islam." *Journal of Near Eastern Studies,* 1/1942, pp. 106-126, 341-368.

4. 'Abd ar-Rāziq, A., *La femme au temps des Mamlouks en Égypte.* Paris, 1974.

5. Abū l-Farağ al-Iṣfahānī., Kitāb al-Āġānī
   a. Vols. 1-20, Būlāq, 1285. Vol. 21, ed. by R. Brünow, Leiden, 1305.
   b. Vols. 1-16, al-Qāhira, 1927-1961.

6. Abū l-Faẓl 'Allāmī., *The Ain-i Akbari.* Vol. I. Trans. by H. Blochmann. Calcutta, 1873.

7. Akram, I. I., Al-ittiğāhāt al-iğtimā'iyya as-sā'ida fī ba'ḍ qiṭā'āt al-muğtama' al-irāqī naḥwa markaz al-mar'a fī l-muğtama'. Risālat Māğistār. Baghdad, 1970.

8. Amdja, K., *Das Buch der Aufklärung über die Geheimnisse der Eheschliessung. 2. Teil* (Kitāb al-iḍāḥ min asrār an-nikāḥ des Aš-Šīrāzī) Medical thesis. Erlangen-Nuremberg, 1976.

9. Anderson, N., *Law Reform in the Muslim World.* 2nd edition. London, 1976.

10. Andrae, T., *Islamische Mystiker.* Stuttgart, 1960.

11. al-Anṭākī, D., Tazyīn al-ašwāq fī aḫbār al-ʿuššāq. Beirut, 1973.

12. al-ʿAqqād, ʿA. M., Aṣ-Ṣiddīqa bint aṣ-Ṣiddīq. al-Qāhira, 1943.

13. Arberry, A. J., *The Poems of al-Mutanabbī.* Cambridge, 1967.

14. Arnold, T. W., *Painting in Islam* (reprint). New York, 1965.

15. Ashtor, E., *A Social and Economic History of the Near East in the Middle Ages.* Berkeley *et al.,* 1976.

16. ʿAṭṭār, Farīd ad-Dīn, The Tadhkiratu l'-auliyá of Shaykh Farídu d-dīn ʿAṭṭār, Vols. 1, 2. Ed. by R. A. Nicholson. Persian Historical Texts 3, 5. London, Leiden, 1905, 1907.

17. Authors, team of, *Geschichte der Araber,* Vols. 1-4. Berlin, 1971-1974.

18. al-Azdī, M. b. A., Ḥikāyat Abī l-Qāsim al-Baġdādī. Ed. by A. Mez. Heidelberg, 1902.

19. al-Batlūnī, Š., "Kitāb tasliyat al-ḫawāṭir fī muntaḫabāt al-mulaḥ wa-n-nawādir." In A. Fischer, *Arabische Chrestomathie aus Prosa-Schriftstellern,* 6th edition. Leipzig, 1953.

20. Beck, L. and Keddie, N., eds., *Women in the Muslim World.* Cambridge, Mass., London, 1978.

21. Bertel's, E. E., *Nisami i Fusuli.* Moscow, 1962. (Bertel's, *Izbrannye trudy*).

22. Blachère, R., "Les principaux thèmes de la poésie érotique au siécle des Umayyades de Damas." In *Annales de l'Institut d'Études Orientales de la Faculté des Lettres de l'Université d'Alger* 5/1939-1941, pp. 82-128.

23. Boyce, A. S., "Moslem women in the capital of Persia." In *MW* 20/1930, pp. 265-269.

24. al-Buḫārī, Kitāb al-ǧāmiʿ aṣ-ṣaḥīḥ. Vols. 1-3, ed. by L. Krehl. Leiden, 1862-1868. Vol. 4, ed. by T. W. Juynboll. Leiden, 1907/1908.

25. Bürgel, J. C., *Drei Hafisstudien.* Bern/Frankfurt am Main, 1975. (Schriften d. literar. Gesellschaft Bern II).

26. —. "Love, Lust, and Longing: Eroticism in early Islam as reflected in literary sources." In as-Sayyid-Marsot, A. L. (ed.), *Society and the Sexes in Medieval Islam.* Malibu, Calif., 1979, pp. 81-117.

242

27. Bulliet, R. W., *The Patricians of Nichapur: A Study in Medieval Social History.* Harvard Middle Eastern Studies 16. Cambridge, 1972.

28. Cahen, C., *Der Islam I. Vom Ursprung bis zu den Anfängen des Osmanenreiches.* Fischer-Weltgeschichte, Vol. 14. Frankfurt am Main, 1968.

29. *The Cambridge History of India,* Vol. 4. "The Mughul period." Planned by W. Haig; ed. by R. Burn. Cambridge, 1937.

30. Chardin, J., *Voyages du Chevalier Chardin en Perse et autres lieux de l'Orient,* Vols. 1-10. Paris: L. Langlès, 1811.

31. Chehata, C., "L'évolution moderne de droit de la famille en pays d'Islam." In *Revue des Études Islamiques* 37/1969.

32. Cooper, E., *The Harim and the Purdah.* Studies of Oriental women (reprint). Detroit, 1975.

33. ad-Darbandī, 'A. S., Al-mar'a al-'irāqiyya al-mu'āṣira. Ğ. 1, 2. Baghdad, 1968, 1970.

34. Derenk, D., *Leben und Dichtung des Omaiyadenkalifen al-Walīd Ibn Yazīd.* Islamkundl. Untersuchungen, Vol. 27. Freiburg, 1974.

35. Dietrich, E., "Eine arabische Eheurkunde aus der Aiyūbidenzeit." In *Documenta Islamica Inedita.* Berlin, 1952, pp. 121-154.

36. Dilger, K., "Ziviltrauung und religiöse Eheschliessung in der Türkei." In WI *N.S.* 17/1976/1977, pp. 194-206.

37. Drewes, G. W. J., "The Beginning of Emancipation of Women in the Arab World." In *Nederlands Arabische Kring* 1955-65. Leiden, 1966, pp. 47-66.

38. Duda, H. W., *Ferhād und Schīrīn. Die literarische Gestaltung eines persischen Sagenstoffes.* Monografie Archívu orientalního, Vol. 2. Prague, Paris, Leipzig, 1933.

39. Edib, H., *Memoirs.* New York. London, 1926.

40. *The Encyclopedia of Islam,* new edition, Vol. 1. Leiden, London, 1960.

41. *Enzyklopädie des Islams,* Vols. 1-4 and Supplementary Volume. Leiden, Leipzig, 1913-1938.

42. Fahmy, M., *La condition de la femme dans la tradition et l'évolution de l'Islamisme.* Paris, 1913.

43. Firdausī, Šāh-nāma, Vol. I, ed. by E. Bertel's. Moscow, 1960.

44. Fück, J. W., "Die Religion des sunnitischen Islams." In *HO*. 1st Section, Vol. 8, 2nd Paragraph. Leiden, Cologne, 1961, pp. 405-448.

45. Fyzee, A. A., *Outlines of Muhamedan Law,* 2nd edition. London *et al.,* 1955.

46. Gätje, H., *Koran und Koranexegese.* Zurich, Stuttgart, 1971.

47. Ğahāngīr, *The Tūzuk-i-Jahāngīrī or Memoirs of Jahāngīr.* Ed. by H. Beveridge. Trans. by A. Rogers. Vols. 1, 2. Oriental Translation Fund Series 19, *N.S.* 22. London, 1909, 1914.

48. al-Ğāḥiẓ, Pellat, C., *Arabische Geisteswelt.* Selected and translated texts of al-Ğāḥiẓ. Zurich, Stuttgart, 1967.

49. —. Ṭalāṯ rasā'il. Ed. by J. Finkel. al-Qāhira, 1344/1926.

50. al-Ğaḥiẓ (Pseudo), al-Kitāb al-musammā bi-l-maḥāsin wa-l-aḍdād. Ed. by G. V. Vloten. Leiden, 1898.

51. Ğamī, *Mewlana Abdurrahman Dschami: Kitāb-i Yūssuf wa-Zulaiḥā. Joseph und Suleicha.* Romantic historical poem, trans. by V.v. Rosenzweig. Vienna, 1824.

52. Gaudio, A., *La révolution des femmes en Islam.* Paris, 1957.

53. al-Ğazālī, *Ghazālī's Book of Counsel for Kings* (Naṣīḥat al-mulūk). Trans. by R. C. Bagley. London, 1964.

54 —, *Von der Ehe. Das 12. Buch von al-Ğazālī's "Neubelebung der Religionswissenschaften."* Trans. and explained by H. Bauer. Islamische Ethik, No. 2. Halle, 1917.

55. Di Giacomo, L., *Une poétesse andalouse du temps des Almohades:* Ḥafṣa bint al-Ḥājj ar-Rukūnīya. Paris, 1949.

56. Gibb, E. J. W., *A History of Ottoman Poetry,* Vols. 1-5. London, 1900-1909.

57. Giffen, L. A., *The Theory of Profane Love among the Arabs.* London, New York, 1971.

58. Goetz, H., "The History of Persian Costume." In A.V. Pope, P. Ackerman, *A Survey of Persian Art,* Vol. 3. Oxford *et al.,* 1939, pp. 2227-2256.

59. —, "Kostüm und Mode an den indischen Fürstenhöfen der Grossmoghulzeit." *In Jahrbuch d. asiat. Kunst,* 1924, pp. 67-101.

60. Goldziher, I., *Muhammedanische Studien,* Vols. 1, 2. Halle, 1889/1890.

61. Granquist, H., *Marriage Conditions in a Palestinian Village,* Vols. 1, 2. Helsingfors, 1931, 1935.

62. Grotzfeld, H., *Das Bad im arabisch-islamischen Mittelalter.* Wiesbaden, 1970.

63. Grunebaum, G. E. von, "Avicennas Risāla fīl-Išq und höfische Liebe." In *Kritik und Dichtkunst.* Wiesbaden, 1955.

64. —, *Der Islam II: Die islamischen Reiche nach dem Fall von Konstantinopel.* Fischer-Weltgeschichte, Vol. 15. Frankfurt am Main, 1971.

65. —. *Medieval Islam,* 2nd edition. Chicago, 1953.

66. Haddad, T., Kitāb Nuzhat al-aṣḥāb fī muʿāšarat al-aḥbāb fī ʿilm al-bāh. Part I, Paragraphs 6-8. Ed., trans., and rev. text. Medical Thesis. Erlangen/Nuremberg, 1976.

67. al-Hamaḏānī, Die Maqāmen des Hamaḏānī. Trans. from the Arabic by O. Rescher. Leonberg, 1913.

68. Hamdī, A. M., Muʿaddāt at-taǧmīl bi-Mathaf al-Fann al-Islāmī. al-Qāhira, 1959.

69. al-Ḥammāš, S., Al-marʾa al-ʿarabiyya wa-l-muǧtmaʿ at-taqlīdī al-mutaḫallif, Beirut, 1973.

70. *Handwörterbuch des Islam.* A. J. Wensinck and J. H. Kramers, eds. Leiden, 1941.

71. Heffening, W., "Zur Geschichte der Hochzeitsbräuche im Islam." In *Beiträge z. Arabistik, Semitistik u. Islamwissenschaft.* Leipzig, 1941, pp. 386-422.

72. Hell, J., "Al-ʿAbbās Ibn al-Aḥnaf, der Minnesänger am Hof Hārūn ar-Rašīds." In *Islamica* 2/1926, pp. 271-307.

73. Hickmann, H., "Die Musik des arabisch-islamischen Bereichs." In *HO,* Section 1, Supplementary Volume 4. Leiden, Cologne, 1970.

74. Hoeltich, F. H., and Waltz, J. C., *Quaestio. Foemina non est homo videbunt publicè in Auditorio JCtorum à D. XIV. Decembris Anno 1672.*

Nunc recusa. Wittebergae, 1678.

75. Hoenerbach, W., "Zur Charakteristik Wallādas, der Geliebten Ibn Zaidūns." In *WI N.S.* 13/1971, pp. 20-25.

76. Hume, E. C., "Woman's part in modern movements in India." In *MW* 22/1932, pp. 361-372.

77. Ibn 'Abd Rabbihi, Kitāb al-'iqd al-farīd. A. Amīn, I. al-Abyarī, 'A. Hārūn, eds. Ǧ. 6. Al-Qāhira, 1949.

78. Ibn Abī Ṭāhir Ṭaifūr, Kitāb balāgāt an-nisā'. Beirut, 1972.

79. Ibn Dāwūd, Kitāb az-zahra. *The first half.* Ed. by A. R. Nykl with I. Tuqan. (The Oriental Institute of the University of Chicago. Studies in Ancient Oriental Civilization, No. 6.) Chicago, 1932.

80. Ibn Ḥair Allāh al-'Umarī, Kitāb ar-Rauḍa al-faiḥā' fī tawārīḫ ah-nisā'. Ed. by R. M. as-Samarrā'ī. Baġdād, 1966.

81. Ibn Ḥallikān, Kitāb Wafayāt al-a'yān wa-anbā' abnā' az-zamān. G. 1-3. Būlāq, 1299.

82. Ibn Ḥanbal, A., Musnad. Ǧ. 1-6. Miṣr, 1313.

83. Ibn Ḥazm al-Andalusī, *Das Halsband der Taube. Über die Liebe und die Liebenden.* Trans. from the Arabic by M. Weisweiler, 4th edition. Leiden, 1942.

84. Ibn Hišām, Kitāb sīrat rasūl Allāh li-bn Isḥāq, Vols. 1, 2, ed. by F. Wüstenfeld. Göttingen, 1858, 1860.

85. Ibn Qayyim al-Ǧauziyya, Kitāb Aḫbār an-nisā'. Beirut, n.d.

86. —, Rauḍat al-muḥibbīn wa-nuzhat al-muštāqīn. Ed. by A. 'Ubaid. Damascus, 1930.

87. Ibn Sa'd, Kitāb aṭ-Ṭabaqāt al-kabīr, Vols. 1-9, ed. by E. Sachau *et al.,* Leiden, 1904-1921.

88. Ibn as-Sa'ī, Nisā' al-ḫulafā' al-musammā ǧihāt al-a'imma al-ḫulafā' min al-ḥarā'ir wa-l-imā. Ed. by M. Ǧawād. al-Qāhira, 1960.

89. Ibn al-Waššā', Kitāb al-Muwaššā. Ed. by R. Brunnow. Leiden, 1886.

90. Jäschke, G., "Die Frauenfrage in der Turkei." In *Saeculum* 10/1959, pp. 360-369.

91. Jorga, N., *Geschichte des osmanischen Reiches,* Vols. 1-5. Gotha, 1908-1913.

92. Juynboll, T. W., *Handbuch des islamischen Gesetzes.* Leiden, Leipzig, 1910.

93. Kaḥḥāla, 'U. R., A'lāmau-nisā' fī 'ālam al-'Arab wa-l-Islām. Ǧ. 1-5. Damascus, 1959.

94. Kai Kā'ūs b. Qābūs, Kitāb-i nasīḥat-nāma ma'rūf ba-Qābūsnāma. Ed. with commentary by S. Nafīsī. Teheran, 1342.

95. Kohn, S., *Die Eheschliessung im Koran.* London, 1934.

96. Kračkovskij, I., "Die fruhgeschichte der erzählung von Mačnūn und Lailā in der arabischen literatur." Trans. into German by H. Ritter. In Oriens 8/1955, pp. 1-50.

97. Kremer, A. von, *Kulturgeschichte des Orients unter den Chalifen,* Vols. 1, 2. Vienna, 1875, 1877.

98. Kitāb-i Kultūm-nāma, *Customs and Manners of the Women of Persia and their Domestic Superstitions.* Trans. by J. Atkinson. London, 1832.

99. Lane, E. W., *Sitten und Gebrauche der heutigen Aegypter,* Vols. 1-3. Trans. from the English by J. T. Zenker. Leipzig, n. d.

100. Le Brun, C., *Voyages de C.L.B. par la Moscovie, en Perse et aux Indes Orientales,* Vol. 1. Amsterdam,1718.

101. Lens, A. R. de, *Pratique des harems marocains: sorcellerie, médicine, beauté.* Paris, 1925.

102. Levy, R., *The Social Structure of Islam.* Cambridge, 1957.

103. Lichtenstädter, I., "Das Nasīb in der altarabischen Qasīde." In *Islamica* 5/1932, pp. 17-96.

104. —, Women in the Aiyām al-'Arab. London, 1935.

105. Littmann, E., *Kairiner Volksleben.* Leipzig, 1941.

106. Maher, V., *Women and Property in Morocco.* Cambridge, 1974.

107. Maḥfūẓ, N., al-Marāyā. al-Qāhira, n. d.

108. Manucci, N., *Storia do Mogor or Mogul India* 1653-1708, Vols. 1-4. Trans. by W. Irvine. Indian Text Series 1. London, 1907-1908.

109. al-Maqqarī, Kitāb nafḫ aṭ-ṭīb min ġusn al-Andalus ar-raṭīb, Vols. 1, 2. Ed. by R. Dozy, G. Dugat *et al.* Leiden, 1855, 1860.

110. el-Masry, Y., *Le drame sexuel de la femme dans l'Orient arabe*. Paris, 1962.

111. Massignon, L., "Der gnostische Kult der Fatima im schiitischen Islam." In *Eranos-Jahrbuch*, ed. by O. Fröbe-Kapteyn. Zurich, 1939, pp. 161-173.

112. al-Mas'ūdī, Murūǧ aḏ-ḏahab. Vols. 1-9. Texts and trans. by C. B. de Meynard and P. de Courtelle. Paris, 1861-1877.

113. Mayer, L. A., *Mamluk costume*. Geneva, 1952.

114. Mernissi, F., *The Effects of Modernization of the Male-Female Dynamics in a Muslim Society: Morocco*. Ph.D. Thesis, Brandeis University, 1974.

115. Mez, A., *Die Renaissance des Islams*. Heidelberg, 1922.

116. Minhāǧ ad-Dīn, Ṭabaqāt-i Nāṣirī, Vols. 1, 2. Trans. by G. Raverty. London, 1881.

117. Montague, M. W., *The Complete Letters*, Vol. 1. Ed. by R. Halsband. Oxford, 1965.

118. Morier, J., *A Second Journey through Persia, Armenia, and Asia Minor*. London, 1818.

119. Munaǧǧid, S., Al-ḥayāt al-ǧinsiyya 'inda l-'Arab. Beirut, 1958.

120. al-Muttaqī, 'A., Muntaḥab kanz al-'ummāl. In the Margin of A. Ibn Ḥanbal: Musnad. Miṣr, 1313.

121. Nafzāwī, *Scheik Nefzaui: Der blühende Garten. Die arabische Liebeskunst*. Trans. by J. Wilkat. Munich, 1966.

122. Niẓāmī, *Leila und Madschnun*. Trans. by R. Gelpke. Zurich, 1963.

123. Nuwairī, Nihāyat al-arab fī funūn al-adab. Ǧ. 2. Al-Qāhira, n.d. (Turāṯunā)

124. Nykl, A. R., *Hispano-Arabic Poetry*. Baltimore, 1946.

125. Olearius, A., *Offt begehrte Beschreibung der Newen Orientalischen Reise. Schleswig*, 1647.

126. —, *Vermehrte Moscowitische und Persianische Reisebeschreibung Zum Andern mahl herausgegeben*. Schleswig, 1656.

127. Paret, R., *Zur Frauenfrage in der arabisch-islamischen Welt*.

Veröffentl. d. Orient. Seminars d. Univ. Tübingen. Stuttgart, Berlin, 1934.

128. —, *Muhammed und der Koran.* Stuttgart, 1957.

129. Pellat, C., *Le milieu basrien et la formation de Ğāḥiẓ.* Paris, 1953.

130. Polak, J. E., *Persien: Das Land und seine Bewohner.* Parts 1, 2. Leipzig, 1865.

131. Prigmore, C. S., *Social Work in Iran since the White Revolution.* Alabama, 1976.

132. Ragai (Shafik), D., *La femme et le droit religieux de l'Égypte contemporaine.* Paris, 1940.

133. ar-Rāġib al-Iṣfāhānī, Kitāb Muḥāḍarāt al-udabā' wa-muḥāwarāt aš-šu'arā' wa-l-bulaġā'. Ğ. 2. Al-Qāhira, 1870.

134. Reintjens, H., *Die soziale Stellung der Frau bei den nordarabischen Beduinen unter besonderer Berücksichtigung ihrer Ehe- und Familienverhältnisse.* Bonn, 1975.

135. Rifā'a Bey aṭ-Ṭahṭāwī, Talḫīṣ al-ibrīz ilā taḫlīṣ Barīz au ad-dīwān an-nafīs bi-īwān Bārīs. Būlāq, 1849.

136. Ritter, H., *Über die Bildersprache Niẓāmīs.* Studien z. Gesch. u. Kultur d. Islam. Orients, Heft 5. Berlin, Leipzig, 1927.

137. —, *Das Meer der Seele.* Leiden, 1978.

138. Rodinson, M., *Mohammed.* Harmondsworth, 1971.

139. Roe, T., *The Embassy of Sir Thomas Roe to India 1615-1619,* 2nd edition. Ed. by W. Foster. London, 1926.

140. Rosenthal, E. I. J., *Political Thought in Medieval Islam.* Cambridge, 1958.

141. Rossi, E., "La sultana Nur Banu moglie di Selim II (1566-1574) e madre di Murad III (1574 to 1595)." In *Oriente Moderno* 33/1953, pp. 433-441.

142. Russell, A., *The Natural History of Aleppo,* Vols. 1, 2. 2nd edition. London, 1794.

143. Sābā, 'Ī., Ġazal an-nisā'. Beirut, 1953.

144. as-Saḫāwī, Aḍ-Ḍau' al-lāmi' li-ahl al-qarn at-tāsi'. Ğ.12. Al-Qāhira, 1355.

144a. Šajdullina, L. I., *Arabskaja ženščina i sovremennosť*. Moscow, 1978.

145. Šalabī, R., Istauṣū bi-n-nisā' ḫairan. Naẓariyyat al-Islām fī šu'ūn al-mar'a. Al-Qāhira, 1975.

146. Schacht, J., ed., *G. Bergsträssers Grundzüge des islamischen Rechts*. Berlin, Leipzig, 1935.

147. Schack, A. F. von, *Poesie und Kunst der Araber in Spanien und Sizilien*, Vols. 1, 2. Stuttgart, 1877.

148. Schimmel, A., *Mystical Dimensions of Islam*. Chapel Hill, 1975.

149. —, "Der Islam im Rahmen der monotheistischen Weltreligionen." In A. Mercier, ed., *Islam und Abendland*. Bern, Frankfurt am Main, 1976, pp. 9-27.

150. Schregle, G., *Die Sultanin von Aegypten. Šaǧarat ad-Durr in der arabischen Geschichtsschreibung und Literatur*. Wiesbaden, 1961.

151. Schwarz, P., *'Umar Ibn Abi Rebī'a. Ein arabischer Dichter der Umajjadenzeit*. Leipzig, 1893.

152. Serjeant, R. B., "Material for a History of Islamic Textiles up to the Mongol Conquest," In *Ars Islamica* 9/1942, pp. 54-92.

153. Smith, M., *Rābī'a the Mystic and her Fellow-Saints in Islam*. Cambridge, 1928.

154. Sourdel-Thomine, J., and Spuler, B., *Die Kunst des Islam*. Propyläen-Kunstgeschichte, Vol. 4. Berlin, 1975.

155. Spies, O., "al-Muǧulṭā'īs Spezialwerk über 'Martyrer der Liebe'." In W. Heffening and W. Kirfel, eds., *Studien zur Geschichte und Kultur des Nahen und Fernen Ostens*. P. Kahle zum 60. Geburtstag. Leiden, 1935, pp. 144-155.

156. Spies, O. and Pritsch, E., "Klassisches islamisches Recht." In *HO*, 1st Section, Supplementary Volume 3. Leiden, Cologne, 1964.

157. Spuler, B., *Iran in frühislamischer Zeit*. Ak. d. Wiss. u. Lit. Veröff. d. Orient. Kommission, Vol. 2. Wiesbaden, 1952.

158. Stern, G., *Marriage in Early Islam*. London, 1939.

159. Stigelbauer, M., *Die Sängerinnen am Abbasidenhof um die Zeit des Kalifen al-Mutawakkil*. Thesis of Vienna University. Vienna, 1975.

160. Sundermann, W., ed., *Lob der Geliebten. Klassische persische*

Dichtungen. Paraphrased by M. Remané. Berlin, 1968.

161. as-Suyūṭī, Kitāb al-Īḍāḥ fī ʿilm an-nikāḥ. No place, n.d. (Lithograph).

162. aṭ-Ṭabarī, Taʾrīḫ ar-rusul wa-l-mulūk, 2nd edition. Ed. by M. A. Ibrāhīm. Ǧ. 1-10. Misr, 1969.

163. at-Tauḥīdī, Kitāb al-Imtāʿ wa-l-muʾānasa, 2nd edition. Ed. by A. Amīn and A. az-Zain. Ǧ. 2. Al-Qāhira, 1953.

164. *Die Erzählungen aus den Tausendundein Nächten,* 3rd edition. Vols. 1-6. Translated into German by E. Littmann. Leipzig, n. d.

165. Tavernier, J. B., *Beschreibung Der Sechs Reisen/welche J.B.T. in Türckey/Persien und Indien, innerhalb viertzig Jahren/durch alle Wege/die man nach diesen Landeren nehmen kan/verrichtet.* Parts 1-4. Transl. by J. H. Widerhold. Geneva, 1681.

166. Timm, K. and Aalami, S., *Die muslimische Frau zwischen Tradition und Fortschritt.* Berlin, 1976.

167. *Tuti-Nameh oder Das Papageienbuch.* Trans. from the Turkish by G. Rosen. Leipzig, 1956.

168. Ullmann, M., "Die Medizin im Islam." In *HO,* 1st Section, Supplementary Volume 6, Paragraph 1. Leiden, Cologne, 1970.

169. Uluçay, Ç., "The Harem in the XVIII Century." In *Akten d. 24. Int. Orientalisten-Kongresses München.* Wiesbaden, 1959, pp. 394-398.

170. Vadet, J. C., *L'ésprit courtois en Orient dans les cinq premiers siècles de l'hégire.* Paris, 1968.

171. —, "Une personalité féminine du Ḥiǧāz au Iᵉʳ/VIIᵉ siècle: Sukayna, petite-fille de ʿAlī." In *Arabica* 4/1957, pp. 262-287.

172. Vagabov, M. V., *Islam i ženščina.* Moscow, 1968.

173. della Valle, P., *Eines vornehmen Römischen Patritii Reiss-Beschreibung in unterschiedliche Theile der Welt.* Geneva, 1674.

174. Walther, W., "Die Frau in Islam." In P. Antes, Der Islam, Religion, Ethik, Politik. Stuttgart, Berlin, Köln, 1991, pp. 98-124.

175. Walther, W., "Altarabische Kindertanzreime." *In Studia Orientalia in mem. C. Brockelmann.* Wiss. Ztschr. Martin-Luther-Univ. Halle-Wittenberg 17/1968, No. 23, pp. 217 to 233.

176. Walther, W., "Altarabische . . .

177. Watt, W. M., *Muhammad at Mekka*. Oxford, 1953.

178. —,. *Muhammad at Medina*. Oxford, 1956.

179. Weisweiler, M., *Von Kalifen, Spassmachern und klugen Harems-damen*. Dusseldorf, Cologne, 1963.

180. Wellhausen, J., "Die Ehe bei den Arabern." In *Nachr. v. d. kgl. Ges. d. Wiss. u. d. Georg-August-Univ. zu Göttingen 1893*, No. 11, pp. 431-481.

181. Wensinck, A. J., *A Handbook of Early Muhammadan Tradition*. Leiden, 1927.

182. Werner, E. and Markov, W., *Geschichte der Türken*. Berlin, 1978.

183. Westermarck, E., *Wit and Wisdom in Morocco*. London, 1930.

184. White, C., *Häusliches Leben und Sitten der Türken*, Vols. 1, 2. Ed. by A. Reumont. Berlin, 1844, 1845.

185. Wiedemann, E., "Aus Nuwairīs Enzyklopädie.Über Parfüms." In *Archiv f. d. Gesch. d. Naturwiss. u. d. Technik*, Vol. 6. Leipzig, 1913, pp. 418-426.

187. —, "Über Parfüms und Drogen bei den Arabern." In *Beiträge z. Gesch. d. Naturwiss.*, 56. Sitz. ber. d. Physikal.-Med. Sozietät in Erlangen, Vol. 48. Erlangen, 1916, pp. 329-339.

188. *Wunderbare Erlebnisse, seltsame Begebnisse. Arabische Erzählungen*. Trans. by H. Wehr. Berlin, 1962.

189. Ya'qūb b. Isḥāq al-Kindī, Kitāb Kīmiyā al-'iṭr wa-t-taṣ'īdāt. Trans. by K. Garbers. Abh. f. d. Kunde d. Morgenlandes 30. Leipzig, 1948.

190. Youssef, N. H., *Women and Work in Developing Societies*. Westport, Conn., 1974.

191. az-Zahāwī, Ġ. Ṣ., Al-Lubāb. Baġdād, 1928.

192. az-Zayyāt, L., Al-Bāb al-maftūḥ. Al-Qāhira, 1960.

Additional Bibliography

FOR THE REVISED 1993 EDITION
BY WIEBKE WALTHER

Abu Nasr, Julinda; Khoury, Nabil F.; Azzam, Henry T., Women, Employment and Development in the Arab World. Berlin, New York, Amsterdam 1985.

Alliata, Vittoria, Harem–Die Freiheit hinter dem Schleier. Frankfurt/M., Berlin 1989.

Degand, Angela, Geschlechterrollen und familiale Strukturen im Islam. Frankfurt/M., Bern, New York 1988.

—, "Wie im Prozeß um einen Esel"– Geschlechterrollen in der islamisch-juristischen Literatur des 7/13. bis 9/15. Jahrhunderts. In: Jochen Martin u. Renate Zöpfel (Ed.s), Aufgaben, Rollen und Räume von Frau und Mann. Bd. 2. Freiburg, München 1989, pp. 643-675.

Delcroix, Catherine, Espoirs et réalités de la femme arabe (Algérie-Egypte). Paris 1984.

Fawwāz, Zainab, Ad-Durr al-manṯūr fī ṭabaqāt rabbāt al-ḫudūr. Al-Qāhira 1896.

Galal, Salma, Emanzipationsversuche der ägyptischen Frau. N. e. 1977.

Ġazālī, Abū Ḥāmid, Muḥammad b. Muḥammad al-, Iḥyāʾ ʿulūm ad-dín. Ǧ. 2. Al-Qāhira n. d., pp.20ff.

Höll, Rosemarie, Die Stellung der Frau im zeitgenössischen Islam, dargestellt am Beispiel Marokkos. Frankfurt/M., Bern u. a. 1979.

Lacoste-Dujardin, Camille, Mütter gegen Frauen. Mutterherrschaft im Maghreb. Zürich 1990.

Malti-Douglas, Fedwa, Woman's Body, Woman's Word. Gender and Discourse in Arabo-Islamic Writing. Princeton 1991.

Meghdessian, Samira Rafidi, The Status of the Arab Woman. A Select Bibliography. London 1980.

Mernissi, Fatema, Der politische Harem. Mohammed und die Frauen. Frankfurt/M. 1989.

—, Die Sultanin. Die Macht der Frauen in der Welt des Islam. Frankfurt/M. 1991.

—, Geschlecht, Ideologie, Islam. Köln 1988.

Minai, Naila, Schwestern unterm Halbmond. Muslimische Frauen zwischen Tradition und Emanzipation. Stuttgart 1990.

Motzki, Harald, . . . Dann machte er daraus die beiden Geschlechter, das männliche und das weibliche (Koran 75:39). –Die historischen Wurzeln der islamischen Geschlechterrollen. In: Jochen Martin u. Renate Zöpfel (Ed.s), Aufgaben, Rollen und Räume . . , pp. 607-642.

—, Geschlechtsreife und Legitimation zur Zeugung im frühen Islam. In: E. W. Müller, Geschlechtsreife und Legitimation zur Zeugung. Freiburg, München 1985, pp. 479-550.

Neusel, Ayla; Tekeli, Sirin; Akkent, Meral, Aufstand im Haus der Frauen. Frauenforschung aus der Türkei. Berlin 1991.

Paris, Mireille, Femmes et sociétés dans le monde arabo-musulmane. État bibliographique. Aix-en-Provence 1989.

Petersen, Andrea, Ehre und Scham. Das Verhältnis der Geschlechter in der Türkei. Berlin 1985.

Pickthall, Muhammad Marmaduke, The Meaning of the Glorious Qur'ān. Tripolis n. d. (Translation approved by the Islamic World Congress).

Richter-Dridi, Irmhild, Frauenbefreiung in einem islamischen Land-ein Widerspruch? Frankfurt/M. 1981.

Ruuh, Andrea B., Family in Contemporary Egypt. Cairo 1988.

Rudd, Inger Marie, Women's Status in the Muslim World. A Bibliographical Survey. Köln 1981.

Sa'dāwī, Nawāl as-, Dirāsāt 'an al-mar'a wa-r-raǧul fī l-muǧtama' al-islāmī al-'arabī. Bairūt 1990 (Al-Mar'a wa-l-ǧins; al-Unṣā hiya l-atl; ar-Raǧul wa-l-ǧins; al-Mar'a waṣ-ṣirā' an-nafsī; al-Waǧh al-āḫar li-l-mar'a al-'arabiyya).

Social Science Research and Women in the Arab World. Paris 1984.

Tarabishi, Georges, Women Against her Sex. A Critique of Nawal El-Saadawi. London 1988.

Utas, Bo (Ed.), Women in Islamic Societies: Social Attitudes and Historical Perspectives. London 1988.

Waddy, Charis, Women in Muslim History. London, New York 1980.

Walther, Wiebke, Die Rolle der Frau/Frauenliteratur, in: -, Identitätssuche–Identitätsfindung durch Literatur. In: Der Deutschunterricht 1(1992), pp. 25-28.

—, Arabische Schriftstellerinnen, in: -, Neuere Entwicklungen in der arabischen narrativen und dramatischen Literatur. In:W. Fischer (Ed.), Grundriß der arabischen Philologie. Suppl. bd. 3. Wiesbaden 1992, pp. 209-242.

—, Das Bild der Frau in Tausendundeiner Nacht, in: HBO 4(1982), pp. 69-91.

—, "Die Frau im Koran und in der Überlieferung", in: Studientagung, Frauen in Entwicklungsländern. Afro-Asiatisches Institut Graz 12.-15.11. 1987, pp. 15-32.

—, *Tausendundeine Nacht. Eine Einführung.* München, Zürich, 1988.

—, "Drei Geschichten aus Tausendundeiner Nacht": "Die Geschichte von der listigen Dalila","Das Märchen vom Prinzen Ahmad und der Fee Peri Banu", "Die Geschichte von Ebenholzpferd", in: *Oriens* 32(1990), pp. 139-77, 476.

—, "Mythen über das erste Menschenpaar, den Sündenfall mit seinen Folgen und die Konstituierung menschlichen Lebens in der islamisch arabischen Literatur", in: Forschungsforum. Orientalistik Berichte aus der Otto-Friedrich-Universität Bamberg 2(1990), pp. 9-17.

—, "Die Frau im Islam", in: P. Antes et al., Der Islam. Religion-Ethik-Politik. Stuttgart, Berlin et al., 1991, pp. 98-124.

Recent English-Language Bibliography on Women in the Middle East

BY FARIBA ZARINEBAF-SHAHR

Abadan-Unat Nermin. "Implications of Migration and Pseudo-Emancipation of Turkish Women." *International Migration Review* 11, no. 1 (1977): 31-58.

—. "The Modernization of Turkish Women." *Middle East Journal* 32, no. 3 (1978): 291-306.

—. "Women in Government as Policy-Makers and Bureaucrats: the Turkish Case." *In Rendel, Women, Power, and Political Systems* (1981).

—. *Women in the Developing World: Evidence from Turkey.* Denver, 1986.

—. *Women in Turkish Society.* Leiden: Brill, 1981.

Abaza, Mona. *The Changing Image of Women in Rural Egypt.* The American University in Cairo Press, 1987.

Abdel-Kader, Soha. *Egyptian Women in a Changing Society,* 1899–1986. Boulder: Lynne Reiner Publisher, 1987.

Abdul, Jawwad, Islah. "The Evolution of the Political Role of the Palestinian Women's Movement in the Uprising." *In The Palestinians: New Directions.* Ed. M. Hudson, Washington, D.C., 1990, 63-76.

Abdul-Reuf, Muhammad. *The Islamic View of Women and the Family.* New York: Speller, 1977.

Abouzeid, Leila. *A Moroccan Woman's Journey toward Independence, and Other Stories.* Trans. from the the Arabic by Barbara Parmenter. Austin: University of Texas Press, 1989.

Abu-Lughod, Lila. *Veiled Sentiments: Honor and Poetry in a Bedouin Society.* Berkeley: University of California Press, 1986.

Abu Nasr Julinda et al. *Women and Development in the Gulf States.* Berlin, New York: Mouton Press, 1985.

256

—; Nabil F. Khoury, Henry T. Assam, eds. *Women, Employment and Development in the Arab World.* Berlin, New York: Mouton Press, 1985.

Abu-Said, Abeer, *Qatari Women Past and Present.* Harlow: Longman Groups, 1984.

Afshar, H. "Women, State, and Ideology in Iran," *The Third World Quarterly* 7 (1985): 256-78.

Aftab, Hussein. *Status of Women in Islam.* Pakistan, 1987.

Ahmed, Leila. "Western Ethnocentrism and Perceptions of the Harem." *Feminist Studies* 8, no.3 (Fall 1982): 521-524.

— "Women and the Advent of Islam." *Signs* 2 (1986): 665-91.

—. "Arab Culture and Writing Women's Bodies." *Feminist Issues* (Spring 1989): 41-55.

Allman, James, ed. Women's Status and Fertility in the Muslim World. New York: Prager Publishers, 1978.

Al-Qazzaz, Ayad. *Women in the Middle East and North Africa: An Annotated Bibliography.* Austin: University of Texas Press, 1977.

Altorki, Soraya and Camillia Fawzi El-Solh, eds. *Arab Women in the Field: Studying Your Own Society.* Syracuse: Syracuse University Press, 1988.

—. *Women in Saudi Arabia: Ideology and Behavior among the Elite.* New York: Columbia University Press, 1986.

Arat, Yesim. *The Patriarchal Paradox: Women Politicians in Turkey.* New York: Fairleigh Dickinson University Press, 1989.

Atiya, Nayra. *Khul-Khaal: Five Egyptian Women Tell Their Stories.* Syracuse: Syracuse University Press, 1982.

Azari, Farah, ed. *Women of Iran: The Conflict with Fundamentalist Islam.* London: Ithaca Press, 1983.

Azmaz, Adviye. *Migration and Reintegration in Rural Turkey: The Role of Women Behind.* Göttingen: Edition Herodot, 1984.

Badran, Margot. "Islam, Patriarchy, and Feminism in the Middle East." *Trends in History* 2, no. 3 (1985): 49-71.

—. "Women and Production in the Middle East." *Trends in History* 2, no. 3 (1982): 59-88.

—. "Dual Liberation: Feminism and Nationalism in Egypt, 1870s-1925." *Feminist Issues* VIII, 1 (1988): 15-34.

— "The Origins of Feminism in Egypt." In Arina Angerman et al., eds., *Current Issues in Women's History.* London: Routledge & Kegan Paul, 1989.

—, "Competing Agenda: Feminists, Islam and the State in 19th and 20th Century Egypt." In Deniz Kandiyoti, ed., *Women, Islam, and the State.* Philadelphia: Temple University Press, 1991.

Baer, Gabriel. "Women and Waqf: An Analysis of the Istanbul Tahrir of 1546." *Asian and African Studies* (Jerusalem) 17, nos. 1-3 (1983): 9-28.

Bates, Ulku. "Women as Patrons of Architecture in Turkey." In Beck and Keddie, *Women in the Muslim World* (1978).

Bayat-Philipp, Mangol. "Women and Revolution in Iran, 1905-1911." In Beck and Keddie, *Women in the Muslim World* (1978).

Benallegue, Nora. "Algerian Women in the Struggle for Independence and Reconstruction." *International Social Science Journal* 35, no. 4 (1983): 703-717.

Bendt, Ingela, James Downing, and Ann Henning. *We Shall Return: Women of Palestine.* New York: Lawrence Hill, 1982.

Betteridge, Ann. "The Controversial Views of Urban Muslim Women in Iran." In *Unspoken World,* ed. by Nancy Falk, 141-55. San Francisco: Harper & Row.

—. "To Veil or Not to Veil: A Matter of Protection or Policy." In Nashat, *Women and Revolution in Iran* (1983).

Bouhdiba, Abdelwahab. *Sexuality in Islam.* Trans. Alan Sheridan. London: Routledge & Kegan Paul, 1985.

Boullata, Kamal, ed. Women of the Fertile Crescent: An Anthology of Modern Poetry by Arab Women. Washington: Three Continents Press, 1978.

Bouthaina, Shaaban. *Both Right and Left Hand: Arab Women Talk About their Lives.* London: Women's Press, 1988.

Bowen, Donna Lee. "Muslim Juridical Opinions Concerning the Status of Women as Demonstrated by the Case of 'Azl." *JNES,* 41 (1981): 323-329.

Browning, Janet. *Atatürks Legacy to the Women of Turkey*. University of Durham Press, 1985.

Cannon, Byron. "Nineteenth Century Arabic Writing on Women and Society: The Interim Role of the Masonic Press in Cairo (1885-1895) *IJMES* 17 (1985): 463-484.

Charrad, Mounira. "State and Gender in the Maghrib." *Middle East Report* 163 (1990): 19-24.

Cole, Juan Ricardo. "Feminism, Class, and Islam in Turn-of-the-century Egypt." *IJMES* 13 (1981): 394-407.

Cooke, Miriam. *War's Other Voices: Women Writers on the Lebanese Civil War*. Cambridge: Cambridge University Press, 1987.

Daleb, Nuha. "Palestinian Women and their Role in the Revolution." *Peuples Mediterraneans* 5 (1978): 35-47.

Danforth, Sandra. "The Social and Political Implications of Muslim Middle Eastern Women's Participation in Violent Political Conflict." *Women and Politics* 4, no. 1 (1984).

Davis, Fanny. *The Ottoman Lady: A Social History from 1718-1918*. Westpoint: Greenwood Press, 1986.

Davis, Susan Schaeffer. *Patience and Power: Women's Lives in a Moroccan Village*. Cambridge: Schenkman, 1983.

Dorsky, Susan. *Women of 'Amran: A Middle East Ethnographic Study*. Salt Lake City: University of Utah Press, 1986.

Dengler, Ian C. "Turkish Women in the Ottoman Empire: The Classical Age." In Beck and Keddie, *Women in the Muslim World*. (1978)

Dogramaci, Emel. *Rights of Women in Turkey*. S.N.J. 1982.

Doubleday, Veronica. *Three Women of Herat*. London: Cape, 1988.

Duben, Alan. "Household Formation in Late Ottoman Istanbul." *IJMES* 22 (1990): 419-435.

Duben, Alan and Cem Behar. *Istanbul Households, Marriage, Family and Fertility 1880-1940*. Cambridge: Cambridge University Press, 1991.

Early, Evelyn. "Baladi Women of Cairo, Egypt: Sociability and Therapeutic Action". Ph.D. Dissertation, University of Chicago, 1980.

Eliraz, Giora. "Egyptian Intellectuals and Women's Emancipation, 1919-

1939." *Asian and African Studies* (Jerusalem) 16 (1982): 95-120.

Engineer, Asghrali. *Justice, Women, and Harmony in Islam.* New Delhi, 1989.

Esposito, John. *Women in Muslim Family Law.* Syracuse: Syracuse University Press, 1982.

—, "Women's Rights in Islam." *Islamic Studies* 14 (75): 99-114.

Farah, Madelain. *Marriage and Sexuality in Islam.* Vol. 1, Part 1. Salt Lake City: University of Utah Press, 1984.

Fathi, Asghar, ed. *Women and the Family in Iran.* Leiden: Brill, 1985.

Fernea, Elizabeth Warnock, ed. *Women and the Family in the Middle East: New Voices of Change.* Austin: University of Texas Press, 1985.

Fernea, Elizabeth Warnock and Basima Qattam Bazirgan, eds. *Middle Eastern Women Speak.* Austin: University of Texas Press, 1977.

— *A Street in Marakesh: Personal Encounter with the Lives of Moroccan Women.* New York: Doubleday and Company, 1975.

Friedl, Erika. "Women and the Division of Labor in an Iranian Village." *MERIP Reports* 95 (1981): 25-56.

Gerber, Haim. "Social and Economic Position of Women in an Ottoman City." *IJMES* 12 (1980): 231-244.

Graham-Brown, Sarah. *Images of Women: The Portrayal of Women in Photography of the Middle East, 1860-1950.* London: Quartet, 1988.

Gran, Judith. "Impact of the World Market on Egyptian Women." *MERIP Reports* 58 (1977): 3-7.

El Guindi, Fadwa. "Veiled Activism: Egyptian Women in the Contemporary Islamic Movement." *Mediterranean Peoples* 22/23 (1983): 79-89.

Günseli, Berik. *Women Carpet Weavers in Rural Turkey: Patterns of Employment, Earnings, and Status.* Geneva: Internal Labor Office, 1987.

Haeri, Shahla. "Power of Ambiguity: Cultural Improvisations on the Theme of Temporary Marriage." *Iranian Studies* 19 (1986): 123-155.

—. *Law of Desire: Temporary Marriage in Shi'i Iran.* Syracuse: Syracuse University Press, 1989.

Haim, Sylvia G. "The Situation of Arab Women in the Mirror of Literature." *Middle Eastern Studies* 17 (1981): 510-530.

Hammam, Mona. "Women and Industrial Work in Egypt: The Chubra El-Kheima Case." *Arab Studies Quarterly* 2 (1980): 50-69.

Hammami, Rema. "Women, the Hijab, and the Intifada." *Middle East Report* 164/165 (1990): 24-28.

Hatem, Mervat. "The Enduring Alliance of Nationalism and Patriarchy in Muslim Personal Status Laws: The Case of Modern Egypt." *Feminist Issues* VI (1986): 19-43.

—. "Toward the Study of the Psychodynamics of Mothering and Gender in Egyptian Families." *IJMES* 19 (1987): 287-305.

Heggoy, Alf Andrew. "Algerian Women and the Right to Vote: Some Colonial Anomalies." *Muslim World* 62 (1972): 323-335.

Hegland, Mary Elaine. "Political Roles of Iranian Village Women." *MERIP Middle East Report* 16 (1946): 14-19, 46.

Hijab, Nadia. *Women Power: The Arab Debate on Women at Work.* New York: Cambridge University Press, 1988.

Hoffman-Ladd, Valerie. "Polemics on the Modesty and Segregation of Women in Contemporary Egypt." *IJMES* 19 (1987): 23-50.

—, "The Religious Life of Muslim Women in Contemporary Egypt." Ph.D. Dissertation, University of Chicago, 1986.

Howard-Merriam, Kathleen. "Women, Education, and Professions in Egypt." *Comparative Education Review* 23 (1979): 256-270.

Hussain, Freda, ed. *Muslim Women.* New York: St. Martin's Press, 1984.

Jansen, Willy. *Women Without Men: Gender and Marginality in an Algerian Town.* Leiden: Brill, 1987.

Kabir, Kausar. *Biographical Dictionary of Prominent Muslim Ladies.* New Delhi: Light and Life Publishers, 1982.

Kagitçibasi, Çigdem. "Status of Women in Turkey: Cross-Cultural Perspectives." *IJMES* 18 (1986): 485-499.

Kamali, Hashim. "Divorce and Women's Rights: Some Muslim Interpretations of Sura 2: 228." *The Muslim World* 74 (2): 85-99.

261

Kanafani, Aida S. *Aesthetics and Ritual in the United Arab Emirates: The Anthropology of Food and Personal Adornment Among Arabian Women.* AUB, 1983.

Kandiyoti, Deniz. "Emancipated but Unliberated? Reflections on the Turkish Case." *Feminist Studies* 13 (1987).

—. "Sex Roles and Social Change: A Comparative Study of Turkey's Women." *Signs: A Journal of Women in Culture and Society* 3 (1977): 57-73.

—. "Slave Girls, Temptresses, and Comrades: Images of Women in the Turkish Novel." *Feminist Issues* VIII, 1 (1988).

—. "End of the Empire: Islam, Nationalism, and Women in Turkey," in Kandiyoti, ed., *Women, Islam, and the State,* 22-48.

—, Major Issues on the Status of Women in Turkey: Approaches and Priorities. Ankara, 1980.

Khatib-Shahidi, Jane. "Sexual Prohibitions, Shared Space, and Fictive Marriage in Shi'ite Iran." In Ardner, Shirley, ed., *Women and Space: Ground Rules and Social Maps,* 112-35.

Keddie, Nikki and Lois Beck. *Women in the Muslim World.* Cambridge: Harvard University Press, 1978.

— "Problems in the Study of Middle Eastern Women." *IJMES* 10 (1979): 225-240.

Khayyat, Sana al- . *Honour and Shame: Women in Modern Iraq.* London: Saqi, 1991. (in progress)

Knauss, Peter. *The Persistence of Patriarchy: Class, Gender, and Ideology in Twentieth Century Algeria.* New York: Praeger, 1987.

Layish, Aharon. *Women and Islamic Law in a non-Muslim State: A Study Based on Shari'a Court in Israel.* Jerusalem: Israel University Press, 1975.

Layne, Linda. "Women in Jordan's Workforce." *MERIP Reports* 95 (1981): 19-23.

Lazreq, Marina. "Feminism and Difference: The Perils of Writing as a Woman on Women in Algeria." *Feminist Studies* 14 (1988): 81-107.

Mahdavi, Asghar. "The Significance of Private Archives for the Study of the Economic and Social History of Iran in late Qajar Period." *Iranian*

Studies 16 (1983): 243-78.

Mahdavi, Shireen. "Women and Ideas in Qajar Iran." *Asian and African Studies* (Jerusalem) 9 (1985): 187-197.

— "Shawhar Ahu Khanum, Passion, Polygamy, and Tragedy." *IJMES* 24 (1988): 113-116.

—. "Taj al-Saltanah, an Emancipated Qajar Princess." *IJMES* 23 (1987): 188-193.

—. "The Position of Women in Shi'i Iran: View of the Ulama." In Fernea, Elizabeth Warnock, ed., Women and Family in the Middle East, 255-72.

Makhlouf, Carla. *Changing Veils: Omen and Modernization in North Yemen.* Austin: University of Texas Press, 1979.

Marcus, Abraham. "Men, Women, and Property: Dealers in Real Estate in Eighteenth Century Aleppo." *JESHO* 26 (1973): 136-163.

Marsot, Afaf Lutfi al-Sayyid. "The Revolutionary Gentlewomen in Egypt." in *Women in the Muslim World,* 261-76.

Masudul, Hasan. *Daughters of Islam: Short Biographical Sketches of 82 Famous Muslim Women.* Lahore, 1976.

Mernissi, Fatima. *Beyond the Veil: Male-Female Dynamics in a Modern Muslim Society.* Cambridge: Schenkman Publishing, 1975.

—. "Women and the Impact of Capitalist Development in Morocco, Part II." *Feminist Issues* 3 (1983): 61-112.

—. *Doing Daily Battle: Interviews with Moroccan Women.* New Jersey: Rutgers University Press, 1989.

El-Messiri, Sausan. "Self-Images of Traditional Urban Women in Cairo." In Beck and Keddie, *Women in the Muslim World* (1978).

Mikhail, Mona. *Images of Arab Women: Fact and Fiction.* Washington: Three Continents Press, 1979.

Minces, Juliette. *The House of Obedience: Women in Arab Society.* London: Zed, 1982.

Mizanoglu, Reddy Nilüfer, Trans. *Twenty Stories by Turkish Women.* Indiana University Press, 1988.

Moghadam, Val. "Women, Work, and Ideology in the Islamic Republic." *IJMES* 20 (1988): 245-263.

Musallam, B. F. *Sex and Society in Islam.* Cambridge: Cambridge University Press, 1986.

Najmabadi, Afsaneh. "Hazards of Modernity and Morality: Women, State, and Ideology in Contemporary Iran," in Deniz Kandiyoti, ed., *Women, Islam, and the State.*

—. "Iran's Turn to Islam: From Modernism to a Moral Order." *MEJ* 41 (1987): 202-17.

Nashat, Guity. *Women and Revolution in Iran.* Boulder, Colorado: Westview Press, 1983.

—. "Women in Pre-Revolutionary Iran: A Historical Overview." In Nashat, *Women and Revolution* (1983).

Nelson, Cynthia. "Public and Private Politics" Women in the Middle Eastern World." *American Ethnologist* 1 (1974): 551-563.

—. "The Voices of Doria Shafik: Feminist Consciousness in Egypt, 1940-1960." *Feminist Issues* VI (1986): 16-31.

Parveen, Shaukat Ali. *The Status of Women in the Muslim World: A Study in Feminist Movements in Turkey, Egypt, Algeria, and Pakistan.* Lahore: Aziz Publishing, 1986.

Peters, Emrys L. "The Status of Women in Four Middle Eastern Communities," in Beck and Keddie, eds., *Women in the Muslim World,* 311-350.

Peteet, Julie. "No Going Back: Women and the Palestinian Movement." *MERIP Reports* 16 (1986): 20-24.

Peteet, Julie and Rosemary Sayigh. "Between Two Fires: Palestinian Women in Lebanon." In Ridd, *Caught Up in Conflict* (1987).

Philipp, Thomas. "Feminism and Nationalist Politics in Egypt," in Beck and Keddie, eds., *Women in the Muslim World,* 277-294.

— "Women in the Historical Perspective of an Early Arab Modernist (Gurgi Zaidan)." *Welt des Islams* 18, nos. 1-2 (1977): 65-83.

Raccagni, Michelle. *The Modern Arab Woman: A Bibliography.* Metuchen, New Jersey: Scarecrow Press, 1978.

Rahman, Fazlur. "A Survey of Modernization of Muslim Family Law." *IJMES* 1 (1980): 451-465.

— "Status of Women in the Qur'an." In Nashat, *Women and Revolution in Iran* (1983).

Ramazani, Nesta. "Behind the Veil: Status of Women in Revolutionary Iran." *Journal of South Asian and Middle Eastern Studies* 4 (1980): 27-36.

Rassam, Amal. "Women and Domestic Power in Morocco." *IJMES* 12 (1980): 171-179.

Rugh, Andrea. "Women and Work: Strategies and Choices in a Lower-Class Quarter of Cairo." In Beck and Keddie, eds., *Women in the Muslim World.*

Sa'dawi, Nawal. *The Hidden Face of Eve: Women in the Arab World.* London: Zed Press, 1980.

Sabbah, Fetna. *Women in the Muslim Unconscious.* Trans. by Mary Jo Lakeland. New York: Pergamon Press, 1983.

Saleh, Sanya. "Women in Islam: Their Role in Religious and Traditional Culture." *International Journal of Sociology of Family* 2 (1977): 193-201.

Sanad, Jamal, and Mark Tessler. "The Economic Orientations of Kuwaiti Women: Their Nature, Determinants, and Consequences." *IJMES* 20 (1988): 443-468.

Sansarian, Elizabeth. *The Women's Rights Movement in Iran: Mutiny, Appeasement, and Repression from 1900 to Khomeini.* New York: Praeger, 1982.

Sayigh, Rosemary. "Roles and Functions of Arab Women: A Reappraisal." *Arab Studies Quarterly* 3 (1981): 258-274.

Sh'arawi, Huda. *Harem Years: The Memoirs of am Egyptian Feminist.* London: Virago, 1986.

Siddiqui, H. Y. *Muslim Women in Transition: A Social Profile.* New Delhi, 1987.

Smith, Jane I, ed. *Women in Contemporary Muslim Studies.* London: Associated University Presses, 1980.

Soffan, Linda Usra. *The Women of the United Arab Emirates.* New Jersey:

Barnes and Noble Books, 1980.

Soughate, Minoo S. "Men, Women, and Boys: Love and Sex in the Works of Sa'di." *Iranian Studies* 17 (1984): 413-452.

Stowasser, Barbara. "The Status of Women in Early Islam." In Freda Hussain, ed., Muslim Women, 11-43.

Sullivan, Earl. Women in Egyptian Public Life. Syracuse: Syracuse University Press, 1986.

—. *Women and Work in the Arab World.* Cairo Papers in Social Science 4. Cairo: American University in Cairo Press, 1981.

Tabari, Azar and N. Yeganeh. *The Shadow of Islam: The Women's Movement in Iran.* London: Zed Press, 1982.

Takieddine-Amyuni, Mona. "Images of Arab Women in Midaq Alley by Naguib Mahfouz, and Season of Migration to the North by Tayeb Saleh." *IJMES* 17 (1985): 25-39.

Tucker, Judith. "Decline of the Family in Mid-Nineteenth Century Egypt." *Arab Studies Quarterly* 3, no. 3 (1979): 245-271.

—. "Problems in the Historiography of Women in the Middle East: The Case of Nineteenth Century Egypt." *IJMES* 15, no. 3 (1983): 321-336.

—. "Marriage and Family in Nablus: 1720-1856, Toward a History of Arab Marriage." *Journal of Family History* 13 (1988): 165-81.

—, *Women in Nineteenth Century Egypt.* Cambridge: Cambridge University Press, 1985.

Vieille, Paul. "Iranian Women in the Politics of Family Alliance and Sexual Politics," in Beck and Keddie, eds., *Women in the Muslim World,* 451-72.

Wani, M. A. *Maintenance Rights of Muslim Women: Principles, Precedent, and Trends.* New Delhi: Genuine Publ., 1987.

Waines, David. "Through a Veil Darkly: The Study of Women in Muslim Societies," *Comparative Studies of Society and History* 24 (4):642-59

Wikan, Unni. *Behind the Veil in Arabia: Women in Oman.* Baltimore: Johns Hopkins University, 1982.

Youssef, Nadia Haggag. "Women and Agricultural Production in Muslim Societies." *Comparative International Development* 3 (1977): 41-88.

About the Illustrations

1. *Abū Zayd and al-Ḥārith arrive in a village.*
   Miniature by Wāsiṭī from: Ḥārīrī, Maqāmāt. Bagdad, dated 635 (1237).
   Size of page 36.5 x 29.4 cm. Bibliothèque Nationale, Paris, MS. arabe
   5847, f. 138 r.

2. *Bahrām Gūr with the Princess of the Green Pavilion.*
   Miniature from: Amīr Ḥusrau Dihlavī, Ḥamsa. Iran, School of Shiraz,
   probably between 1590 and 1600. 14 x 13 cm (without dome).
   Orientabteilung der Staatsbibliothek Preussischer Kulturbesitz, Berlin,
   MS. or. fol. 1615, f. 210 r.

3. *Prince Humāy and Princess Humāyūn in the garden.*
   Miniature from a work by Hvağū-i Kirmānī. Herat, first half of fif-
   teenth century. 29.4 x 17.9 cm. Musée des Arts Décoratifs, Paris,
   In 3727.

4. *Noah's ark.*
   Miniature from: Isḥāq an-Nīšāpūrī, Qiṣaṣ al-anbiyā'. Iran, School of
   Shiraz, last quarter of sixteenth century. 13-9 X 10.5 cm.
   Orientabteilung der Staatsbibliothek Preussischer Kulturbesitz, Berlin,
   MS. Diez A fol. 3, f. 23 r.

5. *Isfandiyār kills a sorceress.*
   Miniature from: Firdausī, Šāhnāma. Iran. School of Isfahan, dated
   1014 (1605). 24.3 x 14 cm. Deutsche Staatsbibliothek. Berlin, MS. or.
   fol. 425 I f. 478 v.

6. *Scene before the gate of a city.*
   Miniature from the Jahāngīr Album. India, 1617/18. Size of pages
   53.5 x 40 cm. Orientabteilung der Staatsbibliothek Preussischer
   Kulturbesitz, Berlin, Libr. pict. A 117, f. 14 r.

7. *Muhammed's first meeting with Khadīja.*
   Miniature from: Isḥāq an-Nīsāpūrī, Qiṣaṣ al-anbiyā'. Iran, around 1560.
   Chester Beatty Library, Dublin, MS. 231, f. 253.

8. *The birth of Christ according to the Koran.*
   Miniature from: Isḥāq an-Nīsāpūrī, Qiṣaṣ al-anbiyā'. Iran, around 1560.
   Chester Beatty Library, Dublin, MS. 231, f. 225.

9. *Entrance to the harem of a palace.*
   Miniature from an album of Murād III. Bukhara style, sixteenth cen-
   tury. 21.1 X 12.6 cm. Österreichische Nationalbibliothek, Vienna, Cod.
   Mixt. 313, f. 29.

10. *Adam and Eve being driven out of Paradise.*
    Miniature from: Fuzūlī, Ḥadīqat as-su'adā'. Turkey, end of sixteenth
    century. Size of page 31 x 21 cm. Bibliotheque Nationale, Paris, Suppl.
    turc 1088, f.9b.

11. *The Queen of Sheba on the throne.*
    Miniature from: Niẓāmī, Maḫzan al-asrār. Iran, middle of sixteenth
    century. 35.2 x 21.1 cm. Bibliothèque Nationale, Paris, Suppl. pers.
    1956, f I.

12. *Sūfī preaching from the pulpit.*
    Miniature from: Ḥusain Baiqarā, Maǧālis al-'uššāq. Iran, middle of six-
    teenth century. 11.1 x 10 cm. Bodleian Library, Oxford, MS. Ouseley
    Add. 24, f 55 v.

13. *Scene from Kalīla wa-Dimna.*
    Book page with miniature. Syria, second quarter of fourteenth century.
    Size of page 29.4 x 22.5 cm. Bibliothèque Nationale Paris, MS. arabe
    3467, f. 61.

14. *Layla and Majnūn at school.*
    Book page with miniature. Iran, Shiraz, dated 984 (1576). Size of page
    41 x 27 cm. Museum für Islamische Kunst, Staatliche Museen
    Preussischer Kulturbesitz, Berlin (West), Inv. No. I 14/62.

15. *The birth of Rustam.*
    Miniature from: Firdausī, Šāhnāma. Iran, School of Isfahan, dated 1014
    (1605). 24.5 X 14.5 cm. Deutsche Staatsbibliothek, Berlin, MS. or. fol.
    4251, f 180 v.

16. *The Iranian King Jamshīd teaches his subjects the various crafts.*

Miniature from: Ṭabarī, Ta'rīḫ. Iran, dated 874 (1470). Chester Beatty Library, Dublin, MS. 144, f. 20.

17. *Doctor in the harem.*

Miniature from: 'Alī Čelebī, Humāyūnnāma. Turkey, end of sixteenth century. 22 x 12 cm. Topkapi Saray Museum, Istanbul, Ḥaz. 843, f. 163 v.

18. *Stoning of an adulterous pair.*

Miniature from: Qiṣṣa-i Amīr Ḥamza. India, probably end fifteenth century. 10 x 15.8 cm. Orientabteilung der Staatsbibliothek Preussischer Kulturbesitz, Berlin, MS. or. fol. 4181, f 11 r.

19. *Ladies preparing a picnic in the country.*

Miniature from: Amīr Ḥusrau Dihlavī, Ḥamsa. Iran, around 1575. 19-6 x 12.5 cm. Bodleian Library, Oxford, MS. Elliott 189, f. 192 r.

20. *Zāl fetches his bride, Rūdābeh.*

Miniature from: Firdausī, Šāhnāma. Iran, probably Shiraz, dated 1002 (1593). 19.5 x 15.5 cm. Deutsche Staatsbibliothek, Berlin, MS. Diez A fol. 1, f. 72 v.

21. *Bahrām Gūr and Āzādeh hunting.*

Miniature from: Amīr Ḥusrau Dihlavī, Ḥamsa. Iran, School of Shiraz, probably between 1590 and 1600. 17 x 13 cm. Orientabteilung der Staatsbibliothek Preussischer Kulturbesitz, Berlin, MS. or. fol. 1615, f. 198v.

22. *Lamentation at the bier of Rustam and Zavāra.*

Miniature from: Firdausī, Šāhnāma. Iran, School of Isfahan, dated 1014 (1605). 24.5 x 14.5 cm. Deutsche Staatsbibliothek, Berlin, MS. or. fol. 4251, f. 519 v.

23. *Harem.*

Miniature. India, end of seventeenth century. 32 x 21.5 cm. Museum für Indische Kunst, Staatliche Museen Preussischer Kulturbesitz, Berlin (West), Cat. No. MIK I 5055.

24. *Emperor Akbar crosses a river with his harem.*

Miniature from: Iqbālnāma-yi Ğahāngīrī. India, seventeenth century. 13.3 x 28.3 cm. Free Library of Philadelphia, Lewis MS. 44, f. 18 r.

25. *In the bazaar.*

Miniature from: Darīr, Siyar-i Nabīy. Turkey, dated 1003 (1594/5). Chester Beatty Library, Dublin, MS. 419, f. 310 r.

26. *Mughal lady with maidservants in the garden of the harem.*
   Miniature. India, end of seventeenth century. 21 x 13.7 cm. Staatliche
   Museen, Berlin, Islamisches Museum, I 4597,f. 25..

27. *A lady in discussion with a sheikh.*
   Miniature. Iran, 1658. 18.5 x 11 cm. Museum des Kunsthandwerks,
   Leipzig, Inv. No. B 11.10c.

28. *The goldsmith, Hasan, is freed from the prison lower by his wife.*
   Miniature from: Amīr H̱usrau Dihlavī, H̱amsa. Signed Hāšim. India,
   School of Jahāngīr, around 1610. 16 x 10.8 cm. Deutsche
   Staatsbibliothek, Berlin, MS. or. fol. 1278, f. 147 v.

29. *Muhammed with his daughter, Fātima, and his wives, Ā'isha and Umm
   Salama.*
   Miniature from: Ḍarīr, Siyar-i Nabīy. Turkey, dated 1003 (1594/5).
   Chester Beatty Library, Dublin, MS. 419, f. 40 v.

30. *Bowl.*
   Faïence. Iran, Ray (?), late twelfth century, Diameter 23 cm, height
   8.8 cm. Smithsonian Institution, Freer Gallery of Art, Washington,
   No. 38,12.

31. *Seated princess with bouquet.*
   Miniature. Iran, Tabriz style, around 1540. 39.7 x 28 cm. Fogg Art
   Museum, Harvard University, Cambridge, Mass., Gift of John Goelet,
   Inv. No. 1958. 60.

32. *The young lute player.*
   Miniature. Turkey, between 1640 and 1650. 22 X 12.4 cm. Bibliothèque
   Nationale, Paris, MS. arabe 6076, f. 2.

33. *Troop of tumblers.*
   Miniature. India, eighteenth century. 27 x 17.7 cm. Museum für Indische
   Kunst, Staatliche Museen Preussischer Kulturbesitz Berlin (West), Cat.
   No. MIK I 5070.

34. *Mughal girl with bird.*
   Miniature. India, middle of eighteenth century. 18 x 9.8 cm. Staatliche
   Museen Berlin, Islamisches Museum, Inv. No. I 4594, f. 15.

35. *Girl writing.*
   Miniature in Isfahan style, around 1600. 13.5 x 9 cm. India Office
   Library, London, Johnson 13-4.

36. *Mughal lady.*
    Miniature, signed Maddhū Ḥurd. India, sixteenth century. Musée Guimet, Paris, Inv. No. 3619 Hc.

37. *Pair of lovers.*
    Miniature by Muʻin Muṣawwir. Iran, dated 1098 (1689). 19.2 x 10.5 cm. Walters Art Gallery, Baltimore, Inv. No. 10 690.

38. *Zāl climbs into Rūdābeh's pavilion.*
    Miniature from: Firdausī, Šāhnāma. Iran, Shiraz, between 1590 and 1595. 40 x 26 cm. British Library, London, MS. Add. 27257, f. 44 v.

39. *Bahrām Gūr with the Princess of the Sandalwood-colored Pavilion.*
    Miniature from: Amīr Ḥusrau Dihlavī, Ḥamsa. Iran. School of Shiraz, probably between 1590 and 1600. 13.4 x 13.4 cm (without dome). Orientabteilung der Staatsbibliothek Preussischer Kulturbesitz, Berlin, MS. or. fol. 1615, f. 226 r.

40. *The black-eyed Talha kills another suitor.*
    Miniature from: Ḍarīr, Siyar-i Nabīy. Turkey, dated 103 (1594/5). Chester Beatty Library, Dublin, MS. 419, f. 91 v.

41. *Couple of lovers.*
    Miniature, signed Riżā-i ʻAbbāsī. Iran, dated 1039 (1630) 18.1 x 11.9 cm. Metropolitan Museum of Art, New York, Francis M. Welch Fund, 1950 Inv. No. 50.164.

42. *Bahrām Gūr with the Princess of the Yellow Pavillion.*
    Miniature by Ṭālib from: Niẓāmī, Ḥamsa. Iran, dated 1077 (1666). Size of page 27.2 X 19 cm. British Library, London, MS. Add. 6613, f. 165 v.

43. *Majnūn dies al Laylāʾs grave.*
    Miniature by Bihzād from: Niẓāmī, Ḥamsa. Iran, around 1495. Size of page 24 x 17.5 cm. British Library, London, MS. Or. 6810, f. 144 v.

44. *Fitna carries the cow on her shoulders.*
    Miniature from: Ibn ʻImād. Rauḍat al-muḥibbīn. Iran, dated 1582. 15.7 x 8.5 cm. Free Library of Philadelphia, Lewis Oriental MS. 78, f 24 v.

45. *The angel Tobias.*
    Miniature, signed Ḥusain. India, sixteenth century. Musée Guimet. Paris, Inv. No. 3619 Ha.

46. *Wall tile with woman's head.*

Clay, glazed. Iran, early seventeenth century. Museum für Islamische Kunst, Staatliche Museen Preussischer Kulturbesitz, Berlin, Inv. No. I 7/71.

Cover: Young woman smoking the hookah.

Miniature by Muʿīn Muṣawwir. Iran, dated 1084 (1673/4). 20 x 10.2 cm. Topkapi Saray Museum, Istanbul, Ḥazine 2142, f. 12 r.

Text Illustrations

44. *Female hunter.*

Reconstructed mural from a Khalifʾs palace in Samarra, ninth century. After: Herzfeld, E. *Die Wandmalereien von Samarra.* Berlin, 1927.

63. *Calligraphic illuminated page with the Basmala.*

Iran, seventeenth century. Staatliche Museen, Berlin, Islamisches Museum. After: Kühnel, E. *Islamische Schriftkunst.* 2nd ed., Graz, 1972.

81. *Bridal procession.*

Turkey, seventeenth century. After: Taeschner, F. *Alt-Stambuler Hof- und Volkskeben.* Hanover, 1925.

90. *Woman crushing corn.*

Miniature from an Indian manuscript, probably by a Persian painter, sixteenth century. British Library, London, MS. Or. 3299. After: Lewis, B. (editor) *The World of Islam.* London, 1976.

98. *Dancer.*

Miniature, India, eighteenth century, signed Kamāl Hileh. Louvre, Paris, Inv. No. 3619.

120. *Obverse and reverse of the Sultana Shajarat ad-Durrʾs dinar.*

Egypt, thirteenth century. British Museum, London. After: Schregle, G. *Die Sultanin von Ägypten.* Wiesbaden, 1961.

124. *Mughal princess on the throne.*

Miniature, India, eighteenth century. 9.7 x 6.4 cm. Staatliche Museen, Berlin, Islamisches Museum, Inv. No. I 4601, f. 18.

170. *Bahrām Gūr and Āzādeh hunting.*

Ceramic tile relief, lustre-painted. Iran, Kashan, thirteenth century. Islamic Museum, Cairo, Inv. No. I 11090.

172. *Laylā and Majnūn have fainted with love.*

Miniature from: Niẓāmī, Ḥamsa. South Iran, middle of the fifteenth century. 3.7 x 8 cm. Deutsche Staatsbibliothek, Berlin, Ms. Sprenger 1475, f. 128r.

193. *Young woman making her toilet.*

Miniature, Turkey, around 1710. 16.2 x 11 cm. Topkapi Saray Museum, Istanbul. After: Stchoukine, I. La peinture turque d'après les manuscrits illustrés. II partie. Paris, 1968.

196. *Lady with maidservant on the way to bathe.*

Turkey, seventeenth century. After: Taeschner, F. *Alt-Stambuler Hof- und Volksleben.* Hanover, 1925.

Sources of Illustrations

Bibliothèque Nationale, Paris, 1, 10, 11, 13, 32

Bodleian Library, Oxford, 12, 19

Breitenborn, Dieter, Berlin, 15

British Library, London, 38, 42, 43

Deutsche Staatsbibliothek, Berlin, 5, 20, 22, 28

Fogg Art Museum, Harvard University, Cambridge, Mass., 31

Freer Gallery of Art, Washington, 30

Hanse, Ingrid, Leipzig, 27

India Office Library, London, 35

İslamisches Museum, Staatliche Museen, Berlin, 26, 34

Metropolitan Museum of Art, New York, 41

Mills, Charles & Son, Philadelphia, 24, 44

Musee des Arts Decoratifs, Paris, 3

Museum für Indische Kunst, Staatliche Museen Preussischer Kulturbesitz, Berlin, 23, 33

Museum für Islamische Kunst, Staatliche Museen Preussischer Kulturbesitz, Berlin, 14, 46

Orientabteilung der Staatsbibliothek Preussischer Kulturbesitz, Berlin, 2, 4, 6, 18, 21, 39

Pieterse Davison International, Dublin, 7, 8, 16, 25, 29, 40

Service de documentation photographique de la Réunion des musées nationaux, Paris, 36, 45

Topkapi Saray Museum, Istanbul, 17

Walters Art Gallery, Baltimore, 37

Index

Index

Chronology of Islamic Dynasties

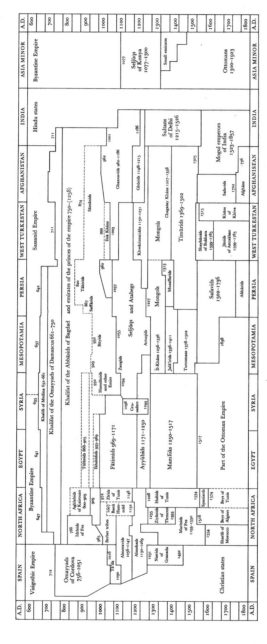

ARABIA
HIJĀZ (Mecca and Medina): Khalifs and Arabian Sharīfs

YEMEN (Southern Arabia): Khalifs and Arabian dynasties, 1174-1536 Ayyūbids, Rasūlids and others, since 1536 Ottomans and Imāms of Sanʿa

SICILY
up to 830 Byzantine, 830-1070 Aghlabids and Fāṭimids, 1070-1194 Normans, later Hohenstaufen, Anjou, Aragon and others

VOLGA STATES
up to thirteenth century Khāns of the Khazars and Bulgars 1236-1558 Mongol Khāns of the Golden Horde and rivals

CRIMEA
1420-1783 Giray Khāns

BALKANS
under Ottoman rule from end of fourteenth or fifteenth century to nineteenth century

HUNGARY
1541-1699 under Ottoman rule